The Operator's Manual
for the New Administration

IBM Center for
The Business of Government

THE IBM CENTER FOR THE BUSINESS OF GOVERNMENT BOOK SERIES

The IBM Center Series on The Business of Government explores new approaches to improving the effectiveness of government at the federal, state, and local levels. The Series is aimed at providing cutting-edge knowledge to government leaders, academics, and students about the management of government in the 21st century.

Publications in the series include:

Collaboration: Using Networks and Partnerships, *edited by John M. Kamensky and Thomas J. Burlin*

Competition, Choice, and Incentives in Government Programs, *edited by John M. Kamensky and Albert Morales*

E-Government 2003, *edited by Mark A. Abramson and Therese L. Morin*

E-Government 2001, *edited by Mark A. Abramson and Grady E. Means*

Human Capital 2004, *edited by Jonathan D. Breul and Nicole Willenz Gardner*

Human Capital 2002, *edited by Mark A. Abramson and Nicole Willenz Gardner*

Innovation, *edited by Mark A. Abramson and Ian D. Littman*

Integrating Performance and Budgets: The Budget Office of Tomorrow, *edited by Jonathan D. Breul and Carl Moravitz*

Leaders, *edited by Mark A. Abramson and Kevin M. Bacon*

Learning the Ropes: Insights for Political Appointees, *edited by Mark A. Abramson and Paul R. Lawrence*

Managing for Results 2005, *edited by John M. Kamensky and Albert Morales*

Managing for Results 2002, *edited by Mark A. Abramson and John M. Kamensky*

Memos to the President: Management Advice from the Nation's Top Public Administrators, *edited by Mark A. Abramson*

New Ways of Doing Business, *edited by Mark A. Abramson and Ann M. Kieffaber*

The Procurement Revolution, *edited by Mark A. Abramson and Roland S. Harris III*

Transforming Government Supply Chain Management, *edited by Jacques S. Gansler and Robert E. Luby, Jr.*

Transforming Organizations, *edited by Mark A. Abramson and Paul R. Lawrence*

The Operator's Manual for the New Administration

Mark A. Abramson

LEADERSHIP INC.

Jonathan D. Breul

IBM CENTER FOR THE BUSINESS OF GOVERNMENT

John M. Kamensky

IBM CENTER FOR THE BUSINESS OF GOVERNMENT

G. Martin Wagner

IBM CENTER FOR THE BUSINESS OF GOVERNMENT

ROWMAN & LITTLEFIELD PUBLISHERS, INC.
Lanham • Boulder • New York • Toronto • Oxford

ROWMAN & LITTLEFIELD PUBLISHERS, INC.

Published in the United States of America
by Rowman & Littlefield Publishers, Inc.
A wholly owned subsidary of The Rowman & Littlefield Publishing Group, Inc.
4501 Forbes Boulevard, Suite 200, Lanham, Maryland 20706
www.rowmanlittlefield.com

Estover Road
Plymouth PL6 7PY
United Kingdom

Copyright © 2008 by Rowman & Littlefield Publishers, Inc.

British Library Cataloguing in Publication Information Available

Library of Congress Cataloging-in-Publication Data Available

ISBN-13: 978-0-7425-6329-2 (cloth : alk. paper)
ISBN-10: 0-7425-6329-4 (cloth : alk. paper)
ISBN-13: 978-0-7425-6330-8 (pbk. : alk. paper)
ISBN-10: 0-7425-6330-8 (pbk. : alk. paper)

Printed in the United States of America

™
The paper used in this publication meets the minimum requirements of American
National Standard for Information Sciences—Permanence of Paper for Printed Library
Materials, ANSI/NISO Z39.48-1992.

*To government executives
in the hope that this manual
will help them succeed.*

TABLE OF CONTENTS

Foreword

Musing about the word "operator," one's thoughts drift to the only true government insiders' use for the word: the one that describes the intelligence officer or special military professional who works in the secret, sometimes dark, and often dangerous world of clandestine intelligence activities.

But wait a minute; that doesn't seem to be among the topics treated in this volume. So we focus on the phrase "operator's manual." Aha, that's it: The analogy is to one of those instruction books that come with complex machines. I am reminded of the four 6-inch binders that came with the 30-foot, jet-powered, state-of the art picnic boat a friend bought recently. These how-to volumes for the craft he christened the *Richard Henderson* were truly impenetrable to those uninitiated in modern maritime ways.

Government is even more complex than the *Richard Henderson,* and so it seems audacious to think that an operator's manual can fit in fewer than 200 pages. But that is what you will find in this book by leaders of IBM's Center for The Business of Government, which has just celebrated its 10th year of running a top-notch research program on management issues in the public sector. The authors presume, with considerable merit, that the past decade has produced a set of management principles that find common application across much of government.

This truth might come as a relief to some readers, people who are newly arriving to staff the next administration. After all, they might understandably believe that government has greatly changed as a consequence of the September 11 tragedy and its aftermath, and continues to evolve as security remains paramount. And, indeed, they would not be far off the mark. The huge Department of Homeland Security, which enveloped 22 agencies, remains a work in progress. The Defense Department, consuming well over half of all federal discretionary spending, is struggling with the difficult job of balancing today's recruiting, retention, and equipment needs against tomorrow's requirements for expensive new weaponry and larger force structures.

By comparison, there has been little change elsewhere in government. To be sure, a few big programs have been launched in this decade, with Medicare's prescription drug subsidies and the No Child Left Behind Act ranking at the top. Much of government remains on autopilot in the kind of "demosclerosis" that my colleague Jonathan Rauch described in his 1999 book, *Government's End: Why Washington Stopped Working.* Programs come but never go, living on in their own protected worlds. No fewer than 92 education programs are on the books, according to the federal website ExpectMore.gov. Many are past their prime, and their sheer number suggests how hard it would be to achieve focus on a few important goals.

The challenge facing many public managers is, in the old cliché, finding ways to do more with less. Much of domestic discretionary spending has been flat or down, with many programs losing purchasing power. Defense programs, too, are short of cash. The outlook is for less, not more, as retirement programs, including Social Security and Medicare, consume ever more resources and federal deficit spending loses its appeal.

Against this backdrop and the growing realization that government cannot by itself solve society's problems, federal officials must make the best of the authority they have. Regulatory powers can sometimes be used to change course. Elsewhere, management can be more important than policy making in a political and fiscal environment not particularly conducive to large new initiatives. And collaboration with people both inside and outside of government becomes ever more important.

To note that large new programs are not in the cards is not to belittle the tasks facing the next cadre of political and career leaders who will be taking over before long. Without a single new program, the government already is huge and occupied with addressing many of our most vexing problems. Improving performance of our existing agencies and programs remains a large and complex endeavor.

Of course, progress has been made, and this volume draws on research that has documented successes. Reformation of the Federal Emergency Management Agency in the 1990s, the advances in medical care made by the Veterans Health Administration, the fascinating public-private network created by the Bureau of Primary Health Care to extend its reach, the recasting of the Internal Revenue Service as guardian of the taxpayer, NASA's recovery from the shuttle *Columbia's* tragic loss, and the creation of the Human Genome Project are among the cases providing grist for the research.

To its credit, the IBM Center has reached out to accomplished academic and journalistic researchers to produce reports, now more than 200 in number. Well-regarded researchers have included Harry P. Hatry of the Urban Institute, Kathryn E. Newcomer and Philip G. Joyce of The George Washington University, Robert D. Behn of Harvard University, Lenneal Henderson of the University of Baltimore, James R. Thompson of the University of Illinois–Chicago, Thomas H. Stanton of Johns Hopkins University, Jacques S. Gansler of the University of Maryland, W. Henry Lambright of Syracuse University, Jonathan Walters of *Governing* magazine, and my colleague Anne Laurent, formerly of *Government Executive*.

Parsing through the reports, and bringing the benefit of their own decades of experience in government administration, the authors have grouped *The Operator's Manual* lessons into eight chapters. Some will strike readers as familiar, applying in any large institution, while others are more peculiar to government and its lingo. Most are illustrated with excerpts from case studies the IBM Center has published over the years, and the reader will find useful lists of laws and resources to guide the way. As a primer, therefore, on techniques leaders can use to achieve better results, and as a guide to deeper research, *The Operator's Manual* delivers a great deal in a compact volume.

Timothy B. Clark
Editor in Chief
Government Executive

Washington, D.C.
April 2008

Acknowledgments

The Operator's Manual for the New Administration represents the collective effort of many individuals over the past 10 years. Since its creation in 1998, the IBM Center for The Business of Government has awarded nearly 300 stipends to more than 250 outstanding researchers across the nation and around the world. This book represents what we have learned from each of them about managing in government. Although they are too numerous to name individually, we wish to thank them collectively for their hard work and efforts, which are reflected in this volume.

Over the past 10 years, we have had the opportunity to work with many outstanding individuals. We would like to thank Albert Morales, current managing partner of the IBM Center, and his predecessor, Paul R. Lawrence, for their leadership during this period. We would also like to thank the current staff members of the Center for their support: Ruth M. Gordon, Michael J. Keegan, Lauren B. Kronthal, and Consueline S. Yaba.

We worked with many fine, young professionals who had the opportunity to be assigned to the Center during its first 10 years: Abby Bailes, Susan Mitchell Gunter, Shirley Hsieh, Shana Montesol Johnson, Lily Kim, Amanda Lopez, Corinne Minton-Package, Shelene DeCoster Morgan, and Kirstin Thomas. We thank them for keeping the Center going and for making our work easier.

In preparing this book, we also called upon Curtis Clark, Bruce McConnell, Carl Moravitz, Frank Reeder, Elise Storck, and Solly Thomas to review chapters. We thank them for their insights, which improved this volume. Blattner Brunner's Nancy Carlsen and Eileen Jinks assisted us tremendously in the production of this book. We also received support from our colleagues at Rowman & Littlefield: Ashlee Mills and Jon Sisk.

It was truly a team effort.

Mark A. Abramson

Jonathan D. Breul

John M. Kamensky

G. Martin Wagner

Introduction

The Operator's Manual for the New Administration is written for newly appointed agency heads—those who lead departments, bureaus, or programs—and their senior management teams, consisting of both political and career executives. It is these teams, augmented by an experienced career staff, that must navigate the seemingly endless rules and procedures of government.

This *Operator's Manual* describes the tools available to new agency heads and their management teams that can assist them in implementing their policy and program objectives. We hope that executives, especially those who are new to the public sector, will find *The Operator's Manual* particularly helpful.

Why an Operator's Manual?

The Operator's Manual is a guide to how government works and, more important from the standpoint of executives, how to make it work to advance policy goals and objectives. We present, in brief and simple terms, descriptions of the most important tools and levers that executives can use to advance agency goals and the president's agenda. *The Operator's Manual* will help executives accomplish their objectives. It will help them better understand the terrain of government, become familiar with the terms and lingo used inside agencies, and know how to effectively use the tools of government.

The concept of an operator's manual for government executives is particularly fitting. Like an automobile, the machinery of government exists to fulfill a purpose beyond itself. In the case of government, it is to implement public policy and programs. The machinery of government is a set of systems by which action is undertaken and results are obtained. The parts in a machine move and mesh, and can be replaced or improved. Government executives need to have a basic understanding of these systems.

However, today's federal government operates quite differently from the past. Executives now need an effective set of tools to manage successfully in the 21st century, and that's what *The Operator's Manual* intends to provide. It is aimed at helping executives understand the tools and know how to leverage them to achieve their *goals*. It is also geared to introducing executives to new tools, such as collaboration, which we think will be increasingly used in the years ahead.

What's in *The Operator's Manual*?

The Operator's Manual provides key information on eight important tools for operating in government today. We selected these tools after extensive discussions to assess the essential background information that government executives need to know. By understanding these tools, government executives can use each one effectively to accomplish their agency's goals and objectives. The tools selected and presented in this volume are:

- **Leadership.** Executives must know how to use their leadership abilities to set strategic direction and motivate their organizations.

- **Performance.** Executives must develop a performance framework that enables them to track the progress of their agencies toward achievement of their goals.

- **People.** Executives must build commitment and engage their workforce in order to succeed.

- **Money.** Executives must know how to get resources and smartly manage them.

- **Contracting.** Executives must know how to effectively manage contracts.

- **Technology.** Executives must know how to successfully leverage information technology in their organizations.

- **Innovation.** Executives must know how to foster innovation in their organizations.

- **Collaboration.** Executives must know how to collaborate effectively in order to respond to national problems that require the participation of many sectors.

We do not rank the eight tools in order of importance. Government executives have to pay attention to and work with all of them. None can be ignored. Each tool complements the others. The challenge facing executives is to bring into line all of these tools to achieve their mission.

How to Use *The Operator's Manual*

This volume consists of eight *Memos,* more than 50 questions and answers, and excerpts

Eight Essential Tools for Achieving Your Goals

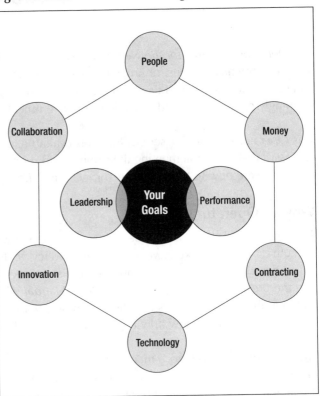

from previously published IBM Center for The Business of Government publications; the IBM Center's magazine, *The Business of Government*; and other publications. Since its creation in 1998, the Center has published more than 200 reports and 17 books. It reflects what we have learned during the past 10 years about managing in government and the major management challenges now facing government executives.

The *Memos* are written in the style of memos that government executives will be receiving from the federal government's central management agencies, such as the Office of Management and Budget. Executives can use this book in several ways. Some might prefer to read all eight *Memos* back-to-back to get an overview of the challenges they face. Others might choose to review an entire chapter based on their interest in specific topics, such as people or contracting. Others might choose to read individual answers to specific questions. A list of questions included in *The Operator's Manual* is presented on pages xiii–xv. All reports that are excerpted in this volume are available in their entirety free of charge at the IBM Center's website: www.businessofgovernment.org. We hope that this volume will be helpful to both new executives coming to Washington in 2009 and experienced executives who are seeking additional insights into managing the operations of government.

A Final Word

The Operator's Manual focuses on the operations of government. A separate volume, *Getting It Done: A Guide for Government Executives,* provides advice on "learning the ropes" and being a successful executive in government. While *The Operator's Manual* deals with the "machinery" of government (such as budgets, personnel, and technology), *Getting It Done* addresses issues related to successfully working and managing in a political environment. We hope that both books will be instructive and useful.

Questions for Newly Appointed Agency Heads Addressed in *The Operator's Manual*

CHAPTER ONE: LEADERSHIP

- What can I learn about leadership and transformation from the experience of James Lee Witt at the Federal Emergency Management Agency? (p. 4)

- What can I learn about leadership and transformation from the experience of Dr. Kenneth Kizer at the Veterans Health Administration, Department of Veterans Affairs? (p. 6)

- What can I learn about leadership and transformation from the experience of Charles Rossotti at the Internal Revenue Service? (p. 8)

- What can I learn about leadership and transformation from the experience of Daniel Goldin at the National Aeronautics and Space Administration? (p. 11)

- What can I learn about leadership and transformation from the experience of Sean O'Keefe at the National Aeronautics and Space Administration? (p. 14)

- What can I learn about leadership from the experience of Dr. Francis Collins, director of the National Human Genome Research Institute at the National Institutes of Health, Department of Health and Human Services? (p. 16)

- How do I develop future leaders? (p. 18)

CHAPTER TWO: PERFORMANCE

- How do I get started on improving performance in my organization? (p. 26)

- After I get started, what are the steps I need to take to ensure successful implementation of performance management in my organization? (p. 28)

- What is a balanced scorecard, and should I consider using it as part of my performance management system? Is it just a private sector tool? (p. 30)

- How do I get my program managers to use outcome information? (p. 34)

- What is program evaluation and how does it differ from performance measurement? How can I use program evaluation? (p. 36)

- I've heard about CompStat and CitiStat. What exactly are these programs and can they be applied to the federal government? (p. 38)

- My organization makes grants to state governments. How can I best engage them in collecting and using performance information? (p. 40)

- Should my organization take the lead in creating a cross-agency measurement system involving several organizations all dealing with a common problem? (p. 42)

- What is Lean Six Sigma and how should I use it? (p. 44)

- What is analytics? Can it be used in my organization? (p. 46)

(continued on pages xiv–xv)

CHAPTER THREE: PEOPLE

- What is workforce planning and should I pay attention to it? (p. 54)

- How do I maximize the use of personnel flexibilities in my own organization? (p. 56)

- What is the difference between performance appraisal and performance management? And how are they both related to pay for performance? (p. 58)

- What is paybanding and is it another tool to transform the organization? Will it help my organization? If I decide to move toward paybanding, how do I go about it? (p. 60)

- What is pay for performance and should I consider it for my organization? (p. 62)

- What are "nonstandard work arrangements" and should I use them in my organization? (p. 66)

- Does government have unions and do I need to spend time on labor relations in my organization? (p. 68)

CHAPTER FOUR: MONEY

- Instead of making budget decisions based on past level of support, is there a way to inject performance information into the budget process? (p. 78)

- My agency, like many other government agencies, is going to have to control its spending more tightly over the next several years. Do you have any suggestions on how we might better control our costs? (p. 80)

- I understand that moving from a "budget control" culture to a "cost management" culture is a major change. Can you tell me more about creating a "cost management" culture? (p. 82)

- I understand that my agency has a number of credit programs that provide loans and loan guarantees. What are some best practices regarding risk management that I should consider? (p. 84)

- I understand that my agency owns some buildings and might have other assets. What can I do to improve my agency's asset management activities? (p. 86)

- As a major provider of grants, what are the key challenges I will face? (p. 88)

CHAPTER FIVE: CONTRACTING

- What are alternative sourcing strategies? I thought my only two alternatives were either to outsource via contract or to continue to perform activities in-house with government employees. (p. 96)

- What is performance-based contracting? What has been the experience of other public sector organizations in using it? (p. 98)

- What is the procurement partnership model? How does it differ from the traditional procurement model? (p. 100)

- What are public-private partnerships? Should I consider them for my organization? (p. 102)

- I understand that competitive sourcing is very controversial. What exactly is it? If I undertake competitive sourcing, what is likely to happen? (p. 104)

Chapter One: Leadership

A key to successfully accomplishing your goals and objectives will be clearly communicating them to a variety of audiences, including both political appointees and civil servants in your own organization.

IBM CENTER FOR THE BUSINESS OF GOVERNMENT
WASHINGTON, DC 20005

MEMORANDUM FOR THE HEADS OF EXECUTIVE DEPARTMENTS AND AGENCIES

SUBJECT: **Leadership**

Your leadership can make all the difference in determining whether you accomplish your goals and objectives.

Effective leaders first gain an understanding of the context of their organization. Understanding the context of your organization includes knowing your mission, stakeholders, constraints, and the political environment facing you.

This *Memo* summarizes 11 leadership lessons that we have learned from observing effective agency heads.

Use different leadership styles. There is no single leadership style on which to rely. You should adjust your own leadership style to the specific situation and environment confronting your organization. There might be times in which the traditional "command and control" leadership style is appropriate, but there are likely to be other times when you will need to practice a more collaborative leadership style. You might also find that your style will need to change as the organization evolves and your external environment changes due to either an anticipated or unanticipated chain of events.

Define and focus on your goals and objectives. In other words, you must define and then tell people what you want to get accomplished. A key to successfully accomplishing your goals and objectives will be clearly communicating them to a variety of audiences, including both political appointees and civil servants in your own organization. Another key will be your ability to focus on a defined set of goals and to avoid being distracted by secondary issues or activities.

Articulate a strategy for moving forward. Everybody will be looking to you for how to act on the organization's mission and vision. Articulating a forward-looking strategy that bridges the gap between policy and action will help ensure that the organization is doing what you want it to be doing. A clear strategy provides a map of how you and your leadership team get to where you want to go, given constraints within your operating environment and the resources available.

Engage employees. Employees have much to offer the organization via their ideas, including innovations, to improve the performance of the agency's programs and activities. Former Internal Revenue Service Commissioner Charles Rossotti suggests that you should develop a policy of "engaging people and then deciding" rather than the traditional practice of "decide, then explain." You will be able to learn much about your agency by going out and listening and engaging with people, especially those on the front lines.

Put customers first. Your agency serves the public. Get out and talk with your agency's customers. Ensure all customers have a voice and that every voice is heard. You will learn surprising things your employees and stakeholders may not tell you. Encourage your senior managers to do the same. Recent technologies allow new ways to constructively engage with your customers. Use them.

Involve key stakeholders. In a similar approach to engaging employees, you must launch an active outreach program to meet with the stakeholders of your organization—interest groups, congressional staff members, and partners (such as nonprofit and private sector companies) with whom your organization collaborates. Include both your advocates and adversaries. The more time spent on outreach will make your job easier in both the long and short term. While you will be tempted to devote more time to players outside of the executive branch of government, don't underestimate the importance of building sound working relationships with key appointees in other agencies both inside and outside of your own department.

Seize the moment. The simple fact about serving as a political appointee is that you do not know from the outset how long you will have the opportunity to serve. You might be asked to serve in another position as the administration matures or you might leave government. Thus, an essential lesson from leaders is that you must "seize the moment" and take full advantage of the environment now surrounding your organization. You must take advantage of the moment and move as quickly as you can to implement your goals and objectives.

Communicate, communicate, and communicate. Leaders emphasize the importance of placing a high priority on communication from day one of their tenure. A major insight from the IBM Center profiles and interviews with leaders is that while all felt they did try to communicate and thought they were reaching their intended audience, nearly all felt in retrospect that they needed to communicate more both in quantity and frequency. The lesson learned is that one announcement or meeting is unlikely to get the job done. As in advertising, repetition is crucial to getting your message out. Leaders find that many employees in their agencies will likely become uncomfortable because change creates uncertainty regarding their future. You must be sensitive to this phenomenon and repeatedly meet with employees (as well as stakeholders) to answer all of their questions and attempt to alleviate concerns to the extent possible.

Create alignment. A key element of leadership is "putting it all together." The accomplishment of your goals and objectives will depend on your ability to align the people in your organization around effective business practices, technology, and organizational structure. Based on your analysis of how well your organization is aligned structurally, you may conclude that reorganization is necessary. We caution you, however, to reorganize as a last resort. Reorganizations are time-consuming, frustrating, and likely to meet with resistance from both inside and outside of your organization.

Expect the unexpected. While you will have your plan in place for the coming years, it is likely that an unexpected event will occur which will require that you adapt and adjust your game plan to new realities and situations. You will need to be resilient in your capacity to overcome obstacles and unexpected problems as they arise.

"Stick with it." None of the above will be easy. You are likely to face opposition that may disagree with your goals and objectives. While you may not know exactly how long you will serve, you must plan for the long term and persevere in your quest for the transformation of your organization. In describing former Under Secretary Ken Kizer's experience in transforming the Veterans Health Administration, Boston University's Gary Young writes, "No transformation will be perfect, and those who oppose the changes will seek to exploit flaws or limitations to derail the effort. Leaders of transformation need to be responsive to legitimate criticisms, but they also must avoid being swallowed up in technical details."

REVITALIZING THE FEDERAL EMERGENCY MANAGEMENT AGENCY

QUESTION: What can I learn about leadership and transformation from the experience of James Lee Witt at the Federal Emergency Management Agency (FEMA)?

ANSWER: James Lee Witt took over FEMA in the early 1990s after a decade in which the performance of the agency was severely criticized. In the aftermath of Hurricane Andrew in 1992, several members of Congress called for the abolishment of the agency.

In their report to the IBM Center, California State University, Bakersfield's R. Steven Daniels and the late Carolyn Clark-Daniels examined the FEMA experience and developed the following lessons:

- **Experience counts—recruit the best.** When appointed, James Lee Witt became the first head of FEMA with prior experience in emergency management. He had served as the head of the emergency management agency in Arkansas.

- **Clarify your mission.** FEMA historically had two diverse missions: emergency management and national preparedness (in response to a nuclear attack). Under Witt, the agency redefined the agency's primary target population to be disaster victims and placed increased focus on its emergency management role.

- **Structure your agency to reflect the agency's mission.** After the mission was clarified, Director Witt redesigned the agency's structure to reflect its emphasis on emergency management regardless of what causes the emergency. Separate directorates were created for Preparedness, Mitigation, and Response and Recovery.

- **Leverage the White House.** Because of its ineffectiveness during the late 1980s and early 1990s, FEMA had become a clear political liability. Because of this, White House support was sought by Witt and received for major changes in the agency. If the consequence of failure in your agency is high (such as the political aftermath following Hurricane Katrina), you will have more leverage with the White House.

- **Use your career staff.** From the beginning of his tenure, Witt concluded that the support of his career staff was crucial to the transformation of FEMA and regaining its credibility. Several key positions went to career officials, and Witt emphasized the importance of his political team and career team working closely together.

- **Don't be afraid of the press.** Director Witt also recognized that it was crucial for the agency to regain its credibility among citizens, as well as stakeholders such as state and local governments. Because of this, he launched a vigorous outreach effort to the press to communicate FEMA changes and its increased capacity and capability to respond to national emergencies.

- **Provide governmental and non-governmental partners a stake in the outcome.** Witt also recognized that the federal government was only one actor in the national emergency network, consisting of state and local governments, the private sector, and the nonprofit sector. In his report to the IBM Center, Georgia State University's William Waugh describes FEMA's increased focus on mitigation, the effort to prevent losses rather than simply being reactive and focusing on disaster recovery. As part of this initiative, Witt created a "safe construction" network consisting of nonprofit organizations (such as the American Red Cross), private sector members (the building and insurance industries), universities, other government organizations (the Agriculture Extension Service), and state and local government organizations.

An Interview with James Lee Witt
Former Director, Federal Emergency Management Agency

From *Transforming Government: The Renewal and Revitalization of the Federal Emergency Management Agency* by R. Steven Daniels and Carolyn L. Clark-Daniels

This interview was conducted when James Lee Witt was director of FEMA.

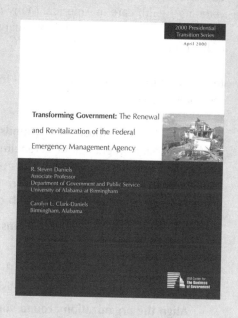

In your role as administrator of the Federal Emergency Management Agency, how do you define your job?

I found that the job came with a lot of responsibility, and I have taken the job very seriously. Shortly after assuming office, I undertook two major initiatives. First, I worked within the agency to strengthen it. I wanted to involve employees in the future of the agency. Second, I refocused the organization on the customer by placing emphasis on those we were serving externally.

As a new agency head, it was my job to describe where FEMA needed to go. After describing where we wanted to go, it was my job to involve the entire organization. I wanted employee input into how we could best meet our goals because I strongly believe in involving our people. I met with FEMA's senior managers during a three-day retreat in which I described where I thought the agency was heading.

Can you tell us more about your efforts to involve your employees?

I made a special effort to visit with employees, both at headquarters and in the regions. I am constantly asking them what they think we should be doing. I also developed an open-door policy: Any employee can make an appointment to see me on Tuesdays to discuss any matter.

How are you transforming FEMA?

As I mentioned before, a major part of the transformation was getting all employees involved. We worked hard at creating a more customer-focused agency. A major initiative was to provide customer service training to all FEMA employees, including senior management. This was a huge undertaking. Our goal was to make FEMA a better agency, a better place to work, and an agency that provided better service to its customers. We were very pleased that our latest customer survey found that over 85 percent of our clients approved of our programs. Another aspect of managing change is constant communication to employees. You have to keep employees informed. I have a director's report that goes out weekly. I have received a very positive response to it. The report, two to three pages in length, describes what is going on in the agency and how we are doing in meeting our goals for the agency.

At the same time that we were involving employees, we were also improving the operations of the agency. We decreased the number of our financial accounts from 45 to 14. We simply had too many accounts. We have also moved to quarterly spending plans, which was a major change from the past when we never quite knew how much money we had remaining. I am now holding our senior managers responsible for their spending. In addition, I'm working closely with our chief financial officer in overseeing the agency's financial management systems. All of our changes at FEMA were based on my trusting my managers. I trusted my people to make the agency work. I gave them authority to do their jobs and I resisted the temptation to micro-manage.

TRANSFORMING THE VETERANS HEALTH ADMINISTRATION

QUESTION: What can I learn about leadership and transformation from the experience of Dr. Kenneth Kizer at the Veterans Health Administration (VHA), Department of Veterans Affairs?

ANSWER: Dr. Kizer took over the VHA in 1994 during a period of intense controversy about the future of veterans' health care in America. Many felt that the agency was out of sync with the prevailing trends in the delivery of health care. In addition, many veterans and many in Congress were dissatisfied with the quality of health care provided by VHA.

In his report to the IBM Center, Boston University's Gary Young examined the VHA experience and developed the following lessons:

- **Appoint leaders whose backgrounds and experiences are appropriate for the transformation.** There was clear agreement that VHA required a transformation. In selecting Kizer, the White House recruited a leader who had experience transforming organizations. Kizer had previously led the California Department of Health Services during a time of change. He also was an expert in innovation related to the financing and delivery of health care services.

- **Follow a focused and coherent transformation plan.** There were four components to Dr. Kizer's transformation plan:

  - **Create a vision for the agency.** This resulted in a series of documents that described the vision and the agency's game plan for accomplishing the vision.

  - **Align the organization around your goals and objective.** Kizer concluded that he could not get "from here to there" with the VHA structure he inherited, which resulted in a new organizational structure for the agency.

  - **Establish an accountability system.** Each of the members of Kizer's leadership team signed a performance contract that stipulated a set of performance goals to which she or he would be held accountable.

  - **Modify agency rules and regulations.** As with the need for a new organizational structure, the leadership team also concluded that the agency needed reforms to a number of long-standing agency rules and regulations.

- **Persevere in the presence of imperfection.** Many of the components of VHA's transformation plan indeed proved to be controversial, with some opposition to the changes within the organization.

- **Match changes in the external environment with changes in the internal environment.** Kizer and his management team worked closely with veterans service organizations and key members of Congress to gain support for his reforms.

- **Develop and manage communication channels from the highest to the lowest levels of the organization.** This is one area in which VHA could have performed more effectively. Communication is crucial during a transformation.

- **Do not overlook training and education.** In his analysis of the VHA experience, Young concluded that training was a key component in gaining the support of employees and assisting them in developing needed skills in a timely manner during the transformation.

- **Balance system-wide unity with operating-unit flexibility.** This is always a challenge: The organization must strike an appropriate balance between system-level coordination and control and operating-unit flexibility.

Kenneth W. Kizer's Key Principles of Transformation

From *Transforming Government: The Revitalization
of the Veterans Health Administration* by Gary J. Young

LEADERSHIP

*Dr. Kizer served as under secretary for health at the Department of
Veterans Affairs. He originally set forth his key principles in* Straight
from the CEO, *edited by G. W. Dauphinais and C. Price (New York:
Simon & Schuster, 1998). The excerpt below is based on Gary
Young's report.*

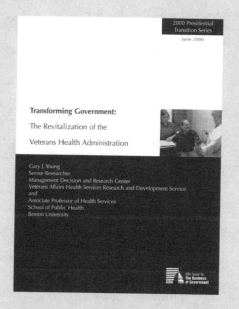

1. **Clearly articulate your vision, intent, and principles of change.**
   The VHA's statement is about "why," not "how." With a clear
   end-purpose in mind, we used certain principles of modern
   health care to lay the framework for transformation at the VHA,
   as well as the new managerial system that would implement it:

   - The VHA is in the business of health care, not of running
     hospitals.

   - Health care is now primarily a local outpatient activity.

   - The VHA's critical mandate is to provide good value.

   - Health care must reorient itself to become more population-
     directed, community-based, and health-promotive.

2. **The process of change should be broadly inclusive.** The top manager should allow all members of the
   organization to have their say in some form or forum—and what they say should be taken seriously and
   sincerely. However, that inclusivity should be flexible enough to embrace partnerships and outside asso-
   ciations that can facilitate the new vision.

3. **Change within an organization must move in harmony with environmental or externally focused
   change.** Top managers, particularly those in the public sector, cannot hope to stand against the
   "forces of nature"—this constitutes bad management. In the case of the VHA, that means being in sync
   with broad trends, such as the national revolution in health care, the explosion of biomedical research
   and knowledge, the shift to an "information society," and the aging of the eligible VHA population.

4. **The top manager must make key personnel decisions.** Bad hires stay around to haunt you; good ones
   make you look good. Here are seven key characteristics of the good hire: committed to change; shares
   the vision; experienced, knowledgeable; innovative, nontraditional; respected; empowered; and willing
   to get his or her hands dirty.

5. **Set high expectations.** People will meet them—unless your system impedes their best efforts.

6. **Focus on rigorous execution, including minimizing errors.** Innovative, nontraditional thinkers will make
   errors because errors are inherent to trailblazing. These should be openly discussed without instilling the
   kind of fear that engenders complacency. However, stupid, careless mistakes should not be tolerated.

7. **Anticipate problems.** Change, by definition, is rarely neutral. It will create new problems—but they
   shouldn't come as a surprise.

RESTRUCTURING THE INTERNAL REVENUE SERVICE

QUESTION: What can I learn about leadership and transformation from the experience of Charles Rossotti at the Internal Revenue Service (IRS)?

ANSWER: Charles Rossotti served as commissioner of the IRS from 1997 to 2002, serving under two presidents of the United States. He took over shortly after a series of congressional hearings in which the IRS was criticized heavily for both ineffectiveness and accusations by citizens of abuse of its authority. IRS had also been intensely scrutinized (and criticized) by the National Commission on Restructuring the Internal Revenue Service, which resulted in legislation to reform the agency.

In his memoir, *Many Unhappy Returns: One Man's Quest to Turn Around the Most Unpopular Organization in America* (Boston: Harvard Business School Press, 2005), Rossotti reflected on what he had learned from the IRS experience. He wrote, "The most important conclusion I can draw from my experience is that it is wrong to assume that a big, entrenched institution that gets into deep trouble cannot be changed for the better. The crisis can be turned into an opportunity. If it is important to do, it can be done." Specifically, Rossotti sets forth the following ingredients for successful transformations:

- **Successful change means improving the way an organization performs its missions on behalf of all of its stakeholders and rejecting an either/or model of performance.** At IRS, Rossotti worked to improve both service and treatment of taxpayers as well as the organization's effectiveness in enforcing compliance with the law.

- **Successful change means getting the right people in the right jobs.** Rossotti put together his team at IRS, which included senior executives from the private sector as well as senior career officials within IRS.

- **Successful change requires the right measurements and incentives.** Rossotti developed a balanced set of measurements for IRS that included feedback from taxpayers and employees, as well as measures of business results.

- **Successful change depends on aligning people, business practices, technology, and organizational structure with the needs of customers.** Rossotti developed a modernization program that addressed all four components.

- **Successful change requires knowing what is really going on where it counts—at the front line.** Rossotti made it a practice to visit IRS offices across the nation to speak directly to IRS frontline workers.

- **Successful change requires open and honest communication inside and outside the organization.** Rossotti writes, "Throughout the change program, I established a policy of 'engage, and then decide' rather than 'decide, and then explain' with stakeholders, including dozens of groups representing taxpayers and employees, congressional committees, and oversight bodies."

- **Successful change requires change, not just communication about change.** After arriving at IRS, Rossotti found that the agency was preoccupied with issuing announcements "about change" but lacked a transformation plan to bring about those changes. Rossotti quickly developed the plan.

- **Successful change depends more on having the right governance, leadership, direction, and authority than on rules and mandates.** Rossotti concludes that effective governance can only be achieved by "well-informed, competent, and diligent people paying serious and sustained attention to the health of the organization, not by the quantity of audits and procedures."

- **Successful change in any organization has its limits—set by the broader constraints of the context within which it operates.**

A Conversation with Charles Rossotti
Former Commissioner, Internal Revenue Service

From *The Business of Government,* Winter 2002

On Arriving at IRS

The first thing to remember is that because of the confirmation process, you have a long windup period, whether you like it or not. I tried to make best use of that period to … take the lay of the land, meet some people, and read a lot of things.…

I had an interview with a bunch of reporters … and I said it was like coming in from a beautiful fall day and then opening a door and having a blast furnace hit you.… it wasn't so much the blast furnace from inside the IRS, as it was all these blasts coming from everywhere else into the IRS. It was definitely a period of crisis in terms of the agency.

One of the things that was evident to me right off the bat was that the IRS was getting a lot of advice.… there were so many studies that had been done over the years … the Vice President's Reinventing Government had done a study, the Presidential Commission had done a study, and there were any number of GAO [Government Accountability Office] reports that had done studies.

I had somebody add up all the recommendations that had been made, and by the time they got to 5,000, I stopped counting. I said, "We're not going to get where we need to go by doing 5,000 line items one at a time.…"

The very first thing that had to be done was to create a sense of stability and say that what we're going to do is sit down and set some priorities … [identifying] some of the things we're going to do—a few things we're going to really do in the short run—to get the place going.

There were a few things that were under way in the problem-solving days … there was a need to have a safety valve to allow people who were coming forward every day and claiming that they were being unable to get their problems resolved, that their lives were being ruined by the IRS. We had to have an outlet for that. There were some other things like

that, which had to be done on a short-term basis. Then the other thing—on a longer-term basis— was to set some strategic priorities over what we were going to do to address the more fundamental problems in an organized way.…

I put it together into a set of priorities of what we needed to do in terms of modernizing the organization, the management structure, and eventually the technology. Those were the initial things: try to get some short-term stability; concentrate on a few things that we could deliver right away; and then try to lay out … a longer-term plan for addressing the bigger issues.

On the Need for Reorganization

[Reorganization] was a little bit controversial in the sense that it is a pretty expensive, disruptive thing to do and it doesn't immediately deliver any benefits to anybody. The question was, why focus on something like that, which is more internal than external. That was a pretty big choice.

… from what I know today … it was the right decision. One of the reasons I believe previous attempts at modernizing the technology … did not go very well was precisely because they were viewed as a technology program. There are a lot of people in a lot of places, including the government, that make the mistake that you can "modernize the technology" and leave everything else the same.

… there isn't any point in modernizing technology if you leave everything else the same.… If you just keep everything the same and modernize the technology, you have some new disk drives and maybe more reliable computing, but you don't really resolve anything. On the other hand, if you're going to put in technology to improve the way the business works, you can't be isolated in the IT area.…

If nothing else, getting control over the information system resources [was essential] in order to create an appropriate level of standardization and management to set the groundwork for reorganization.... One [reason for modernization] is to have a business owner that was properly aligned to be their customer, the proper customer to be the partner in modernizing the way business is done; and the other being to modernize the IT operations itself so that we had an appropriate management structure to manage it.

On His Role Leading IRS

It is different compared to being a CEO in business, because [there] you have to work with investors and securities analysts and the general public and the press, but it's a much smaller factor as compared with your customers and your employees.... in any public agency, especially one like the IRS, we have a multitude of stakeholders, including six congressional committees that oversee us....

We have, in addition to those governmental stakeholders, an enormous array of stakeholders [in the public]. In fact, everybody in the economy is a stakeholder ... [and] they're organized into a lot of different groups. We have numerous practitioner groups like the AICPA [American Institute of Certified Public Accountants] and the CPAs, we have many business groups like small-business groups, large-business groups, industry groups.... People forget that we [also] regulate the tax-exempt sector, which is a whole world unto itself with its own set of issues.

One of the jobs of the commissioner is to try to not only recognize those interests, but to keep people aligned as much as you can; to keep yourself aligned and to keep aligned with them in a way that is constructive, because one thing for sure is that almost any of them can slow you down or stop you in your tracks or really make life difficult if they want to....

So that is an extremely important role ... it's certainly one that takes a lot of time. But I'll say this—it takes a lot more time if you don't tend to it, because then what you have is the unplanned time that you didn't count on.... My view has been to try to get a clear set of messages of what we're trying to do, and basically ... we tell the same thing to everybody, because I can't see how you can tell one person one thing and tell somebody something else. If you do that, you're not going to get anywhere.

On the Differences Between Management in the Public and Private Sectors

I think there are a lot of things that are similar.... There are [also] some things that are different. And one of them, of course, is the public visibility that you have. You really are operating in a fish bowl, and that is something that is a unique management challenge. Because one of the implications of that is the question, "How do you handle mistakes?...There is never going to be a major systems project, even small systems project, that doesn't have blind alleys and mistakes and false starts, and there just isn't ever going to be one no matter how skilled you are. The kind we're doing at the IRS, which is a rare one where you're sort of replacing the whole infrastructure as well as specific applications, is obviously pretty complex.

So how do you handle mistakes?... In the private sector world, you have them and you react to them and you do whatever you want to do. Here [in government], you've got to deal with them in the environment where you've got everybody watching you and writing about your mistakes while it happens. So, that's a ... challenge that's certainly unique.

Another thing is that you have more rules [in government]. And that's not only true of technical modernization, that's true of everything. You have personnel rules, you have procurement rules, you have budgeting rules. You have rules for just about everything....

LEADERSHIP

REMAKING THE NATIONAL AERONAUTICS AND SPACE ADMINISTRATION

QUESTION: What can I learn about leadership and transformation from the experience of Daniel Goldin at the National Aeronautics and Space Administration (NASA)?

ANSWER: Dan Goldin had the longest tenure of any NASA administrator since the creation of the agency in 1958, serving for nine and a half years under two presidents of the United States. Over that nine-year period, Goldin dealt with numerous controversial issues and problems, such as repairing the Hubble telescope, finding funding for the International Space Station, and responding to several mission to Mars failures. In his report to the IBM Center (2001), Syracuse University's W. Henry Lambright set forth seven lessons based on his case study of the Goldin years at NASA:

- **Who is appointed the agency executive matters.** The key to success in many agencies is matching up both the leader and his or her leadership team with the challenges facing the agency. In the case of Goldin, the agency clearly needed a change agent and a change agenda. Lambright writes, "He was a good match for the organization and his times."

- **Make the most of a mandate for change.** There was agreement that NASA needed change. There was much unhappiness with NASA in Congress. Goldin used this "mandate" to push significant policy and management changes within NASA during his tenure.

- **Adopt a general strategy of what needs to be done.** In simple terms, this means having a plan and a set of priorities. Prior to his confirmation hearings, Goldin used that time to talk with knowledgeable individuals about NASA and to determine a strategy and a plan for bringing change to the agency.

- **Implement a change process quickly, instilling urgency and gaining as much organizational support as possible.** You will need to use your judgment here. A key factor in your success (or lack of success) will be your ability to move quickly and urgently—while at the same time gaining support for change among your management team and the larger organization. You will be walking a fine line between pushing hard, but yet not "too hard" and alienating your workforce.

- **Turn crisis into opportunity.** A crisis can indeed be helpful to you. In the case of Goldin, he had numerous crises (the future of the space station, the Hubble telescope) that he could "use" to push his change agenda. Lambright writes, "Crisis allows the leader to pull power up to himself. Because he spans the boundary across organization and environment, he is in a strategic position to seize the initiative. He can use a crisis to go beyond incremental to radical change."

- **Build on success.** In football, they call this "putting points on the board." It is often useful to put together some "small wins" quickly in order to both build credibility for yourself and to gain momentum.

- **Be aware of the limits of change and modify strategies when flaws are detected—preferably before they lead to setbacks.** If you stay for the entire four years of the first term of the new administration (or longer), you will most likely encounter some failures along the way. Lambright cautions, "The aim is to minimize the failures through realism.... It is also to learn from mistakes and make timely corrections in hardware, management, and, if need be, the [leader's] personal style in dealing with the agency."

A Conversation with Daniel S. Goldin, Former Administrator National Aeronautics and Space Administration

From *The Business of Government,* Fall 2001

On His Major Accomplishment at NASA

Freeing up the NASA people to dream, telling them that failure is okay in spite of the constant hammering they take. I remember early in my tenure, I was going home at about 9 o'clock, 9:30 at night. There were still offices lit at NASA headquarters and, contrary to popular belief, federal employees are terrific. They work long, hard hours, and it's very easy to take shots at them, and with NASA, it's an even bigger bull's-eye.

One of NASA's employees said to me, "I'm so depressed. The harder I work, the more we get criticized." And I said to him, "There is a new kid in town. You'll work hard, you'll get criticized, but you'll have fun because failure will be acceptable and you can dream again."

And I feel, based upon what NASA has done, the employees are really dreaming. That in my mind is more important than anything else. There were good people at NASA before I came, there are good people there now, and there will be outstanding people when I leave.

All that a leader can do is create an environment, pick good people, nurture and train those people, and support the hell out of those people and take personal responsibility for the problems so those people aren't afraid to fail. That in my mind is the most enjoyable thing that I had at NASA.

On Arriving at NASA

I felt that NASA, in a very honest attempt to deal with their environment, had gone into a survival mode. What was important then was how many jobs did people win in what part of the country—rather than what those jobs were about—and that more and more their budget was going into operations in near-term things because of the criticism over the *Challenger,* the Hubble being blind, *Galileo* being deaf, and I could go on and on.

People lost their confidence and were doing more and more mundane things. The space station was

dead man walking. They spent $8 billion or $10 billion in eight years. There wasn't a piece of hardware, but the contractors were having a good time. I could cry.

So I resolved that I would free up NASA employees from these burdens and try and get a process in place that would focus on performance, not style, that would focus on what needs to be done to fix things instead of putting our heads in the sand and transitioning NASA from near-term safe things into long-term high-risk things.

On Risk-Taking at NASA

… the most important message I wanted to get … failure is good. Failure is really the process that you learn.

… 10 out of 10 failures is bad. On the other hand, zero out of 10 failures is worse, zero failures out of 10 attempts, because if you tried 10 things and had zero failures you set such mediocre goals you don't deserve being part of the space program. Getting that message across was the fundamental essence of what faster, better, cheaper was, and I came with this passion to do it.

If you have a few big things managed by a few powerful individuals, you suppress the creative process. Second, if you have a few big things managed by a few powerful individuals, you are terrified of failure because you risk the whole program.

So the concept of faster, better, cheaper that's not well understood is to get a large number, a diversity in number and function, so no one failure takes you down, and then to empower a broad range of people and develop the next generation and create competition of ideas, not emotions, within the organization.

On Accountability

Hyman Rickover was criticized for his success, but he had as a statement … that fundamentally you don't know who is responsible unless you can take your finger and point at that person and that person says "I'm responsible."

And one of the problems I had when I arrived at NASA, I tried to find out who was responsible for anything. People do a wonderful job and, again, these are good people. These are not bad people. But people were so afraid of failure no one wanted to say I'm responsible when something occurred.

So I decided I would tell them hey, look, when there is a major problem don't worry. The administrator will say he's responsible. I have a letter of resignation in my desk and the very minute it's necessary because I serve the American people I'm ready to go. I won't fight to stay. You've got to have the ability to do that, and once you do that everything is okay.

© 2001 IBM Center for The Business of Government

On Working with Congress

… the big lesson that I learned out of this job is we have a wonderful democracy. From the outside looking in, you don't see how well it works. And a democracy doesn't need everyone supporting you, and you don't need cheerleaders to make a democracy work. In fact, you need skeptics.

So if you go to the hearings—I go up on the Hill— we don't have cheerleaders. I could assure you that, but that's good. That's not bad. And in fact there is a story that I recollect. We faced the senator from Arkansas, Dale Bumpers. I mean, he got pretty graphic on the floor of the Senate about how upset he was with the space station.

And after the next to the last vote before he left the Congress I had been looming outside the Senate chambers watching the vote. And I walked up to him and I said, "How are you doing, Senator Bumpers?" He said, "Dan, you're talking to me?" I said, "Yes." He said, "I always go after the space station." I said, "Senator Bumpers, do you know what you don't realize? More than anyone else, with your criticism of the space station you have made us more determined to do a better job."

And people always think of the debate up on Capitol Hill as being bad. It's good. Go to some other countries and see where everyone talks together and votes together, and you lose the ability for a democracy.

Having the open press, having the press criticize us, it gets depressing for the employees, but I keep telling them this is good; this is not bad. Because if you believe in what you're doing, deeply believe in what you're doing, you have a passion for what you're doing. You're not doing this to get promoted. You're not doing this to get a job after you leave the government. You're doing this for the benefit of the American people. You could stand up to the criticism, and the criticism makes you better.

Now, that takes an enormous amount of time, but that's called listening to your customer, and it is the job of the NASA administrator to understand what the customer wants. Now, the customer is the American people. I can't talk to each American person, but by talking to all of their representatives in the Congress and going to the districts and meeting with people, I got a sense of what the American people wanted and expected from NASA.

On Working in a Public Environment

It's more difficult than running a corporation without that glare…. I don't think there is any other place that has the kind of scrutiny that NASA does…. I would stack our employees against any corporation in the world, because they have a thick skin because of the public scrutiny…. this is a system full of checks and balances and don't fight the checks and balances.

CHANGING LEADERSHIP STYLES AT THE NATIONAL AERONAUTICS AND SPACE ADMINISTRATION

QUESTION: What can I learn about leadership and transformation from the experience of Sean O'Keefe at the National Aeronautics and Space Administration?

ANSWER: The major lesson from the O'Keefe years at NASA is that you will be living in a rapidly changing environment in which the unexpected might (or is likely to) happen. In his report to the IBM Center (2005), W. Henry Lambright found that O'Keefe's three years at NASA could be divided into three distinct periods, each being characterized by a different set of challenges:

- **Period One: As consolidator and incremental innovator.** When he first arrived at NASA, O'Keefe's initial challenge was responding to the projected cost-overruns of the International Space Station. O'Keefe's experience as the deputy director of the Office of Management and Budget in the first year of the administration had prepared him to fix the accounting and management practices within NASA.

- **Period Two: As crisis manager.** In February 2003 (a little over one year after O'Keefe became NASA administrator), the *Columbia* shuttle came apart and seven astronauts died. Lambright writes, "O'Keefe, the self-effacing financial manager, was immediately thrust into the national spotlight. He had to respond to a major disaster."

- **Period Three: As steward of the president's vision.** The last year of O'Keefe's tenure was spent implementing the president's "space exploration vision" to the moon, Mars, and beyond.

Thus, O'Keefe's tenure is characterized by an ability to rapidly shift from managing in one situation to managing in a dramatically different environment. The key lesson, according to Lambright, is that managers must be prepared for the unexpected. Key leadership lessons can be gleaned from each of O'Keefe's periods:

- **Period One:** In this period, O'Keefe was "Mr. Fix-it." In that role, the following lessons are instructive:

    - **Mitigate the immediate problem, but monitor the solution over time.** O'Keefe's initial priority was fixing the space station cost over-run (and NASA's credibility), which he did.

    - **Communicate a vision.** While focusing on "fixing" problems, O'Keefe also presented his programmatic vision for the agency, which stressed a scientific role in NASA exploration.

    - **Deal with the next worst problem.**

- **Period Two:** In this period, O'Keefe was nearly a full-time "crisis manager" focused on determining the cause of the *Columbia* tragedy and then making appropriate changes in NASA based on findings from the Columbia Accident Investigation Board (CAIB). Lessons from this period include:

    - **Take charge of a crisis—be decisive, open, and consistent.**

    - **Use crisis to leverage transformative change.**

- **Period Three:** In this period, O'Keefe's management challenge was implementing the vision set forth by the president in his January 2004 speech. Lessons from this period include:

    - **Get a presidential policy off to a fast start.** If your agency becomes a presidential priority, you will clearly need to devote a significant amount of your attention to ensuring that the policy is successfully implemented.

    - **Avoid distractions.** This will be a challenge throughout your time in government. It is easy to get distracted by side issues and you must continue to focus on the priorities of the president.

Turning Crisis into Opportunity

From *Executive Response to Changing Fortune: Sean O'Keefe as NASA Administrator*
by W. Henry Lambright

If there was any silver lining coming from the *Columbia* cloud, it was that there was a new consensus that NASA needed change, and O'Keefe was able to push change related to safety. He was setting up the new Engineering and Safety Center at Langley as a check on the program offices. He had the Stafford-Covey group, now grown to 26 strong…. He hired a well-known consulting organization to help him with the longer-term and deeper cultural change that CAIB said was needed at NASA. He said he would borrow a culture-change technique from the Marine Corps called "repeated rhythmic insult." All these moves aimed at enhancing the power of safety interests at NASA.

But now O'Keefe saw the chance for even broader change—transformation—linked to the call for a new vision from Congress, media, and many of his own advisors. CAIB said that an underlying problem causing the *Columbia* disaster was NASA's attempt to do too much with too little in the way of funding. The shuttle budget had been particularly squeezed as NASA sought to build a space station, pursue a viable space science effort, and create a shuttle successor launch system—all at a time of overall agency downsizing. The funding problem was due to the absence of a "compelling vision" of the future. To risk human lives to go into low Earth orbit just didn't seem worth it. In fact, this call for a new vision suggested to O'Keefe a window of opportunity for long-term NASA recovery.

O'Keefe now pursued two kinds of recovery strategies. One was short term: return to flight of the shuttle. Unfortunately, even the short-term plans were beginning to stretch longer. In early October, it was reported that instead of spring 2004, the shuttle might not go up until September 2004. CAIB had set forth 29 requirements NASA had to meet, and what NASA did would be reviewed by the Stafford-Covey team. Some of these requirements were technical changes to be surmounted before return to flight; others could happen later. Many would be difficult indeed, such as the capacity to repair the shuttle in space, particularly away from the space station. Cultural change fell into the very long-term, non-technical recovery mode.

But real long-term recovery also required a goal that would give NASA greater public support and additional funds, the opportunity to go beyond recovery to revitalization. What should that be? In the 1990s, Dan Goldin, O'Keefe's predecessor, championed a manned Mars mission as NASA's next big goal. But he could not sell that to the Clinton White House and he did not particularly try to do so. The Clinton administration would support only unmanned Mars flights. First, said President Clinton, finish the space station; then we'll discuss more distant human spaceflights.

The senior George Bush had proclaimed moon-Mars as a goal back in 1989, but that objective disappeared quickly from his and the nation's agenda. From the standpoint of congressional and public opinion, such a goal was premature and dismissed by most observers as empty rhetoric. O'Keefe felt the *Columbia* accident made a big decision that might adhere this time more possible. In 1989, there was no space station. In the 1990s, one had been built and orbited the Earth. There was much more work to do on the station, but the end was in sight. A space station in orbit was the major achievement of Goldin, albeit over cost and incomplete. O'Keefe had in his first year presented a modest agenda. He now decided the time was ripe to try for a big decision.

LEADING OTHERS INVOLVED IN THE HUMAN GENOME PROJECT

QUESTION: What can I learn about leadership from the experience of Dr. Francis Collins, director of the National Human Genome Research Institute at the National Institutes of Health (NIH), Department of Health and Human Services?

ANSWER: In many ways, Dr. Francis Collins represents a new type of leader in government. In addition to leading his own organization (initially, the National Center for Human Genome Research and later "upgraded" to full institute status as the National Human Genome Research Institute), Collins led an international coalition consisting of other government organizations, the private sector, and the academic community. Nearly one-third of funding for the Human Genome Project (HGP) came from the Department of Energy, requiring close coordination between NIH and Energy. Funding was also provided by the Wellcome Trust, a philanthropy in England that became a joint sponsor of the project. In addition, Collins developed an effective working relationship with J. Craig Venter, head of the private sector firm Celera, in what was often viewed as a "race" between the public and private sectors to sequence the human genome. Partners from other nations were involved in the project as well.

Collins thus faced the challenge of not only leading within his own agency but also leading many other key organizations that did not "report" to him. In his report to the IBM Center (2002), W. Henry Lambright sets forth the following key lessons from the experience of Collins in leading the Human Genome Project:

- **The importance of leadership.** Leadership was crucial. Collins faced the challenge of reorienting HGP from a loose consortium into a tight alliance with a small circle of performers and decision makers. Instead of relying on the traditional "command and control" leadership style, Collins relied on a more collegial, collaborative style of leadership.

- **The importance of goals.** In describing his experience leading the Human Genome Project, Collins frequently cites the importance of goals in the success of the project (see page 17). Lambright concurs with Collins' assessment that large projects need clear, unmistakable goals. Lambright writes that a clear goal "provides a constant point of reference against which to measure, direct, prioritize, and modify actions by various individuals and organizations involved."

- **The importance of political support.** In any government endeavor, political support is crucial. NIH leadership, including the NIH director and Collins, worked closely with the White House and Congress in gaining support and continued funding for HGP.

- **The importance of management.** The management of the Human Genome Project was a major challenge. The way in which government would pursue HGP was not clear at the start. It constantly evolved over the years, starting with funding by the Department of Energy followed by the designation of NIH as the "lead agency" for HGP. For most of its project life, HGP was managed as a loosely coupled international consortium located in six countries, with multiple sponsors and performers. After assuming leadership of the project, Collins concluded that the management of the genome project was too loose and too uncoupled. He then developed a more centralized management model.

- **The importance of competition.** Lambright concludes that competition, both internal and external, was a critical factor in HGP's success. It was initially bureaucratic competition with the Department of Energy that induced NIH to launch HGP. The external competition came from Celera. With the addition of Celera in the game, HGP moved into "crash project mode" and Celera became the measure against which HGP would be judged. Lambright writes, "Whether or not HGP wished to be in a race, it was in one."

A Conversation with Dr. Francis S. Collins, Director, National Human Genome Research Institute, National Institutes of Health

From *The Business of Government,* Winter 2002

On 'Managing' Talent

What helps in terms of managing ... was the unquestionable shared commitment to the goal. If I had tried to manage a project where there was uncertainty about the value of what we were trying to do, it would have been very difficult to keep those opinions from gradually beginning to erode the determination of the team to do this together. But that never wavered. There was never a question about whether this was worth doing.

I also had the benefit of an incredible group of advisers who were willing to put a lot of their time into overseeing the effort and giving me advice about whether we were on the right track. We also were much benefited by the NIH system of how you do science, which is: You don't give a lot of money to anybody until they have been peer reviewed. And that gave an opportunity both to nurture the centers that were doing well and were ready to expand, and, frankly, it gave me the clout necessary to shut down the centers that were not performing. And we shut down quite a few. That was a painful part of the enterprise, but you have to do that in a project of this magnitude if you expect to deliver.

On the Importance of Deadlines in Management

The genome project has benefited from the beginning from having this explicit set of goals—and there was quite a long list of them—and having each of those goals attached to a timetable, a set of intermediate milestones, ways of checking the quality of the data that was being produced, and enforcing that that quality was being maintained, and making sure that costs had been projected and were closely tracked as well. I have been enormously benefited by having a talented staff of Ph.D. scientists who have been involved in all of that tracking, and particularly making sure that we weren't slipping on any of those milestones. And that has helped immeasurably in gaining credibility for a project which, at the beginning, had its doubters in terms of "big science" being applied to biology.

That same mentality needs to be applied to many other aspects of genome research that we support in the next decade, although I should quickly add that is not appropriate for a lot of other medical research that is critically important for the benefits of all this to play out. In the same breath that I am saying we need those milestones for an organized genome-project-style management, we probably don't want them when you are talking about trying to get the investigators in this country to come forward with their best and brightest blue-sky ideas. There, you want to really let their creativity drive the process, which is what most of NIH's research funds are devoted to. But for some parts of the enterprise—and particularly the parts that we are likely to support, whether it's sequencing additional genomes like the chimpanzee, which we are about to embark upon; or whether it's a haplotype map; or whether it's trying to understand how all the genes turn on or off in an organized way instead of just doing it in a cottage-industry fashion—we will continue to be driven by that very managerial approach that sets milestones and timetables. I think everybody is now getting pretty used to that.

DEVELOPING LEADERS

QUESTION: How do I develop future leaders?

ANSWER: Your legacy will depend in part on your ability to develop and nurture future leaders to sustain your goals and objectives. This important role, developing a cadre of future leaders, is frequently overlooked in government. It is worth your devoting time and effort to this endeavor.

The rhetoric of the private sector places greater emphasis on this role. University of Michigan's Noel Tichy writes in *The Leadership Engine* (New York: HarperCollins Publishers, 1997):

> Winning companies win because they have good leaders that nurture the development of other leaders at all levels of the organization. The key ability of winning organizations and winning leaders is creating leaders....

> The ultimate test for a leader is not whether he or she makes smart decisions and takes decisive action, but whether he or she teaches others to be leaders and builds an organization that can sustain success even when he or she is not around.

In his report to the IBM Center, Ray Blunt describes roles that leaders can play in growing future public service leaders.

- **Growing leaders through personal example: As an *exemplar*.** This role often receives little attention. Throughout your tenure, the entire organization will be watching you and observing both your management style and your management decisions. This will be especially true of your mid-level managers. Blunt writes, "Leaders are followed more for who they are as observed by their behavior than for what title they have or how expert they are." Blunt cautions that people will learn leadership from you whether you intend for them to or not.

- **Growing leaders through relationships: As a *mentor*.** There is often confusion about the role of serving as a mentor. While there are *formal* mentorship programs in many organizations where senior individuals are assigned to mentor future leaders, there is also *informal* mentoring that takes place frequently in all organizations. At its core, mentoring involves your spending some time over the course of your tenure with individuals within your organization that you deem to have high potential. At a minimum, serving as a mentor could include meeting or having lunch with a high-potential individual (or individuals) several times over the course of the year. The goal of these encounters is to share your experiences on becoming a leader and to answer questions from the mentee both about the mentee's own career and your career.

- **Growing leaders through experiences or development programs: As a *coach* or *teacher*.** There are several components to these roles and you can select the one which works best for you:

  - **Forming coaching relationships.** This could involve selecting a high-potential individual to serve as a special assistant in your office on either a rotating or fixed-term basis. During the period in which that individual works in your office, you can set aside time to provide feedback and advice to the individual on how he or she is doing.

  - **Participating in executive development programs in your agency.** Jack Welch, the well-known former chief executive officer of General Electric, received much acclaim for participating every two weeks in GE's leadership program in Crotonville, New York. He met with participants in the program, talked about his career and his vision for GE, and answered questions. You can do the same. Just ask your chief human capital officer to book you at the next session of your agency's executive development program. In addition to providing you with an opportunity to meet face-to-face with your agency's future leaders, you will also likely enjoy the experience.

Getting Started on Developing Leaders

From *Growing Leaders for Public Service* by Ray Blunt

Making It a Priority: Take Stock of Your Time, Then Make the Time

… leaders who grow leaders start by setting an example, blocking time for this important task. Perhaps the greatest message you can give as a leader that you are making it your priority to serve the needs of the next generation is how you use your time.

To start, go back over your calendar for the past 30 days and see how you have spent your time. How much of it was spent on what was most urgent: your "in box," interrupting phone calls or visits, extended meetings about budget issues, correspondence, etc.? How much of your time was spent with your peers or with top executives, Congress, or OMB? If you are like most senior leaders, you will find that, as St. Augustine observed, "the urgent will drive out the important."

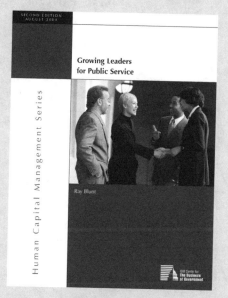

Finding and Preparing Your Leadership Stories

Effective leaders convey their own learning through stories—the lessons of their experience…. this is the heart of extending leader learning—teachable experience. Stories wrap the two central facets of leader learning into a package—experience and example—and make it a memorable and practical package.

… we learn and remember information and even plan strategically by ingesting knowledge and storing it in the form of stories. So storytelling should be an integral part of your leadership coaching, mentoring, and teaching. But where do the stories themselves come from? Perhaps you think that you don't have any. Then a first step might be to see what were your own leader learning points.

To start, get a large spiral notebook to use as a journal for notes about what you have learned and want to pass on. On the first page of the journal, draw a horizontal line across the middle. At the top of the upper section write "Highs" in the center. Near the bottom of the page in the lower section, in the center, write "Lows." The horizontal line represents your career or perhaps even your life. The upper portion, the relative "Highs," represents significant challenge, excitement, high achievement, recognition, a great event, or a satisfying accomplishment—personally or professionally. The lower portion, the relative "Lows," represents failure, disappointment, tragedy, a setback, a bad boss, a bad relationship, a dead-end job, boredom, getting fired or demoted, etc.

Once you have identified these key events across the span of your career and personal life, reflect on each one. For each high and each low, begin to draw out the lessons from it that may have informed or reshaped the way you now lead. If it is true that the emotionally impacting events of our lives lead to leader learning—even career setbacks and bad bosses—then these lessons are critical and constitute the learned wisdom that we each possess about leadership.

Each of these events is a story that can be told to others as an illustration of a key learning in your life. It is a story that links ideas and experiences together with a "moral" or a central learning for others. Not only does this give you insight about how you learned leadership—lessons to pass on—but it gives you ideas about how you might challenge others to learn as well and apply these lessons to their lives.

For Additional Information on Leadership

Government Reorganization: Strategies and Tools to Getting It Done (2004) by Hannah Sistare

This report examines various approaches to how government can undertake reorganization initiatives. The report examines four principal reorganization strategies that policy makers have used in the past: commissions, presidential reorganization authority, executive-branch reorganization staff, and congressional initiatives. In addition, four new strategies are identified: virtual reorganization through e-government, virtual reorganization through coordinating councils, reorganization by commission, and reorganization by legislative authorization.

Making Public Sector Mergers Work: Lessons Learned (2003) by Peter Frumkin

This report discusses the challenges of mergers and consolidations of government agencies. The report provides guidance to policy makers on how to analyze proposed mergers and presents practical advice to agency and department managers on how to respond to the many challenges created when several independent public organizations suddenly become one.

Managing Across Boundaries: A Case Study of Dr. Helene Gayle and the AIDS Epidemic (2002) by Norma M. Riccucci

A major challenge facing the public sector in the years ahead will be to manage across boundaries. To better understand the challenge of boundary-spanning leadership, this report profiles Dr. Helen Gayle, former director of the National Center for HIV, STD, and TB Prevention (NCHSTP) at the Centers for Disease Control (CDC). In her role as director of the Center, Dr. Gayle was responsible for working closely with the United Nations and other international organizations and nations in combating the AIDS epidemic.

Moving Toward More Capable Government: A Guide to Organizational Design (2002) by Thomas H. Stanton

This report provides a resource for policy makers in federal agencies and the Congress who are considering whether to create or restructure a government agency or instrumentality. The report provides insights to public sector executives on how various tools and changes in government organizations can be applied to developing creative solutions and interventions to national problems.

Trans-Atlantic Experiences in Health Reform: The United Kingdom's National Health Service and the United States Veterans Health Administration (2000) by Marilyn A. DeLuca

This report is a comparative study of the National Health Service in the United Kingdom and the Veterans Health Administration in the United States, and examines how two large public systems responded to the challenge of health reform. The study evaluates the reform impacts on health service delivery in each setting, explores how implementation was managed, and describes the effects on organization, workforce, and culture.

For Additional Information on Leadership

The Challenge of Managing Across Boundaries: The Case of the Office of the Secretary in the U.S. Department of Health and Human Services (2000) by Beryl A. Radin

In this report, Professor Radin presents seven case studies of how one cabinet department—the United States Department of Health and Human Services—effectively used a portfolio of crosscutting mechanisms to address specific issues or problems facing the department. Radin argues that in the 21st century, contemporary organizations will have to find new organizational mechanisms to address constantly arising crosscutting issues and problems. The movement toward flatter, less hierarchical organizations will require new ways to share responsibility and jointly problem-solve within organizations.

Leadership for Change: Case Studies in American Local Government (1999) by Janet Vinzant Denhardt and Robert B. Denhardt

This report profiles three outstanding local government executives—Robert O'Neill, Jan Perkins, and Phil Penland—who have served in various local governments over the years. The study profiles the change activities of these city/county managers as they sought to transfer a set of values and a methodology for leading change into a new setting. Case studies are presented on the change activities of each of these managers, drawing out lessons from their experiences that might suggest a new model of leading change in American local governments.

Transforming Government: Creating the New Defense Procurement System (1999) by Kimberly A. Harokopus

This report focuses on the government leaders within the Department of Defense and the White House who transformed the weapons procurement process from a rule-bound, inflexible, and inefficient system to a more subjective, cost-effective, and innovative public acquisition process. The study seeks to discover how these public sector leaders injected private sector business methodologies into the traditional federal bureaucracy and offers an illustration of how this government team exemplified leading widespread change and instilling innovation.

Managing Decentralized Departments: The Case of the U.S. Department of Health and Human Services (1999) by Beryl A. Radin

Since its creation in 1953 as an amalgam of several existing agencies, the U.S. Department of Health and Human Services (originally the Department of Health, Education and Welfare) attempted to find the appropriate balance between centralized functions in the Office of the Secretary and autonomy to the various agencies and bureaus contained within its boundaries. Over the years, the pendulum has swung back and forth between an emphasis on centralization and decentralization. This report examines the efforts by former Secretary Donna Shalala to delegate many functions to the operating components, while attempting to devise processes that emphasize coordination and crosscutting approaches as appropriate.

For Additional Information on Leadership

The Importance of Leadership: The Role of School Principals (1999) by Paul E. Teske and Mark Schneider

This report examines how public school leaders affect change by transforming the environment and culture of schools, turning rule-bound organizations, often more concerned with the needs of staff, into responsive organizations more concerned with student needs and performance. The study identifies high-performing schools and includes a series of interviews to understand the leadership tools and service delivery techniques that lead to higher performance.

Chapter Two: Performance

You do have a bottom line and will have to manage to it. However, your bottom line is different; it's the results of your organization.

IBM CENTER FOR THE BUSINESS OF GOVERNMENT
WASHINGTON, DC 20005

MEMORANDUM FOR THE HEADS OF EXECUTIVE DEPARTMENTS AND AGENCIES

SUBJECT: **Performance**

One of the many myths about government that you have probably encountered is that "government doesn't have a bottom line." By this, folks usually mean that government doesn't make a profit.

You do have a bottom line and will have to manage to it. However, your bottom line is different; it's the results of your organization. Former government executive Chris Wye writes, "Political leaders are triply vested—as American citizens, appointed public servants, and members of an incumbent political party—with bottom line responsibility for the performance of the policies, programs, and activities entrusted to their care."

Assess Your Performance Framework

Harvard University's Robert Behn describes a performance framework as a way of thinking about the leadership challenge of producing specific results in organizations based on a collection of general, cause-and-effect principles, supported by some operational hints for implementing these principles. Much of your first year in office should be devoted to understanding the performance framework of your organization so that you can track progress on your organization's performance and results. You won't be starting from scratch. Your predecessors also tracked performance. Your job is now to make sure that the information currently being collected by your organization is useful to you in both your decision-making capacity and performance manager role. Due to the numerous demands on your time, you should select three to five priority areas on which you will personally monitor your organization's performance. You should place your emphasis on your most important organizational goals. However, your organization will also be addressing a wider range of goals, many of which will not require your attention but still must be done.

Under the Government Performance and Results Act, enacted in 1993, each federal agency is required to develop both multi-year strategic and annual performance plans that include agency goals and measures. One of your first requests to your staff should be to review your organization's existing strategic plan. Over the next year, you may need to revise the strategic plan to link to the president's priorities. You will also benefit from the experience your staff has gained over the last decade in both strategic planning and performance management. Technology has also enhanced organizational capability to use performance management to track organizational progress toward agency goals as reflected in the organization's strategic plan.

Implement Your Performance Framework

Behn describes three components of performance management that you should put in place to ratchet up your organization's performance:

- Create or enhance the performance framework: What would it mean to do a better job?

- Drive performance improvement: How can you mobilize your people?

- Learn to enhance performance: How will your organization change to do better?

Behn offers "better practices" for you to use in implementing your organizational performance framework. You should:

- **Clarify and articulate your organization's mission.** Behn recommends that you "proclaim—clearly and frequently—what the organization is trying to accomplish." A key to your success will be ensuring that you "get the mission right" and then articulate it.

- **Identify your organization's most consequential performance deficit.** Your task here, as described by Behn, is to "determine what key failure is keeping the organization from achieving its mission."

- **Establish a specific performance target.** This involves specifying what new level of success you desire for your organization.

- **Clarify the link between target and mission.** This involves clearly articulating how meeting the performance targets you establish will help your organization accomplish its mission.

Use Performance Information

After your performance framework is in place and you are comfortable with the information your organization is producing, you will find that you can use performance information in many ways. The Urban Institute's Harry Hatry, Elaine Morley, and Shelli Rossman, along with former University of Southern California professor Joseph Wholey, identify four ways in which you can use performance information in your organization:

- **Trigger corrective action.** In your managerial role, you can use the information collected to make changes in your organization's performance to eliminate performance deficits.

- **Motivate your employees.** As discussed in the *Memo on People*, one of your key responsibilities is motivating and rewarding your employees. Performance management will tell you which of your managers are exceeding the performance targets you established and should be recognized and rewarded.

- **Plan and budget.** As discussed in the *Memo on Money*, one of your major challenges will be using performance information in the budget process to allocate resources within your organization.

- **Identify and encourage "best practices."** Based on the information you collect, you will begin to see that some components of your organization might be performing better than others. This will give you the opportunity to share the best practices of high-performing components with other components that might not be performing as well.

There is an old saying that "if you don't know where you are going, you will never get there." This is truly the case of managing in government. If you do not have a performance framework (which includes your goals and objectives) in place, you will not be able to track where you are heading and agency progress toward achievement of your goals. In order to track agency progress, you will need to either put a performance management system in place or use the system now in place.

GETTING STARTED ON PERFORMANCE MANAGEMENT

QUESTION: How do I get started on improving performance in my organization?

ANSWER: According to Harvard University's Robert Behn, the first question that agency heads and their leadership teams must address is, "What would it mean to do a better job?" In his report to the IBM Center (2006), he writes, "Different people will make this call differently. In some circumstances, the answer may appear obvious. In others, it may be open to much debate. But this debate should not go on forever. If the organization is actually to improve performance, it cannot go on forever."

Behn, like many other performance experts, advocates the "get started" approach. As noted in the *Memo on Performance*, Behn sets forth "better practices" needed to create a performance framework for your organization:

- **Clarify and articulate the organization's mission.** This practice involves two key activities to achieving your goals: strategy and performance. You must articulate your organization's mission and then quickly begin to track the performance of your organization against that mission. Your articulation of the mission must go beyond the traditional "mission statement," which you may have seen when you walked into the building.

- **Identify the organization's most consequential performance deficit.** You and your team will be facing many challenges during your tenure. According to Behn, "This is the first challenge to the organization's leadership—to figure out, from the variety of problems inhibiting its ability to produce results, that one performance deficit (or, at most, a very few) on which the organization should now focus its intelligence and energies."

- **Establish a specific performance target and performance metrics.** Whatever target you select, you must also do the following:

  - You must specify the target in sufficient detail to ensure that a vast majority of people will agree when it has been achieved.

  - You must attach a specific deadline to the target. You should also request intermediate milestones on the organization's progress toward achieving your goal and you should ensure that the milestones are "real."

  - You must clearly identify a person who is accountable for delivering results.

- **Clarify the link between target and mission.** It is not enough simply to articulate a mission, identify a performance deficit, and establish performance targets. You must also link the target and mission. This is a crucial step. Behn writes, "Unfortunately, most actions taken by most public agencies are not connected … closely to their mission. The causal link between the actions taken by the agency to close its performance deficit and the achievement of its mission may be indirect, vague, poorly understood, or nonexistent."

A related perspective is provided by former government executive Chris Wye. Wye recommends that an effective strategy for getting started is to select one or two management or performance areas that will receive your priority attention. These might be, points out Wye, areas of your special expertise or interest. In his report to the IBM Center (2004), Wye writes, "Focusing on a small number would help to assure that something gets done. Let it be known that these are the things you are interested in. Let it be known that you see this as your 'long term' contribution to the institution of government, not related to party politics or policies. And then ask for help. You'll probably be pleasantly surprised by the enthusiastic response from career professionals."

A Primer on Recent Management Reform Legislation

From *Performance Management for Political Executives:*
A "Start Where You Are, Use What You Have" Guide by Chris Wye

The last two decades have given rise to a series of legislation aimed at improving the performance of government. Key pieces of legislation include the following:

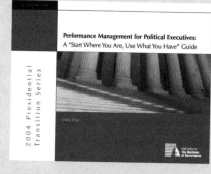

1990: The Chief Financial Officers (CFO) Act

Intended to strengthen financial accountability in the government, the CFO Act created chief financial officers in the largest federal agencies who are responsible for managing agency financial matters, required the Office of Management and Budget (OMB) to develop a five-year financial plan and report for the government, and required agency CFOs to conform their financial plans to the government-wide plan. The act also created the Chief Financial Officers Council, chaired by the Office of Management and Budget.

1993: The Government Performance and Results Act (GPRA)

The centerpiece of recent performance legislation, GPRA requires agencies to set goals and measure performance toward them. Each agency must prepare a five-year strategic plan, updated every three years, an annual plan, and an annual report. OMB is required to prepare a government-wide plan. A unique feature of GPRA is its strong focus on outcome measures.

1994: The Government Management Reform Act (GMRA)

Designed to strengthen the CFO Act of 1990, GMRA extended the act by requiring an audit of each agency's financial statement as well as of the government-wide financial statement.

1996: The Clinger-Cohen Act

The Clinger-Cohen Act created the position of chief information officer in the largest federal agencies. CIOs are required to implement a "sound and integrated information technology architecture." The act empowers OMB to issue directives to CIOs, effectively giving OMB a leadership and coordinating responsibility position.

1996: The Federal Financial Management Improvement Act (FFMIA)

Again tightening agency financial management, FFMIA requires that agency annual financial statements include a report showing where their financials are in compliance with federal financial requirements, accounting standards, and the U.S. Government Standard General Ledger.

1998: Government Paperwork Elimination Act (GPEA)

Intended to encourage the use of electronic, web-based applications, the GPEA requires agencies to offer an electronic option for information gathering or use, and also requires agencies to accept electronic signatures.

2002: The Chief Human Capital Officers Act (enacted as part of the Homeland Security Act of 2002)

The act requires the heads of 24 executive departments and agencies to appoint or designate chief human capital officers (CHCOs). Each CHCO serves as his or her agency's chief policy advisor on all human resource management issues and is charged with selecting, developing, training, and managing a high-quality, productive workforce. The CHCO Act also established a Chief Human Capital Officers Council to advise and coordinate the activities of member agencies on such matters as the modernization of human resource systems, improved quality of human resource information, and legislation affecting human resource operations and organizations.

Implementing Performance Management

QUESTION: After I get started, what are the steps I need to take to ensure successful implementation of performance management in my organization?

ANSWER: Your greatest challenge will be to manage the tension between the use of performance management to increase accountability and improve performance, on the one hand, and employees' fears that the performance management system will be used to penalize them for not achieving targets, on the other.

In her report to the IBM Center (2006), University of Massachusetts Boston's Shelley Metzenbaum cautions, "less attention should be paid to incentives and far more to ensuring the active and effective use of outcome-focused goals and measures." Metzenbaum recommends that linking rewards and penalties to goal attainment be used with caution. This contrasts to some degree with private sector business models, which emphasize incentives, both positive and negative. In government, the potential range of financial incentives is much more limited.

Your ultimate success will depend on how well you implement performance management in your organization and balance the tension described above. In her report, Metzenbaum sets forth five building blocks essential to successful implementation of performance management:

- **Set clear, measurable goals.** In their IBM Center reports, both Behn (2006) and Metzenbaum (2006) agree on the importance of measurable goals. Metzenbaum emphasizes that these goals be specific, challenging, and outcome-focused. She also emphasizes that some of the goals should be "stretch goals" and writes, "If individuals and organizations met all of their targets all the time, it would suggest that they had chosen timid targets and missed the performance-driving power of a stretch target."

- **Use measurement for feedback, insights, and decisions.** The success of your performance management system will ultimately depend on how you use the information it provides and how your use of that information is perceived within your organization. Used as an improvement tool, performance measures can motivate progress toward goals; illuminate by providing information on what might be the problems causing "performance deficits"; communicate progress to program managers, employees, customers, and stakeholders; and inform choices by consumers.

- **Provide one-to-one verbal feedback to unleash the power of goals and measures.** Your job is not just to receive information about performance, but to use that information to provide feedback to your management team. In many ways, you assume the role of coach by inspiring your team to keep trying to meet the specific, challenging goals facing them and making adjustments as necessary. Metzenbaum writes, "Well-delivered verbal feedback boosts confidence that a goal can be met, stimulates ideas and specific plans about how to meet it, and reinforces the importance of specific goals."

- **Use group feedback to encourage interactive inquiry.** During your meetings with your leadership team, performance information can be used to tackle three operational challenges: making mid-course corrections to goals, target, strategies, and commitments; making mid-year budget adjustments; and making mid-course staffing and skill adjustments.

- **Use externally provided incentives cautiously.** Metzenbaum argues that if improperly designed, incentives "introduce unhealthy fears that compromise discoveries that lead to performance gains."

You will also have to ensure that the management culture of the organization is open to using the above building blocks to support better performance. For example, ensuring that bad news leads to performance improvement is as much a cultural matter as it is an organizational matter.

What Is Accountability?

From *Performance Accountability: The Five Building Blocks and Six Essential Practices*
by Shelley H. Metzenbaum

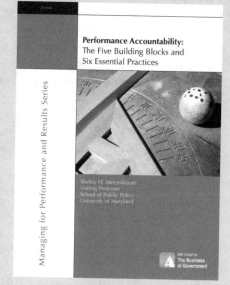

What does it mean to "hold someone accountable"? What does it mean for government agencies and employees to be answerable to someone and for what and to whom do they need to account? Presumably, it means in part the desire of citizens and their elected officials to be able to identify who is responsible for an organization's outputs or outcomes and for its successes and failures. But then what? When people talk about holding someone or some organization accountable, what happens?

Unclear accountability expectations—who is accountable to whom for what and what consequences arise when accountability expectations are not met—are problematic because they introduce fear into performance management, which is the use of goals and measures to manage. That fear, in turn, creates problems such as measurement manipulation, timid targets, outcome avoidance (resulting in an affinity for output targets), and claim games where some rush to claim credit for accomplishments while others run from it, fearful of provoking resentment among their peers. Occasionally, measurement systems even implode, seemingly overburdened by their own weight.

These problems arise for three primary reasons: vague accountability expectations, inadequate feedback and inquiry to probe the insights revealed by performance measures, and misguided notions of how and when to use incentives. Past experience and research suggests that many of these problems can be averted, performance improved, and accountability strengthened, but only if agencies and their watchdogs adopt an inquisitive, non-punitive approach to performance management.

Four Categories of Accountability

Fiscal accountability: Government spends its money as authorized, with as little waste as possible.

Ethical accountability: Government agencies operate honestly, without conflict of interest, self-dealing, other forms of fraud, or abuse of the power of governmental authority.

Democratic accountability: Government agencies do what their citizens want and need, engaging citizens and their elected representatives in understanding trade-offs and making well-informed choices among competing priorities. Government agencies treat people civilly and courteously, unless there are strong justifications not to, so people do not resent or resist government because it has acted in a rude, slow, or inappropriate manner.

Performance accountability: Government agencies and their employees work intelligently and diligently to deliver effective and cost-efficient government programs.

Using Balanced Scorecards

QUESTION: What is a balanced scorecard, and should I consider using it as part of my performance management system? Is it just a private sector tool?

ANSWER: In brief, a balanced scorecard is a family of measures that allow a 360-degree assessment of an organization. The balanced scorecard originated in the private sector as a tool for corporations to go beyond strictly financial measures to also consider customer, stakeholder, internal business process, and employee perspectives. In their report to the IBM Center, DePaul University's Nicholas Mathys and Kenneth Thompson summed up their view of the balanced scorecard as "a tool for translating an organization's strategy into action through the development of performance objectives and measures in order to fulfill its mission."

The use of balanced scorecards is increasing in the public sector. In the federal government, both the Defense Finance and Accounting Service (DFAS) in the Department of Defense and the United States Postal Service, for example, use balanced scorecards as management tools within their organizations.

In describing the usefulness of the balanced scorecard to DFAS since its implementation in 2001, Director Zack Gaddy said, "The balanced scorecard has turned our vision and strategy into a meaningful set of performance measures and targets. It has become a management and diagnostic tool that measures our performance at multiple levels, and we use it to assess the health of our organization and demonstrate our progress on completing key initiatives."

The United States Postal Service (USPS) has also had a positive experience with balanced scorecards. USPS began its current performance measurement system in 2003, now called the National Performance Assessment, which is a web-based measurement and reporting tool that consolidates performance data from across the organization. In their 2006 Annual Progress Report, USPS wrote, "These data are translated into balanced scorecards that report on corporate and unit indicators. The balanced scorecard serves as the foundation for engaging more than 73,000 executive and administrative employees in discussions around individual and organizational performance."

While the concept of the balanced scorecard began in the private sector, the experience of DFAS and USPS demonstrate that it can be a valuable public sector tool as well. While private sector bottom line "shareholder value" will clearly not be the primary focus of the balanced scorecard in government, Mathys and Thompson conclude that "program performance, efficient use of resources, and satisfaction with service by the public" are highly important and can be tracked by a balanced scorecard.

Comparing Balanced Scorecards in the Private and Public Sectors

Features	Private Sector	Public Sector
Focus	Shareholder value	Mission effectiveness
Financial goals	Profit; market share growth; innovation; creativity	Cost reduction; efficiency; accountability to public
Efficiency concerns of clients	No	Yes
Desired outcome	Customer satisfaction	Stakeholder satisfaction
Stakeholders	Stockholders; bondholders	Taxpayers; legislators; inspectors
Who defines budget priorities	Customer demand	Leadership; legislators; funding agencies
Key success factors	Uniqueness; advanced technology	Sameness; economies of scale; standardized technology

Source: Nicholas J. Mathys and Kenneth R. Thompson, "Using the Balanced Scorecard: Lessons Learned from the U.S. Postal Service and the Defense Finance and Accounting Service," IBM Center for The Business of Government, 2006.

Using Balanced Scorecards as a Management Tool

From *Using the Balanced Scorecard: Lessons Learned from the U.S. Postal Service and the Defense Finance and Accounting Service* by Nicholas J. Mathys and Kenneth R. Thompson

While many organizations use the balanced scorecard (BSC) as an *evaluative* tool, we strongly support the notion of a BSC as a *management* tool. What is the difference? As an evaluative tool, the focus is more on using the scorecard for the assessment of (individual) performance, which leads to many different sorts of behavioral consequences that may not support organizational performance improvement. For example, increased pressure to reach targets often will lead to increased pressure to reduce those same targets in order to increase the likelihood that targets will be reached. As a management tool, BSC focuses on improving organizational performance and clarifying where the organization should focus its efforts toward mutual problem solving. As a by-product, BSC acts as a guidepost that also helps to improve individual performance.

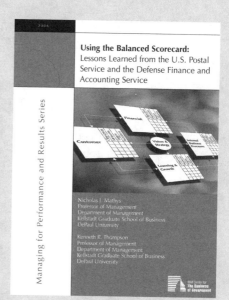

Poor Feedback Is a Chief Cause of Poor Performance

According to a Conference Board study, "poor and insufficient feedback" was the number one cause of poor performance in the workplace and resulted in 60 percent of performance problems. This factor was 20 percent higher than the next cause. The study further states that proper performance feedback requires performance expectations to be communicated and understood, and to lead to *mutual* agreement on problem solving. With BSC, there is a clear set of goals aligned to the vision and strategy of the organization. This allows management to communicate objective expectations for performance, while also allowing a greater understanding of those objectives. This empowers both management and staff to make agreed upon improvements.

BSC allows managers to get and give feedback from all units and all levels of the organization; this results in focusing resources where they are needed most and where they will be most effective in changing overall performance. BSC allows an organization to avoid such costly misallocations while reaping the benefits of proper allocation. Because of the focus of this approach, questions will be asked such as "How does this allocation or program expenditure relate to improving our key internal processes?"—which are then related to improve financial and customer satisfaction measures.

Scorecards Improve Feedback and Planning

In addition, because of the quantified measures and target of performance created in a BSC system, fact-based management can replace intuition or the educated guess. Management develops a greater ability to trace its actions, and the actions of a particular unit, to business outcomes. Conjecture and the causes of poor projections are reduced significantly. In fact, it has been found that when more non-financial measures are used, earnings projections become more accurate. This forward perspective shift contributes to a new management style, one in which future outcomes can be anticipated.

The BSC also allows best practices to be identified. As inefficiencies are uncovered, high-performance areas can be defined and the successful activities of these high performers adopted in areas where appropriate.

Understanding Balanced Scorecards

From *Using the Balanced Scorecard: Lessons Learned from the U.S. Postal Service and the Defense Finance and Accounting Service* by Nicholas J. Mathys and Kenneth R. Thompson

What Is a Balanced Scorecard in the Private Sector?

Reliance exclusively on financial performance measures is similar to "trying to drive an automobile by looking in the rearview mirror rather than the road ahead." The balanced scorecard, or BSC, is an attempt to achieve a more proactive, forward view to managing an organization while still taking into account traditional measures. It does this through a "balanced" perspective of measures that assess the effectiveness in meeting the organization's vision and strategy. Four areas are considered in David P. Norton and Robert S. Kaplan's model: Financial, Customer, Internal Business Processes, and Learning and Growth. Visions and strategies are translated into objectives, measures, targets, and initiatives that answer the questions in each of the four categories:

- For the *financial category*, the main question is: "To succeed financially, how should we appear to our shareholders?"

- For the *customer category*, the focus is: "To achieve our vision, how should we appear to our customers?"

- The *internal business process category* focuses on the question: "To satisfy our shareholders and customers, what business processes must we excel at?"

- The *learning and growth category* focuses on answering the question: "To achieve our vision, how will we sustain our ability to change and improve?"

Why Is Linking or Aligning Performance Measures Important in the Private Sector?

Performance measures provide the link between strategies and actions. Many businesses have strategic plans and business strategies. The real issue is how to implement these strategies in a meaningful way, in a way that is shown to affect the success of the business. However, that success has to be measured. To do this, the BSC links these strategies to organizational operations. Essentially, BSC serves to link the long-term goals of an organization with short-term operational control by means of a cause-and-effect model. It attempts to determine on a daily, monthly, and annual basis what is working to achieve organizational success (cause) and what, in fact, is limiting that success and should be changed. It not only does this at a high management strategy level, but also communicates this down to an operational level.

To do this, the balanced scorecard needs to be considered more in terms of a hierarchical relationship that aligns elements of the organization into a cohesive set of actions to meet the desired strategy. For a for-profit organization, this would place elements more in a hierarchical relationship.... [Kaplan and Norton] viewed that through strategic mapping, the scorecard items were hierarchically related.

- *Vision and strategies* are met through meeting *financial outcome goals*.

- *Financial outcome goals* are related to meeting *customer satisfaction measures*.

- Both improving *customer satisfaction and financial outcomes* are directly related to effective and efficient *internal business process management*.

- *Learning and growth* aspects are focused on improving *internal business processes* in order to improve output goals.

A Strategic Focus on Outcomes: A Global Trend

From *Moving from Outputs to Outcomes: Practical Advice
from Governments Around the World* by Burt Perrin

Over the last decade, countries around the world have undertaken reforms with the aim of improving the relevance and effectiveness of public services and the quality of public sector management. A key aspect of most reform processes is a focus on results and, in particular, on outcomes.

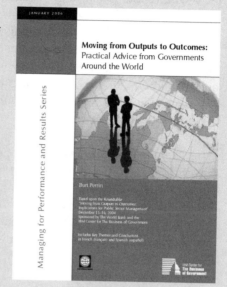

Until recently, the performance of public sector programs, and of their managers, has been judged largely on inputs, activities, and outputs. This approach, however, has come into question. One of the major factors behind many reform initiatives is a concern that government too often is preoccupied with process and following rules, and it is not clear what *benefits* are actually arising from public sector expenditures and activities.

External influences also have played a role in stimulating movement toward a results orientation. An outcome focus increasingly is a prerequisite for financial and other forms of support. For example, as both Ireland and Spain have indicated, one pressure for a results orientation came from the European Union (EU). Leadership from the EU has influenced the administrative systems of the 10 new Member States, mainly from Eastern Europe, and is a major factor influencing reform in other countries that are interested in future membership or closer relations with the EU. Both Spain and Ireland touch upon the role the EU has played in influencing directions in their countries. The World Bank and other development banks, along with many multilateral and bilateral donors, are increasingly demanding an outcome orientation, along with appropriate monitoring and evaluation systems, as a condition of financial and other forms of support.

External pressure can come as well from the other direction, such as from civil society. A number of countries emphasized the importance of the demands of civil society for tangible results that helped lead to their outcome approach. Civil society attention has also been cited as an important factor in sustaining the efforts and in providing a democratic basis for reform efforts linked to the needs and desires of the citizenry.

A number of benefits to an outcome-oriented approach have been identified. For example, it can serve as a frame of reference to ensure that inputs, activities, and outputs are appropriate. It represents a means of demonstrating the value and benefits of public services to citizens and to the legislature. At least as important, an outcome focus is an essential component of a learning approach that can identify how policies and program approaches may need to be adjusted, improved, or replaced with alternatives. It is essential not only to demonstrate that outcomes have occurred, but that the interventions in question have contributed to these in some way.

USING OUTCOME PERFORMANCE INFORMATION

QUESTION: How do I get my program managers to use outcome information?

ANSWER: Your organization collects much information from a variety of sources. The challenge today is no longer in collecting information; the challenge now lies in using the information that is regularly collected. While you will be consuming some of this information, your job is ensuring that your program managers increasingly use this information. In their report to the IBM Center, Harry Hatry, Elaine Morley, Shelli Rossman, and Joseph Wholey write, "a major use, if not the major use, of regularly collected outcome information should be by program managers themselves to improve the effectiveness of the programs." The effectiveness of programs can be improved by taking corrective actions based on the information collected.

Hatry and his co-authors place much emphasis on program managers *collecting* and *using* outcome information. The authors define an outcome as "an event, occurrence, or condition that is outside the activity or program itself and is of direct importance to program customers or the public." Outcome data is clearly not new to the federal government. Over the years, the government has collected outcome data such as number and rates of traffic accidents; incidence of various diseases; rates of infant mortality; employment and unemployment data; number of reported child abuse cases; school dropout rates; and number and rates of reported crime.

It is clearly easier to collect and use "output" measures. Output measures are defined by Hatry and his co-authors as completed products and services delivered, such as the amount of work done within the organization or by contractors. An example of an *output* measure is the number of childhood immunization shots given. In addition, your job will be to continually push your program managers to collect and use *outcome* measures, such as the reduction of childhood diseases prevented by immunizations.

None of this will be easy. While increased emphasis has been placed on outcome data in recent years, collecting and actually using outcome data is still a challenge. To increase the use and utility of outcome information in your organization, Hatry and his co-authors recommend that you ask your program managers to:

- **Break out (disaggregate) the outcome information you receive by important customer and service characteristics.** You could break out your customers by geographical location, age, gender, income group, race/ethnicity, educational level, and household size.

- **Provide data that is timely.** You should ask your managers to develop procedures to obtain outcome information more quickly after the period for which the data is being reported.

- **Present outcome data in user-friendly format.** Examples of user-friendly format include bar charts or other easily understood graphic presentations.

- **Include data from previous time periods (such as the last year or two) in outcome information reports.** This will enable you and your managers to see trends in outcomes over time, which will help you identify where outcomes are declining and what actions may be needed.

- **Provide training for your staff on the uses of outcome information.** Spend time understanding and evaluating the chain of causality between the outputs of your agency and the outcomes you want to achieve.

How Federal Programs Use Outcome Information

From *How Federal Programs Use Outcome Information: Opportunities for Federal Managers*
by Harry P. Hatry, Elaine Morley, Shelli B. Rossman, and Joseph S. Wholey

As outcome information increasingly becomes routinely available to federal program managers, they are likely to use the information routinely in their decisions, such as to help them allocate their inevitably limited resources.

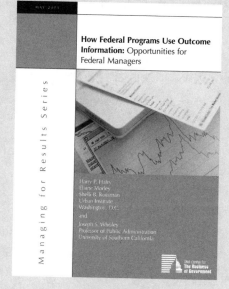

Uses of Outcome Information by Federal Agencies

Trigger corrective action

- Identify problem areas and modify service provision/operational practices

- Identify root causes of problems and develop action plans to address them

- Trigger enforcement activities

- Identify grantee technical assistance and compliance assistance needs

- Develop training or guidelines for regulated entities

- Identify staff training needs and provide training

- Reduce or de-fund poor performers (grantees or contractors)

- Require grantees to provide corrective action plans

- Evaluate the extent to which changes in practices and policies have led to improvements in outcomes

- Identify the need for policy or legislative changes

- Identify underserved "client" groups

Identify and encourage "best practices"

- Identify successful grantee practices

- Disseminate good practices information

Motivate

- Motivate staff

- Develop employee performance agreements

- Use as basis for "How are we doing?" meetings

- Recognize and reward high-performing federal offices or employees

- Recognize and reward high-performing grantees or regulated entities

- Motivate grantees or regulated entities

Plan and budget

- Allocate resources and set priorities

- Develop plans and set targets

- Justify requests for funds

- Determine grantee funding

- Inform budget projections

USING PROGRAM EVALUATION

QUESTION: What is program evaluation and how does it differ from performance measurement? How can I use program evaluation?

ANSWER: Here is how the Government Accountability Office defines performance measurement and evaluation:

- **Performance measurement** is the *ongoing* monitoring and reporting of program accomplishment, particularly progress toward pre-established goals.

- **Program evaluations** are individual systematic studies conducted *periodically* or on an ad hoc basis to assess how well a program is working. Program evaluation typically provides a more in-depth examination of program performance than performance measurement and allows for an overall assessment of whether a program is working and identifies adjustments that may be needed.

In their report to the IBM Center, Kathryn Newcomer and Mary Ann Scheirer write that program evaluation studies can be used by you and your team in support of the following components of performance management:

- **For strategic and program planning.** Program evaluation can support your implementation of the Government Performance and Results Act, specifically in developing strategic plans and annual performance plans.

- **For improving program delivery.** Program evaluation can assist in your program management activities by using strategies and data feedback to inform decision making on delivering existing services and designing and implementing new services.

- **For accountability.** Program evaluation can be used in reporting performance data in GPRA annual performance reports and other reports to oversight bodies, such as Congress and the public.

- **For attributing results to the agency's programs.** Program evaluation can provide research and evaluation to analyze the causal effectiveness of the programs and strategies whose "results" are reported in other documents.

Your program evaluation staff can be instrumental in: (1) designing and providing you with ongoing performance information, and (2) designing and overseeing in-depth evaluation studies. In your new position, Newcomer and Scheirer recommend that you and your management team:

- **Conduct an inventory of the evaluation skills within your organization.** By conducting this inventory, you should find out where your performance management skills are located and whether their efforts are being coordinated. For example, is your performance evaluation staff also involved in preparation of your organization's GPRA strategic and annual plans?

- **Assess whether your organization is allocating adequate resources to performance management.** Does your organization have adequate resources (staff and money) to produce both ongoing performance information and special program evaluation studies for you? This assessment might also include collecting resource information on activities related to "evaluation," such as statistical units, research units, and information technology groups.

- **Institute and support ongoing teams that bring together evaluators from technical offices, program management, and performance planning and reporting staff.** These groups should be used to transfer knowledge throughout your organization about feasible uses of evaluation methods, as well as performance success stories.

Using Program Evaluation to Support Performance Management

From *Using Evaluation to Support Performance Management: A Guide for Federal Executives* by Kathryn E. Newcomer and Mary Ann Scheirer

A central theme of performance measurement is to collect useful evidence, usually quantitative data, about the delivery and results of agency actions. This process is often called evidence-based management in the health services context. The tools of program evaluation and the skills of program evaluators can contribute substantially to the multiple steps needed for institutionalizing useful performance measurement systems.

Federal agency officials suggested that evaluation is not only a set of specific, discrete studies of programs, but is an ongoing function served by both performance measurement and more targeted studies. Interviewees acknowledged that focused evaluation studies are needed to provide more in-depth understanding of program implementation, to supply evidence of the causal links assumed to connect outputs with intended outcomes, as well as to examine the contextual background for ongoing performance data. Performance measurement provides the central core of routinely collected evaluative data about program operations and outcomes. Additional evaluation studies provide complementary evidence and logical frameworks for increasing the depth of knowledge for interpretation of the performance data.

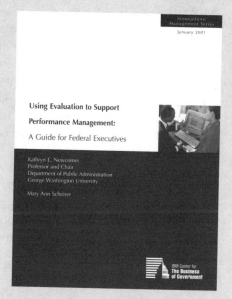

Performance management involves more than simply recording measures of program performance and reporting them upwards to oversight bodies and public stakeholders. Several steps are needed to develop and collect performance measures that can be useful to management in decision making:

- Programmatic stakeholders must come together to reach agreement on strategic and performance objectives and the strategies for achieving them.

- Indicators must be defined for program components that capture program outputs (e.g., the extent of services provided) and/or outcomes (e.g., behaviors of beneficiaries influenced by the services).

- Data sources must be developed or discovered for those indicators.

- Data must be collected with systematic methods, often in multiple jurisdictions (e.g., states, grant-funded projects, etc.).

- Data must be aggregated and reported in user-friendly formats.

- The data must be used by program managers and decision makers to assess and improve results.

- Data quality must be addressed at every step of its journey from original collection to final reporting.

All of these steps are taken in relation to an agency's program strategies and activities to address the problem or content domain targeted in the agency's mission.

Understanding the Performance "Stat" Movement

Question: I've heard about CompStat and CitiStat. What exactly are these programs and can they be applied to the federal government?

Answer: Throughout this section, we have discussed the challenges of linking performance information to performance outcomes. The performance "stat" movement is an excellent example of how public sector organizations have successfully linked the two. The movement started in the New York City Police Department (NYPD) under the leadership of then-Commissioner William Bratton. Commissioner Bratton, with the assistance of the late Jack Maple, created CompStat (which originally stood for computer statistics) in 1994. In his report to the IBM Center, Iona College's Paul E. O'Connell describes CompStat "as a highly sophisticated performance measurement system ... based on the compilation, distribution, and utilization of 'real time' data to allow field managers to make better-informed and more effective decisions."

O'Connell reports that Bratton concluded that he needed data to be collected and analyzed in a timely manner if effective crime-reduction strategies were to be implemented by the NYPD. Over time, meetings to discuss the crime data collected by precinct evolved to formal twice-weekly meetings in which all levels of the department participated to identify precinct and citywide crime trends, which resulted in the redeployment of resources and the assessment of crime control strategies. The CompStat program received nationwide publicity, resulting in numerous visits to CompStat meetings by public sector leaders from across the nation.

The CompStat concept, characterized by the collection of data discussed and analyzed at the regular meetings, spread quickly to other jurisdictions in the 1990s. In New York City, the Corrections Department, the Department of Parks and Recreation, and the Department of Health all created their versions of CompStat. In 2000, the newly elected mayor of Baltimore, Martin O'Malley, hired a former NYPD official as his police commissioner who implemented a CompStat program in the Baltimore police department. The success of this initiative led Mayor O'Malley to seek the assistance of Jack Maple to help develop a CompStat-like program for the entire city of Baltimore, which was termed CitiStat.

CitiStat, like CompStat, also received much attention from managers across the nation. Mayor O'Malley, now governor of the State of Maryland, developed four tenets for CitiStat: accurate and timely intelligence; rapid deployment of resources; effective tactics and strategies; and relentless follow-up and assessment.

The concept of the stat model is clearly applicable to the federal government and to you as the leader of your organization. In his 2007 report to the IBM Center, Robert Behn emphasizes that a stat program should be viewed as a leadership strategy in which the organization's leader uses performance measurement "to focus the personal attention, the management energy, the operational tactics, and the creative talents of the people" in the organization to produce clearly specified results. The common feature of all the stat programs is the organization's leader meeting with his or her management team to focus attention and assess progress toward the organization's goals.

What Exactly Is CitiStat?

From *What All Mayors Would Like to Know About Baltimore's CitiStat Performance Strategy*
by Robert D. Behn

CitiStat is a leadership strategy that any leader can employ to mobilize agencies to produce specific results. The obvious and operational components of CitiStat are its meetings and questions, its targets and data. But these visible features are only the vehicles by which the mayor focuses the personal attention, the management energy, the operational tactics, and the creative talents of the people in individual city agencies on the task of producing clearly specified results.

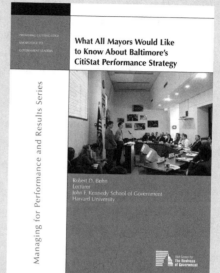

Consequently, one way for a mayor to think about CitiStat might be: A city is employing a CitiStat performance strategy if it holds an ongoing series of *regular, periodic meetings* during which the mayor and/or the principal members of the mayor's leadership team plus the individual director (and the top managers) of different city agencies *use data* to analyze the agency's past *performance*, to establish its next *performance* objectives, and to examine its overall *performance* strategies.

This characterization is not a very demanding one. Technically, all that it requires is "an ongoing series of regular, periodic meetings" plus the actual "use" of some "data"—all designed to improve the "performance" of city agencies. Given, however, that these meetings are "ongoing," "regular," and "periodic," one subtle feature of CitiStat is often missed by casual observers: This ongoing discussion of performance involves much persistent follow-up on past performance deficits and previous commitments to fix specific problems, as well as follow-up on decisions, commitments, and established expectations for future performance improvements.

In practice, however, CitiStat is much more complex. The key aspect of this way of thinking about public management is the clear, express, detailed focus on performance. This focus is revealed in the effort to learn what the data reveal about the achievements and deficiencies of past performance; in the establishment of specific targets for future performance; and in the development, testing, evaluation, and adjustments of operational tactics that can build on past achievements, remedy past deficiencies, and bring about future improvements. Thus, CitiStat is more than meetings and data. It requires:

- **Targets** (which provide benchmarks for judging successes and failure)
- **Tactics** (which focus organizational efforts on achieving the targets)
- **Data** (which track the performance of agencies and subunits)
- **Analysis** (which, using the data, identifies the causes of both success and failure)
- **Question**s (which reveal what agencies are doing and not doing to achieve their targets)
- **Learning** (which comes from these analyses, questions, and answers)
- **Collaboration** (which helps the mayor's staff and the agency's director and managers to determine what to do next)
- **Experimentation** (which creates new ways of achieving success)
- **Meetings** (which regularly review agency progress, targets, analyses, and strategies)
- **Thinking** (which can suggest how the entire approach can be improved)

STRATEGIES FOR COLLECTING INFORMATION FROM GRANT PROGRAMS TO STATES

QUESTION: My organization makes grants to state governments. How can I best engage them in collecting and using performance information?

ANSWER: If your organization works closely with the states, you will face the challenge of developing an appropriate and effective working relationship with them. This relationship may include the submission of performance information to you. Working across levels of government always involves a political dimension. You should be aware of the politics of the state with which you are working and the state's political relationship with the federal government. In her report to the IBM Center (2003), Shelley Metzenbaum presents the following key questions that need to be answered by you and your organization:

- Should your agency adopt clearly defined outcome goals for states or require states to adopt them?

- Should your agency require public reporting on progress toward those goals? Should your agency require performance reporting that is comparable for all states?

- Should your agency enter into formal performance agreements with each state encompassing these goals and measures? What should your agency do with the performance measures, once reported? How should your agency handle goals that states have already set for themselves?

Based on her analysis of the use of state performance data by four federal agencies, Metzenbaum reaches a positive, though cautious, conclusion, "While often politically controversial at the state level, federally mandated goals for states can be powerful motivators when linked to the promise of significant rewards or the threat of significant penalties. The promise of a reward or the threat of serious penalties linked to goal attainment can add to the motivational value of measures as long as those being measured do not feel so strongly threatened that they try to have the goals repealed or destroy the measurement system, either by dismantling it or by undermining it with inaccurate and untimely measurement submission."

Metzenbaum provides a series of recommendations for organizations that are collecting performance information from states:

- **Collect, organize, and make information readily available.** You should annually compile state information into a single compendium that is available in print form, accessible online through a single portal, produced on a regular schedule, and broadly disseminated.

- **Create robust measurement systems and use data that are standardized and normalized across states.** The goal is that information submitted from each state has the same meaning and is characterized in units that enable appropriate comparison.

- **Require measurement.** Standardized state performance measurement is most likely to happen if Congress mandates its generation, collection, and dissemination.

- **Involve those being measured.** You should routinely engage states as co-owners of performance data and as decision makers in developing tools to enhance the use of data.

- **Encourage analysis.** You should conduct your own analysis of state data and encourage third-party analysis.

- **"Market" the results.** You should make information dissemination a priority and make data available in a customer-friendly and audience-focused format.

- **Motivate with comparison and rewards, but carefully.** Your organization should hone its skills to provide balanced presentations of comparative performance information.

- **Share best practices.** Finally, you should serve as a valuable expert resource for state and local governments by assisting them in the search for effective practices.

Case Studies in Using State Performance Information

From *Strategies for Using State Information: Measuring and Improving Program Performance* by Shelley H. Metzenbaum

Environmental Protection Agency: Shifting from Activities to Outcomes

This case study looked at an agreement crafted between the U.S. Environmental Protection Agency (EPA) and the states, called the National Environmental Performance Partnership System (NEPPS). NEPPS was adopted as an overlay to over a dozen separate federal environmental laws, many of which establish specific environmental goals as well as measurement requirements for states. Over time, EPA's management of these laws, with the exception of the mandate that all states attain national ambient air quality standards, had evolved in a manner that emphasized processes over environmental performance. NEPPS was embraced by EPA and state environmental agency leaders as a way to make clear that, instead of EPA's historical emphasis on assuring state completion of a negotiated number of explicitly specified activities, the federal agency could use environmental progress and compliance outcomes as the dominant criteria for program accountability. Further, state leaders were encouraged to do the same in their own program management.

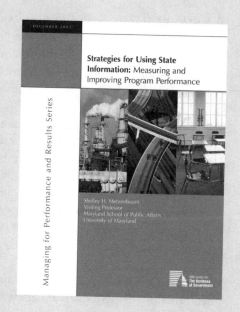

Department of Transportation: Sharing Information and Balancing Mandates

Two agencies of the U.S. Department of Transportation (DOT), the Federal Highway Administration (FHWA) and the National Highway Traffic Safety Administration (NHTSA), established themselves as expert resources for state and local governments. They collect and disseminate written materials on state practices and progress. In addition, they identify more effective practices worthy of replication. Compilation of state information in an easy-to-find and easy-to-use format; analysis tailored to meet the needs of specific audiences—especially the states and others whose actions directly affect the rate of progress; problem and success identification; aggressive packaging and dissemination of the raw information, analysis, and materials supporting programs demonstrated to be effective; ongoing evaluation at multiple levels; and co-ownership of decision-making responsibilities characterize the successful work of FHWA and NHTSA with the states.

Department of Education: Federal Report Cards Motivate and Analysis Illuminates

In the U.S. Department of Education (ED), the department's release of the "Wall Chart" in 1984 and, more recently, reports released by a nonprofit association using data assembled with ED funding illustrate the power of comparative measurement across jurisdictions whether within a state, among states, or internationally. The first example demonstrates how comparative measurement can motivate improved performance. It also underscores the power and possibility of state political leaders collectively endorsing comparative measurement after years of opposition. The second underscores the value of the federal government gathering and organizing state performance data. It shows how, just by gathering and organizing information and making it easy to use, the federal government can stimulate external analyses to find effective government programs worthy of replication.

THE CHALLENGE OF CROSS-AGENCY MEASUREMENT

QUESTION: Should my organization take the lead in creating a cross-agency measurement system involving several organizations all dealing with a common problem?

ANSWER: Thus far in this section, we have been focused primarily on the role of performance measurement in the management of your own organization. A major challenge for the next administration is the federal government's ability to measure progress toward administration goals, which include measuring the contribution of individual agencies toward larger government-wide goals. Baltimore's CitiStat initiative discussed on pages 38–39 is a good example of cross-agency measurement.

The government's most extensive experience with cross-agency measurement systems to date was the use of a Performance Measurement and Evaluation (PME) system in the late 1990s by the Office of National Drug Control Policy (ONDCP). In their report to the IBM Center, Patrick Murphy and John Carnevale write, "This ambitious undertaking would require coordinating with the more than 50 agencies and departments involved in drug control efforts. In the end, the process would utilize the input of over 250 people representing numerous government agencies and other organizations. To organize the effort, the ONDCP constructed a complex set of steering committees and working groups designed to address the specific tasks of developing a performance measurement system."

While the ONDCP experience was cumbersome and time-consuming and had its share of critics, government-wide performance data was collected and shared by the executive and legislative branches of the federal government, as well as state and local governments. The imposition of "stretch goals" and intergovernmental goals proved controversial. A compromise was struck. Murphy and Carnevale write, "The ONDCP agreed to present the PME system and its performance targets as part of the *national* strategy. Responsibility for reaching the targets, therefore, would not fall solely on the federal agencies. Instead, state and local governments would have to cooperate as well if the objectives were to be realized. This realization, in fact, led to the ONDCP beginning to reach out to state and local governments in an attempt to more completely integrate their efforts. Consequently, the federal office formed performance partnerships with the states of Oregon and Maryland and the city of Houston. These partnerships focused on monitoring specific outcomes in these jurisdictions."

Much was learned from the ONDCP experience that can be applied by a new administration. While highly challenging, a government-wide performance management system was put in place that can be replicated in the future by other agencies working together to track national progress on achieving national goals.

Understanding Challenges Facing Cross-Agency Measurement

From *The Challenge of Developing Cross-Agency Measures: A Case Study of the Office of National Drug Control Policy* by Patrick J. Murphy and John Carnevale

By most accounts, the Performance Measurement and Evaluation system has been deemed an impressive and credible attempt to introduce accountability into the management of federal drug policy. It is clearly the most extensive and institutionalized effort to measure performance for a crosscutting program in the federal government. To create it, the ONDCP had to face substantial challenges with measuring performance in general, as well as the added complication of working across organizational lines.

The ONDCP set out to develop a performance measurement system. In addition to the systemic problems of building performance and accountability systems, however, the office had the additional challenge of constructing a system that cut across traditional organizational and functional lines in the federal government. Accountability in this context means that programmatic responsibility extends beyond departmental lines.

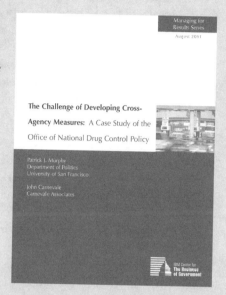

Challenge One: Breadth of Effort

First, the absolute breadth of what constitutes the federal drug control effort is impressive, complicating efforts to measure performance. Federal drug control policy is a conglomeration of agency programs in several functional areas (treatment, prevention, domestic law enforcement, international, and interdiction), for which many different agencies are responsible. Included under the rubric of drug control are law enforcement programs designed to investigate, arrest, prosecute, and incarcerate individuals violating drug laws.

To implement this collection of programs, federal anti-drug activities involve over 50 different federal organizational entities. Twelve of the 14 Cabinet departments are represented as well as two independent federal agencies.

Challenge Two: Little Formal Authority

A second factor making the task of performance measurement more difficult is that, despite its "czar" designation, the office possesses relatively little formal authority. The Congress has charged the ONDCP with drafting a strategy that establishes policy goals and priorities for the nation's drug control efforts. The office is also responsible for coordinating and overseeing the implementation of that strategy. To carry out these responsibilities, however, the office is granted rather limited authority (P.L. 105-277). The role of the ONDCP director in the formulation of a drug control budget is the most clearly defined of the office's powers. The ONDCP is required to certify agency budget requests as to their adequacy in support of the national drug control strategy. The director can also request the reprogramming of funds from one agency to another.

Challenge Three: Diffuse Federal System

A third element complicating the ONDCP's development of a performance measurement system stems from the fact that illicit drug control is a national program—that includes states, localities, and nonprofit partners—that is relying upon a federal structure for much of the program implementation and service delivery. Drug control efforts are not unique in this regard, as many federal programs are structured similarly. Nevertheless, trying to assess the performance of government efforts over which federal control is limited serves to compound an already difficult problem.

Understanding Lean Six Sigma

QUESTION: What is Lean Six Sigma and how should I use it?

ANSWER: In his report to the IBM Center, Rensselaer Polytechnic Institute's John Maleyeff describes the evolution of Lean Six Sigma, a process improvement methodology that combines tools from both Lean (also called Lean Manufacturing) and Six Sigma. Lean has traditionally been associated with reducing waste in the system, while Six Sigma is associated with improving quality and reducing defects. Lean Six Sigma encompasses common features of both, such as an emphasis on customer satisfaction, a culture of continuous improvement, the search for root causes, and comprehensive employee involvement. In each case, a high degree of training and education takes place, from upper management to the shop floor.

Defining Lean

According to Maleyeff, Lean can be defined as a management approach that seeks to maximize value to customers, both internal and external, while simultaneously removing wasteful activities and practices. Maleyeff writes, "It is based on the management system used at Toyota Motor Corporation, with Shigeo Shingo and Taiichi Ohno generally considered to be its architects. Womack, Jones, and Roos, in a world-wide study of automobile manufacturing, used the term Lean to describe the activities that seek to minimize waste, such as excess inventory and defective products. Their study concluded that Lean was preferable to 'mass production' prominent in the United States and Europe." Lean focuses on the separation of "value-added" work from "non-value-added" work.

Defining Six Sigma

The goal of Six Sigma is to apply scientific principles to reduce variation and thus eliminate defects in products and service offerings. The term "sigma" refers to a statistical measure of variation and the number "six" refers to the relationship between process variation and product specifications. When first applied as a metric by Motorola, the goal was to achieve Six Sigma quality by limiting defects to no more than 3.4 defects per million products.

Maleyeff writes, "The statistical roots of the term Six Sigma have become less important as Six Sigma has evolved into a comprehensive management system. Many practitioners, however, continue to view Six Sigma as a set of techniques that promote variance reduction."

Lean Six Sigma Builds on Practical Lessons Learned from Previous Eras of Operational Improvement

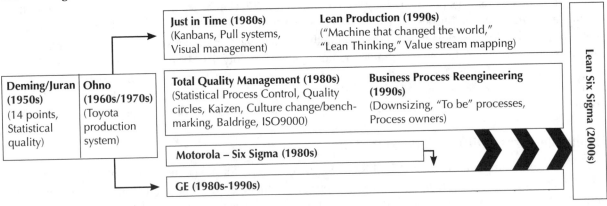

Source: IBM Institute for Business Value, Driving Operational Innovation Using Lean Six Sigma.

Getting Started on Lean Six Sigma Initiatives

If you decide to implement a Lean Six Sigma initiative, your personal commitment is crucial. If it is clear that you are committed to the initiative, participation and support for the initiative within your organization is likely to be much higher than otherwise. In his report to the IBM Center, Maleyeff writes, "Management commitment to a Lean Six Sigma process improvement program must go beyond slogans, banners, or motivational speeches. The leadership team should exude a constancy of purpose, along with discipline and patience that allows the program to take root."

Maleyeff found that there are two crucial steps in launching a Lean Six Sigma program: (1) creating the infrastructure, and (2) implementing the initiative. You must be involved in both steps in order to ensure the success of the initiative.

During the creation of a Lean Six Sigma infrastructure, you must:

- **Build trust.** The creation of a Lean Six Sigma initiative is likely to create concern, perhaps even fear, among employees due to job insecurity and the anticipation of change in the organization. You must communicate directly the importance of the initiative and your willingness to engage employees in the process. If your organization has a union, you should work closely with them in launching the initiative. (See page 68 for a discussion of working with unions).

- **Institute culture change.** This is clearly a long-term initiative. By focusing on program improvement, you will be starting to change the organization's culture to become more results-oriented.

- **Communicate the vision to all stakeholders.** As noted above, communication will be crucial to the success of the initiative. In addition to communicating with employees, you must also communicate with all of your organization's stakeholders.

During Lean Six Sigma implementation, you must:

- **Create a centralized focal point.** A key to the success of the program will be your selection of a program administrator dedicated to firmly establishing the program within your organization and working directly with you on it. You do not need to create a new "office" to run the initiative, but you might create a steering committee that you chair.

- **Encourage involvement across the organization.** You are the only one who can do this. You must ensure that there is a good working relationship between all the units within your agency. You may wish to have liaisons from each of your units who will serve as the "champions" for Lean Six Sigma within their organizations.

- **Ensure staff capability.** You will need to rely on staff that have been trained in Lean Six Sigma or you will have to send key individuals in your organization to receive such training. External consultants are also an option. In addition, you should consider agency-wide training in Lean Six Sigma so that your entire organization understands the key concepts involved.

STRATEGIC ANALYTICS IN GOVERNMENT

QUESTION: What is analytics? Can it be used in my organization?

ANSWER: In brief, analytics is the extensive use of data, statistical and quantitative analysis, explanatory and predictive models, and fact-based management to drive decisions and actions. Strategic analytics, as described by Tom Davenport and Sirkka Jarvenpaa in their report to the IBM Center, are useful inputs into decisions. Analytics is a subset of what has come to be called *business intelligence*: a set of technologies and processes that use data to understand and analyze organizational performance.

Analytics can be a useful tool for you in managing your organization. There are now a variety of analytical applications, or tools, which can be grouped under the term analytics. Some of these applications are used for internal analytics (financial, research and development, human resources) and some for external analytics (customers, suppliers). Your organization is already collecting much data, but may not be using or analyzing that information to its fullest extent.

Analytical applications range from relatively simple statistical and optimization tools in spreadsheets (Excel being the primary example) to statistical software packages (e.g., Minitab), to complex business intelligence suites (SAS, Cognos, Business Objects), predictive industry applications (Fair Isaac), and the reporting and analytical modules of major enterprise systems (SAP and Oracle).

In earlier incarnations, analytics was called operations research and has long been used in the Department of Defense for military analysis and supply chain analysis. In addition to continuing to use analytics in those areas, the military today is using analytics to analyze the military recruitment process and using geodemographic data to identify potential recruits.

Two other diverse arenas in government that are using analytics are health and government revenue management. In the health arena, the Department of Veterans Affairs is now using analytics extensively to study the quality of patient care, as well as applying evidence-based medicine to diagnosing and treating patients.

In the government revenue arena, extensive use of analytics is now being seen in both state government and the U.S. Internal Revenue Service. Tax organizations are using analytics for revenue analysis, compliance reviews to discover nonfilers and make audit and collection decisions, fraud detection, and customer services for taxpayers. In the *Money* section, two other areas ready for analytics are discussed: identifying risks in federal credit programs and analyzing the life cycle and costs of managing federal assets.

Your job will be to assess the state of the use of analytics in your organization. Analytics can be an effective component of your performance management system. You will have to make sure, however, that your organization has a well-trained cadre of analysts ready to use analytics. Davenport and Jarvenpaa write, "Analytical professionals—those who can develop new algorithms and quantitative models—are already present in some data-intensive agencies, such as the Bureau of Labor Statistics.... And as analytics becomes embedded into key governmental processes, those who work with them on the front lines—for example, call center agents who discuss tax returns—will need to be generally aware of, if not expert on, the analytical tools used to carry out an agency's work with citizens."

The Use of Strategic Analytics in Government: Fraud Prevention

From *Strategic Use of Analytics in Government* by Thomas H. Davenport and Sirkka L. Jarvenpaa

Since health care payments are among the largest government payments to citizens, they are also often the domain for fraud. While Medicare fraud prevention is to some degree a focus for the federal government in the United States, prevention and reduction of Medicaid fraud is a much greater focus at both the federal level (the Deficit Reduction Act of 2005 increased penalties for Medicaid fraud and required organizations receiving substantial Medicaid payments to describe their policies for preventing fraud), and particularly at the state level, where Medicaid programs are administered. Many states have fraud prevention initiatives under way, and analytics is a key tool for identifying payments that may be fraudulent.

As a prominent example, New York State is the largest provider in the U.S. of Medicaid services, at $44 billion per year, and has a strong focus on analytics for fraud prevention. The New York State Office of the State Comptroller identified more than $150 million in Medicaid claim overpayments in 2005 and 2006 after analyzing historical claims data in the eMedNY data warehouse. These analyses identified duplicate payments, overpayments to health care providers, non-billing to Medicare, and miscoding of diseases and payments.

Because Medicaid payments in New York State are distributed through county governments, particular counties also have analytical fraud prevention initiatives under way. Onondaga County, for example, is using business intelligence and analytics tools to identify patients whose Medicaid prescription totals warrant fraud investigation. Nassau County on Long Island has launched two multimillion-dollar investigations based on data compiled using business intelligence tools to identify potential Medicaid fraud by county residents. County officials believe that they have saved millions of dollars in savings since 2003, when they began to use the software tools to analyze Medicaid claims. Nassau County is also using analytical software to identify fraudulent transportation claims for Medicaid reimbursement and saw claims decrease by $1 million after the initiative began.

Stephen Acquario, executive director of the New York State Association of Counties, believes that business intelligence and analytics are confirming that fraud and misuse are contributing to the substantial growth of Medicaid claims. "Anecdotes are no longer going to be the norm," he said. "Now, through statistical-driven reporting … we're able to back up what we had suspected in ways we were not able to do in years past."

The Department of Veterans Affairs also employs analytics for fraud reduction through the Veterans Benefits Administration (VBA). The VBA matches income data with the Internal Revenue Service and the Social Security Administration to ensure the people who receive VA pensions (which are dependent on having low incomes) aren't getting more income than they are reporting. The VBA also analyzes high-value claims checks, which typically go to people who have had long-standing disabilities but have recently filed a claim. The organization produces a dashboard that the heads of regional offices use to adjust resources, and also has a dashboard that managers use to evaluate performance and manage their parts of the business.

For Additional Information on Performance

Engaging Citizens in Measuring and Reporting Community Conditions: A Manager's Guide (2007) by Alfred T. Ho

This report presents two case studies (Des Moines, Iowa, and Boston, Massachusetts) where government agencies and citizen groups reported on government's performance. Each of the cases reflects different strategic approaches to reporting government performance. The report discusses how government officials can engage the public more directly in performance measurement and reporting initiatives.

The Management of Regulation Development: Out of the Shadows (2007) by Cornelius M. Kerwin

This report examines the use of regulations in government. The report provides an overview of how individual policy tools such as regulation operate, how to measure their performance and effectiveness, which actors participate in implementing them, and what features are necessary to ensure accountability and oversight.

Improving Service Delivery in Government with Lean Six Sigma (2007) by John Maleyeff

This report is a comprehensive review of how public sector managers can use Lean Six Sigma to improve the execution and delivery of results. The report sets forth specific actions that public sector managers can take in starting and implementing Lean Six Sigma projects.

The Philadelphia SchoolStat Model (2007) by Christopher Patusky, Leigh Botwinik, and Mary Shelley

This report presents a case study of Philadelphia's SchoolStat program. The program is an adaptation of the successful CompStat model, developed by New York City's Police Department. The report describes how the model was adapted for a school district, what improvements occurred in the performance of the Philadelphia School District after it was implemented, and which features of the approach contributed to improvement.

Performance Leadership: 11 Better Practices That Can Ratchet Up Performance (2006, 2nd ed.) by Robert D. Behn

This report offers an approach to performance leadership that encompasses 11 "better practices" that have been used by successful public managers over the years. The approach focuses not on individual attributes and virtues, but rather on leadership activities or practices that can spur improvements in program performance.

For Additional Information on Performance

Implementing OMB's Program Assessment Rating Tool (PART): Meeting the Challenges of Integrating Budget and Performance (2006) by John B. Gilmour

This report examines how the Office of Management and Budget's Program Assessment Rating Tool (PART) has been implemented in the federal government. The report discusses how federal agencies have responded to the requirements of PART and the strategies that they have employed. The report presents four challenges that confronted both agencies and OMB and describes approaches that agencies took to meet these challenges.

Collaboration and Performance Management in Network Settings: Lessons from Three Watershed Governance Efforts (2004) by Mark T. Imperial

This report describes how performance measures and monitoring processes were developed and implemented in three watershed management programs. The report includes a description of the collaborative approach used by citizens and government in coming to agreement on the performance measures to be used.

Linking Performance and Budgeting: Opportunities in the Federal Budget Process (2004, 2nd ed.) by Philip G. Joyce

This report presents an overview and history of performance budgeting in the federal government, including a description of how performance information can be used at the various stages of the budget process: preparation, approval, execution, and audit and evaluation. The report describes how performance-based information is used at the department and agency level.

E-Reporting: Strengthening Democratic Accountability (2004) by Mordecai Lee

This report traces the history of public reporting on government performance and how technology now allows government leaders to dramatically expand citizen access to government performance. The report presents criteria for assessing how well federal, state, and local agencies report their performance to the public, as well as providing examples of best practices in e-reporting. The report includes recommendations on how public managers can assess their own reporting and how they can emulate best practices.

Staying the Course: The Use of Performance Measurement in State Governments (2004) by Julia Melkers and Katherine Willoughby

This report provides an overview of performance management in state government. The report describes how state budgeting systems have evolved to incorporate measurement of program activities and results. The report also describes which components of performance measurement and performance-related initiatives have been most useful in state government.

For Additional Information on Performance

Performance Management for Career Executives: A "Start Where You Are, Use What You Have" Guide (2004, 2nd ed.) by Chris Wye

This report describes how career executives can overcome common problems in the design, alignment, use, and communication of performance measures and information. It provides a series of antidotes to the problems frequently encountered by career executives in implementing performance management. The report offers specific advice on actions and approaches career executives can take.

The Baltimore CitiStat Program: Performance and Accountability (2003) by Lenneal J. Henderson

This report examines Baltimore's CitiStat program in the area of housing and community development. The report describes how Baltimore developed its performance goals, objectives, and outcome measures with the cooperation of federal and state agencies that provide additional funding for municipal programs.

The Potential of the Government Performance and Results Act as a Tool to Manage Third-Party Government (2001) by David G. Frederickson

This report describes the implementation of the Government Performance and Results Act in five federal health care agencies. The report addresses the ability of the federal government to effectively hold third parties accountable for performance. Third parties are organizations outside of the federal government that have responsibility for implementing federally funded programs, such as state and local governments, nonprofit organizations, and universities.

Using Performance Data for Accountability: The New York City Police Department's CompStat Model of Police Management (2001) by Paul E. O'Connell

This report examines the New York City Police Department's model of police management known as CompStat. The report identifies the management practices that are associated with CompStat and documents the process of dissemination and adoption of CompStat by other police departments across the nation.

Corporate Strategic Planning in Government: Lessons from the United States Air Force (2000) by Colin Campbell

This report analyzes and evaluates the corporate strategic planning initiated by the United States Air Force. The report discusses the legacy left by the inception of corporate strategic planning in the Air Force in the 1990s and identifies how Air Force leadership adapted to change in a dynamic world.

Chapter Three: People

Having your employees committed and engaged in the work of your organization is critical to your success as a leader. And creating that commitment and engagement is a key role of any good leader.

IBM CENTER FOR THE BUSINESS OF GOVERNMENT
WASHINGTON, DC 20005

MEMORANDUM FOR THE HEADS OF EXECUTIVE DEPARTMENTS AND AGENCIES

SUBJECT: **People**

Achieving your goals will depend on the hundreds, if not thousands, of people in your organization. While it has become a cliché to say that an organization's most valuable resource is its people, the statement is true.

As you begin to address the people dimension of your job, you will be working in two distinct time frames: the near term, meaning your first six months or so, and the longer term.

Focus on Near-Term Activities

You have an important job to do and you need to get action quickly on the president's agenda. While you and your immediate team will be talented and will work long hours, your immediate team will not be able to accomplish your goals by themselves. Your challenge will be to tap into the skills, talent, ideas, and strong work ethic of the career civil service. To succeed, you will need to rely on the career civil service to help you accomplish your goals.

Your near-term people agenda will be to assess the "state" of the career service in your organization by asking two crucial questions:

- Do you have people with the right skills in place within your organization to get the job done?

- What do your organization's annual employee surveys tell you about your organization? Are your employees engaged in their work? Is there trust and confidence between your employees and their supervisors?

The answers provided to the first question should reflect the status of your organization's workforce. You should probe to find out whether you have *people* with the right *skills* in the right *job* performing their assignments. If the answers are not to your satisfaction, there are many immediate steps you can take to remedy this situation. Your short-term discussions should provide you with a good understanding of your organization and the longer-term challenges the institution may now be facing.

Your answers to the second question are something you can act upon immediately. Having your employees committed and engaged in the work of your organization is critical to your success as a leader. And creating that commitment and engagement is a key role of any good leader. Creating trust and confidence between employees and supervisors is also critical, but that may take time. Still, that will be an important investment of your time to ensure the work of your organization will be done effectively.

Invest in Long-Term Initiatives

After you complete your near-term assessment of the effectiveness of the people in your organization and their levels of commitment, you can then turn to more complex people issues that typically face every agency. These are crucial to the longer-term effectiveness of your organization and its ability to sustain the president's agenda.

- **Managing workforce planning.** Building on the plan you inherited will be one of your most important long-term initiatives in order for you to leave behind a strong institution. Given the anticipated retirement of many "baby boomers" during your tenure, you will have the unique opportunity to reshape the skill mix of your organization to better fit its mission and strategy for the next decade.

- **Managing talent strategically.** As an outgrowth of your workforce planning, you will need to develop and implement strategies to recruit, retain, develop, and manage your employees. Agencies currently have a number of hiring strategies under way including partnerships with universities, job fairs, and other outreach programs; the use of hiring flexibilities such as recruitment, retention, and relocation bonuses; re-employed annuitants; student hiring programs; and direct hire authority. You should aggressively use these hiring flexibilities.

  In addition to these hiring flexibilities, agencies have implemented learning and leadership development programs such as the Candidate Development Program, emerging-leaders programs, and other succession planning initiatives. Agencies have also implemented other programs to retain employees including child care, student loan repayments, telework, and other work life initiatives. Your chief human capital officer will be able to brief you on current strategies, as well as how well these strategies are working.

- **Managing for better performance.** Your agency should have a performance management system that is designed to link employee performance plans with the agency strategic plan. As a result, employees should have performance plan goals that align with and support the organizational goals. Similarly, employee ratings should be linked to the overall performance of the agency. Some agencies have legislation that authorizes a pay-for-performance system, perhaps including paybanding.

  A pay-for-performance system could serve as an effective complement to your initiatives to drive performance and accountability. You will need to decide whether the nature of the work of your organization lends itself to pay for performance including paybanding. If you do decide that your agency needs pay for performance or paybanding to improve performance, then you will need to work with the Office of Personnel Management (OPM) and the Office of Management and Budget (OMB) to seek legislation.

Develop Effective Relationships

To accomplish your goals, you will need to create an effective working relationship with a variety of different groups, including individuals inside and outside your own organization. Within your own organization, it is crucial that you develop a good working relationship with your own employees. An important group of your employees is union members. Your chief human capital officer (CHCO) should be able to tell you how many unions and union members are in your organization, as well as the extent of their influence and the "state" of labor relations in your organization. Based on the experience of many previous agency heads in government, spending an appropriate amount of time with your union representatives to forge an effective working relationship can be beneficial.

You will also need to work closely with key government staff outside of your own organization. Specifically, you will have to work closely with two central management agencies: OPM and OMB. Both are intimately involved in a variety of people issues, such as pay, employment ceilings, and the number of Senior Executive Service "slots" within your organization.

PEOPLE

WORKFORCE PLANNING

QUESTION: What is workforce planning and should I pay attention to it?

ANSWER: Workforce planning, as defined by the National Academy of Public Administration, helps identify the human capital required to meet organizational goals and develop strategies to meet these requirements.

Your agency has a strategic plan, which contains your organization's business plan. Your challenge is to align that plan with your organization's people. Simply put, do you have the right *people* with the right *skills* in the right *job* at the right *time* performing their assignments?

You will have a major opportunity over the next four years (and perhaps the next eight) to reshape your organization's people via an effective workforce planning initiative. Much has been written about the antici- pated forthcoming retirement "wave" of the baby boomers. While it is unclear how many will actually retire after becoming eligible, it is safe to say that your workplace will look far different four years from now. This should be viewed as an opportunity to reshape your workforce to be more closely aligned to your strategic plan and contain the appropriate skill sets for the 21st century.

You will need to make sure that a credible and effective workforce planning initiative is in place. A key member of your management team will be your chief human capital officer, who will be responsible for overseeing workforce planning in your organization. You will also need to ensure that workforce planning is under way and that it links to your organization's strategic plan.

Where do you get started on workforce planning? In her report to the IBM Center, University of Baltimore's Ann Cotten sets forth the following key steps:

- **Step One:** You must first find out whether your organization is already undertaking a workforce planning effort. If such an initiative is under way, ask to be briefed on it and probe about its linkage to your strategic goals for the organization. If workforce planning is not under way, get it started.

- **Step Two:** As part of its workforce planning initiative, your organization should be conducting internal and external environmental scans to identify workforce trends in a proactive manner before they become prob- lems for your organization. Do specific professions in your organization face a shortage of workers in the future? You might call upon your organization's strategic planners to assist in the environmental scans.

- **Step Three:** Focus your workforce planning efforts in areas where the most benefit will be achieved. Ann Cotten writes, "By targeting workforce planning efforts in the areas of strategic importance—those mission-critical positions that are instrumental to the organization's success and where the organiza- tion is experiencing problems recruiting or retaining employees with the needed skills or abilities— organizations will achieve the best return on investment."

- **Step Four:** You must have an appropriate system in place to collect and report on key workforce indicators. If your organization is not already collecting data about the number of employees and contractors, it must begin to do so. Data should be collected on the number of permanent employees (full or part-time), tempo- rary employees, employees with nonstandard work arrangements, and contractual employees.

Assessing Future Workforce Needs

From *Seven Steps of Effective Workforce Planning* by Ann Cotten

In the public sector, projecting future workforce needs is a relatively new phenomenon. The assessment requires leaders to think critically about how the organization will do business in the future. Assessments can be complex, data-driven models for organizations with sound workforce data or more qualitative estimates developed by the organization's leadership team for organizations that lack strong workforce data. Regardless of the technique used, one maxim applies: Bad assumptions create bad models. Therefore, it is important to vet the model's assumptions thoroughly.

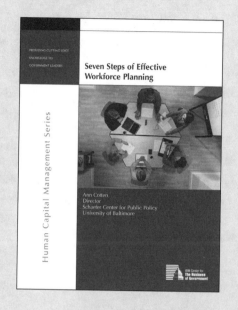

The workforce demand forecast is an estimate of the number and mix of employees that an organization will need in the future. Particular attention should be paid to identifying and projecting mission-critical occupations. The forecast has two components: first, the estimated workload and related staffing requirements; and, second, the likely competencies and skill sets needed. Guidance for both is provided by the strategic plan.

Workforce supply is, at its most basic level, the current workforce plus new hires less projected separations at some specific date in the future, as shown in the figure below. For some organizations, projected workforce supply will be the result of a sophisticated mathematical model. For others, it will be an educated guess based upon data collected in the environmental scan. For most, it will be somewhere in between.

No matter the level of sophistication, all models need to consider the same elements when projecting the future workforce composition: the inventory of the current workforce; the rate at which employees in specific occupations and at various leadership levels will leave the organization; what types of skills and abilities the organization will be able to attract; how the permanent workforce can be supplemented; and how the skill set of those who remain will or can change.

Projecting Workforce Supply

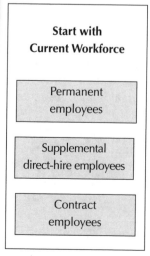

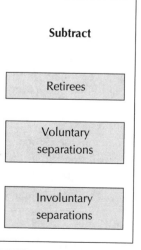
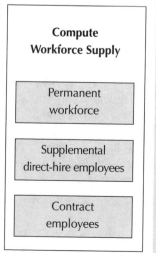

Start with Current Workforce	Add	Subtract	Compute Workforce Supply
Permanent employees	New hires	Retirees	Permanent workforce
Supplemental direct-hire employees	Transfers	Voluntary separations	Supplemental direct-hire employees
Contract employees	Supplemental direct-hire employees	Involuntary separations	Contract employees
	Contract employees		

PEOPLE

PERSONNEL FLEXIBILITIES

QUESTION: How do I maximize the use of personnel flexibilities in my own organization?

ANSWER: Your workforce planning initiative is your first step in effectively aligning your people to your agency's mission, goals, and strategy. Your organizational strategy should drive your human resource reform initiatives.

The extent of your human resource reform effort will depend, in part, on the "starting place" of your organization when you take over and the public and congressional attitudes toward your organization. When the new commissioner of the Internal Revenue Service (IRS) took over in 1997, he found an agency very unpopular in Congress and heavily criticized for its management practices and personnel. As an outgrowth of the National Commission on Restructuring the Internal Revenue Service, Congress passed the IRS Restructuring and Reform Act of 1998 (RRA '98), which granted IRS a variety of new human resource flexibilities aimed at improving the organizational, including its people, capability of IRS.

Your challenge will be twofold: to use the flexibilities you currently have, and to determine if you need additional flexibilities beyond the authorities you have in place. The table on page 57 is significant because of the 15 actions taken by IRS to make its personnel system more flexible, only five required congressional authorization. The table sets forth the following key aspects to transforming human resources in your organization:

- **Developing an effective human resource infrastructure**, including a competency-based personnel system and deploying workforce planning tools (see pages 54–55).

- **Transitioning the workforce to a new structure**, including making managers recompete for positions, and using buy-out and early retirement authorities.

- **Renewing the workforce for improved performance**, including using critical pay authorities to recruit needed talent, succession planning, and modern recruitment techniques, as well as expediting the hiring process.

- **Investing in employee training and development for enhanced capacity**, including expanding job scope for frontline workers, providing world-class training, and supporting employee development and growth.

- **Heightening performance and maintaining accountability**, including developing technical leaders, linking pay to performance through paybanding, and distinguishing levels of performance through a performance management system.

In many ways, the IRS initiatives can serve as your "playbook" for identifying flexibilities you might deploy in your organization to accomplish your mission and goals. After you review what human resource initiatives are currently in place within your organization and you are briefed on your organization's workforce planning efforts, you will then face a series of choices as to whether you need to work with the Office of Management and Budget and the Office of Personnel Management to request additional human resource flexibilities to accomplish your mission.

Examples of additional flexibilities include critical pay authorities (to hire needed expertise at higher pay levels), buy-out and early retirement authority (to reduce your personnel levels and/or reshape the skill set of your employees), a payband system (to base pay on qualifications and skills rather than longevity), and a streamlined hiring process (to give your managers more flexibility in hiring).

If you conclude that your people needs require more flexible 21st century personnel practices, there is much that you can do to change your agency's personnel practices. You must, however, be prepared to make the business case that your mission requires such actions.

Human Resource Initiatives at the Internal Revenue Service

From *Modernizing Human Resource Management in the Federal Government: The IRS Model*
by James R. Thompson and Hal G. Rainey

The table below distinguishes the various elements of the IRS HR model according to:

- Those implemented pursuant to special flexibilities provided under RRA '98, and

- Those implemented pursuant to generally available authorities.

Apparent from the table is that the majority of changes under way fall into the second category and, hence, are suitable for widespread adoption within the federal government.

Human Capital Series

APRIL 2003

Modernizing Human Resource Management in the Federal Government: The IRS Model

James R. Thompson
Director of Graduate Studies and
Associate Professor
Department of Public Administration
University of Illinois-Chicago

Hal G. Rainey
Alumni Foundation Distinguished Professor
School of Public and International Affairs
University of Georgia

IRS Human Resource Initiatives

	Implemented Pursuant to RRA '98 Flexibilities	Implemented Pursuant to Generally Available Authorities
Developing a Modernized Human Resources Infrastructure		
Structuring the Human Resource Function for Mission Accomplishment		✓
Creating a Competency-Based Personnel System		✓
Utilizing Workforce Planning Tools to Drive Recruitment and Development Processes		✓
Transitioning the Workforce to a Modernized Structure		
Making Managers Compete for Positions in the New Organization		✓
Shaping the Workforce through Buy-Out and Early Retirement Authority	✓	✓
Renewing the Workforce for Improved Performance		
Using Critical Pay to Recruit Technical and Organizational Leaders	✓	
Planning and Managing Leadership Succession		✓
Employing Modern Recruitment Techniques		✓
Expediting the Hiring Process through Category Rating	✓	
Investing in Employee Training and Development for Enhanced Capacity		
Expanding the Job Scope for Frontline Positions		✓
Partnering in the Provision of World-Class Training		✓
Supporting Employee Development and Growth		✓
Heightening Performance and Maintaining Accountability		
Developing Technical as well as Organizational Leaders: the Senior Leadership Service	✓	
Linking Pay to Performance through Paybanding	✓	
Distinguishing Levels of Performance through the Performance Management System		✓

PEOPLE

Managing for Better Performance

QUESTION: What is the difference between performance appraisal and performance management? And how are they both related to pay for performance?

ANSWER: There are important distinctions between performance appraisal and performance management. Performance appraisals focus on the year-end rating made by a manager of an employee. These ratings can be used in the performance-based pay systems discussed on page 62.

In contrast, performance management is a broader, more comprehensive process. As described by Howard Risher and Charles Fay in their report to the IBM Center, performance management is future oriented since it starts with performance planning discussions at the beginning of the year. Risher and Fay write, "It [performance management] focuses on planned performance, with a goal of improvement over the prior year. Ratings are still required in the process, but are a natural step in the usual year-end review of organization performance."

In order for your performance appraisal system and any pay-for-performance systems to be successful, you must have a performance management system in place. The recent experience of the Department of Homeland Security has demonstrated this. A senior executive at the Department of Homeland Security concluded that the department "needs to have a good performance management program in place before pay can be linked to it."

The goal of performance management is to link the relationship between your agency's goals and achievements to staff performance ratings. The goal, according to Risher and Fay, is clear: "There should be a strong relationship between the performance ratings of the employees in the department and the effectiveness of that department." An effective performance management system is crucial to linking pay and bonus decisions to performance appraisals.

A clear lesson learned about performance management in recent years is the need to involve employees in defining successful performance. American University's Robert Tobias recommends engaging employee representatives in all stages of a performance management system—initial planning, implementation, monitoring, and subsequent modifications. Such engagement, according to Tobias, creates a much better chance of achieving the goal of a performance management system: improved individual and organizational performance.

Based on an analysis of the Office of Personnel Management's annual Federal Human Capital Survey, Tobias found that when employees understand the linkage between their efforts and the desired agency outcomes, their engagement and productivity increase. Tobias writes, "Employee involvement in identifying agency output goals will bring to light any difficulty in achieving those goals, and will show how employees can contribute to their attainment." Tobias also believes that employee participation allows managers to leverage employees' desire to make a difference by accomplishing agency goals.

Eight Management Practices That Contribute to a Performance Culture

From *Managing for Better Performance: Enhancing Federal Performance Management Practices*
by Howard Risher and Charles H. Fay

- **Leaders as champions.** Leaders across the organization need to explain, in most cases repeatedly, why the new practices are necessary, how they are expected to benefit the organization, and how they are expected to affect employees. This is a walk-the-talk, beat-the-drums mission to convince people that change is necessary.

- **Linkage of work to mission.** Employees want to feel their work efforts are contributing to the success of their organization. That means they need to understand the mission and to have a "line of sight" that enables them to see how their work output is linked to the achievement of goals. Cascading goals help to solidify that linkage.

- **Performance tracking and dialogue.** The common practice in a goal-based environment is to track performance over time, to take corrective action when necessary, and to communicate the results widely. Employees want to know how their employer is performing, and regular communication keeps employees involved. The Total Quality Management (TQM) movement prompted employers to post performance data so everyone could keep track of how well they were doing. Practices like that reinforce the focus on performance.

- **Cascading goals.** This argument has been in management textbooks for decades. Each level of an organization defines goals that are linked to the goals above and below. It may be difficult to define performance goals at lower levels, but even the lowest-level employees will be more engaged if they see the cascading goals.

- **Investment in talent.** Organizations that want to perform at high levels need well-qualified people. They need to invest in the development of individual skills, and they need to ensure that the most qualified people are promoted. Organizations that commit to talent management send the message that performance is important.

- **Recognition and rewards.** It may be difficult to gain adequate support for pay for performance, but every organization has a reasonably long list of ways that employees are recognized and rewarded. Recognition and reward practices should be evaluated occasionally to decide if they are serving the needs of the organization. One purpose is to recognize that high-performing employees and their accomplishments are to be celebrated.

- **Manager accountability.** Managers should be held accountable for managing the performance of their people. That has to be a primary role for frontline managers, and that is reinforced when their pay increases (and other rewards) depend on how well they perform this role. That should be a theme throughout their training. They need to understand the performance management process, but even more important is their commitment to help their people improve. They need to provide guidance and coaching advice, and those competencies should be a priority.

- **Employee engagement.** Finally, we know from research by The Gallup Organization that employee engagement is associated with significantly better performance. A survey to learn how employees feel about their organization, their jobs, and their supervisors will provide a picture related to employee engagement.

PAYBANDING

QUESTION: What is paybanding and is it another tool to transform the organization? Will it help my organization? If I decide to move toward paybanding, how do I go about it?

ANSWER: According to James R. Thompson of the University of Illinois at Chicago, in his report to the IBM Center (2007), "The essential concept behind paybanding is that, for the purpose of salary determination, positions are placed within broad bands instead of within narrow grades." This is in contrast to the traditional 15-grade General Schedule (GS). Payband systems usually have six steps instead of 15 grades. This allows organizations more flexibility in hiring and promoting individuals within broad bands instead of narrow pay grades. In the traditional General Schedule, promotions (for instance, from a GS-14 to a GS-15) are linked to assuming a supervisory position. In a paybanding system, an individual can be promoted based on technical expertise and not the number of employees supervised.

Thompson also notes that a second distinguishing feature of payband systems is that, in general, there are no "steps" within the band. Under the General Schedule, employees automatically move up one pay step each year, two years, or three years. With paybanding, as described by Thompson, the intent is that an employee's progress through the payband is on the basis of performance rather than longevity.

Whether paybanding can help your organization largely depends on the mission of your organization. Organizations consisting of knowledge workers, such as scientific research agencies, have found that payband systems work well for them. As many organizations move away from the traditional 20th century hierarchical model of command and control, paybanding systems appear to be effective in managing knowledge workers in flat organizations.

Receiving approval to move to paybanding will require some work on the part of your organization. There are two paths you can take to receiving approval for the change to paybanding: (1) work with OPM and OMB to seek approval from Congress, as was requested by the Internal Revenue Service and the Department of Defense laboratories; or (2) seek approval from OPM under its demonstration project authority, as was requested by the National Institute of Standards and Technology.

Thompson offers six recommendations to guide you in the design and implementation of a new pay and performance system once you have decided to move to a payband system:

- **Determine system objectives.** The design of a pay system requires that trade-offs be made among three competing objectives: efficiency, equity, and employee acceptance.

- **Determine the principles that will guide pay system design prior to deciding pay system specifics.** This entails deciding on three key design issues: the degree to which the system will be performance-oriented, the degree to which lower-level managers will be given discretion in administering the system, and whether or not the system will be market-based.

- **Decide the extent to which cost control is an objective.**

- **Take contextual factors into account.** As noted above, the adoption of paybanding will allow your organization to move from the "one size fits all" General Schedule to a system specifically designed to fit the mission and needs of your organization.

- **Attend to the cultural aspects of performance-oriented payband systems.**

- **Train managers in the administration of performance-oriented payband systems.**

Why Paybanding?

From *Designing and Implementing Performance-Oriented Payband Systems*
by James R. Thompson

A 2004 report by the National Academy of Public Administration lists the following as reasons "why employers shift to broadbanding":

- **Paybanding "supports organizational change."** This is the case because the rigidities of a conventional system such as the General Schedule greatly complicate attempts to redefine jobs or reduce hierarchical layers. The breadth of the bands in a payband system means that in many instances jobs can be redefined without affecting the salary or status of the incumbent. In 2001, the IRS effectively employed its new payband system to mitigate the impact of its delayering exercise on managers. Approximately 400 mid- and top-level management positions were eliminated in the process of collapsing management layers by half. Managers who had previously been segregated into GS-14 and GS-15 grades were placed into a single "senior manager" band, thereby eliminating hierarchical distinctions and permitting the agency greater flexibility in making assignments.

- **Payband systems are more compatible with "high-performance work systems" than are traditional pay and compensation systems.** Among the distinguishing features of high-performance work systems, according to Nadler and Tushman, are employee empowerment, redesigned processes, the organization of work by teams, broad jobs, and flexible organizational boundaries. Such systems emphasize flexibility in job assignments and de-emphasize both vertical and horizontal boundaries within the organization. Attention is directed less to the "job" as defined in a narrow, bureaucratic way than to meeting the needs of the "customer," however that is achieved. Paybanding is compatible with this organizational model in that it places greater emphasis on the individual rather than on the job for pay-setting purposes.

- **Paybanding "encourages lateral movement" in delayered organizations.** As organizations reduce the number of hierarchical layers, they simultaneously truncate career ladders. Paybanding makes it possible for those who may not be able to move upward in the organization to nevertheless increase their salaries by expanding the scope of their responsibilities. Payband systems sometimes provide for a "dual track" whereby technical experts can be compensated at the same level as managerial personnel.

- **By allowing line managers more responsibility in pay and classification matters, payband systems contribute to a reduction in administrative costs and to a shift in roles for human resource management (HRM) personnel.** Most payband systems provide managers with expanded authority in pay matters and hence there is less need for HRM officials to serve in a policing role. There is also less of a need for classification experts to determine appropriate grade placements.

- **Paybanding avoids the dysfunctional consequences of traditional grade and step systems.** This is perhaps the most compelling argument in support of paybanding. The importance of the grade assignment in traditional systems in conjunction with the emphasis on "job" over "person" provides incentives to "game" the classification system, that is, to reward the incumbent of a job for good performance by getting his or her job reclassified. Also, the priority given "internal equity," that is, the determination of salary levels primarily on the basis of comparison to other internal jobs, rather than to "external equity," the amount paid similar positions on the outside, can lead to excessive salary costs.

PERFORMANCE-BASED PAY

QUESTION: What is pay for performance and should I consider it for my organization?

ANSWER: Pay for performance is one of the most controversial elements of a performance management system, especially in the public sector. The private sector has had more experience with pay-for-performance systems and is generally more positively disposed to such pay systems than the public sector.

The issue of pay for performance is, however, receiving increasing attention because both the Department of Homeland Security and the Department of Defense received legislative authorization to develop their own pay systems. Other departments, such as the Department of State, have requested pay-for-performance systems. Other government organizations, such as the Government Accountability Office and Internal Revenue Service, have already implemented pay-for-performance systems. In addition, both the Senior Executive Service (SES) and the Senior Foreign Service have moved to pay-for-performance systems.

What is pay for performance? The most common definition is that it "links pay, in whole and/or in part, to individual, group, and/or organizational performance." In stark terms, pay for performance contrasts with "longevity-based pay increases" in which individuals receive annual pay raises based on length of service.

In government, pay for performance is usually discussed in the context of annual salary increases. In the private sector, it is common to have both annual salary increases based on performance and bonuses on top of the annual increases. While members of the Senior Executive Service are eligible for bonuses, the use of bonuses for those not in the SES is inconsistent throughout government. It is also important to recognize that there are various types of bonuses available to organizations: individual bonuses (such as "spot" bonus awards, year-end incentive awards, technical achievement awards, and key contributor awards) and group awards (gain-sharing plans and goal-sharing plans).

As with many of the ideas discussed in this volume, a key question is always what to do first. In his 2004 report to the IBM Center, Howard Risher recommends the following steps to get started:

- **Your initial steps should be to document, evaluate, and understand current reward practices in your agency.** The review should consider the existing performance management system as well as cash awards. You should ask managers and employees how they view these practices. The assessment should also look at the ratings and awards in your agency over the past year or two.

- **If you decide to proceed with performance pay, you must play a prominent role in planning and overseeing the change to the new system.** While your role may be limited to attending key meetings or adding key statements to communications, your participation is essential and must be highly visible.

- **You should appoint a key senior member of your team to be responsible for managing pay and performance in your organization, including moving to a new system.** This individual must be highly respected within your organization.

- **Be prepared for the design and implementation of a pay-for-performance system to take time.** It can't be done overnight and will require much consultation and engagement with employees within your organization.

Senior Executive Service Pay and Performance Regulations

From *Pay for Performance: A Guide for Federal Managers* by Howard Risher

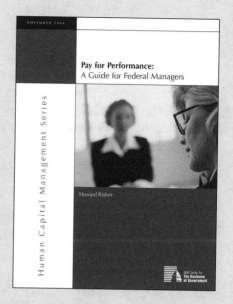

In 2004, the Office of Personnel Management issued regulations creating a new performance-based pay system for the Senior Executive Service that established a solid linkage between the compensation of senior federal executives and their performance. The changes are the most sweeping since the SES was established almost 25 years ago.

Now both salary increases and annual performance bonus awards depend on performance. For the first time, agency performance has to be a factor in compensating executives.

Under these regulations, SES salaries can increase from the old maximum, $145,600, to the new ceiling, $158,100. The combination of salary and bonuses can now go as high as $203,000, the salary of the vice president of the United States. These ceilings are adjusted annually.

To be eligible for the higher pay ceilings, an agency's performance management system has to be certified by OPM that it satisfies nine criteria related to the performance expectations defined for executives as follows:

- **Alignment:** performance expectations linked to the agency's mission, strategic goals, and annual performance plan

- **Consultation:** performance expectations based on executive input

- **Results:** performance expectations that are "measurable, demonstrable or observable, and focus on tangible outputs, outcomes, milestones or other deliverables"

- **Balance:** performance expectations that include measures or indicators of "results, customer/stakeholder feedback, quality, quantity, timeliness, and cost effectiveness ... and competencies or behaviors that contribute to and are necessary to distinguish outstanding performance"

- **Assessments and guidelines:** agency head provides an assessment of the agency's performance as well as the performance of each major program and functional area relative to its Government Performance and Results Act goals to be used in rating executives

- **Oversight:** agency head provides rigorous oversight of SES appraisal system

- **Accountability:** performance ratings reflect the individual's performance as well as the agency's performance

- **Performance differentiation:** the appraisal process "results in meaningful distinctions in performance"

- **Pay differentiation:** pay must reflect "meaningful distinction among executives based on their relative contribution ..."

The funds available for performance awards are unchanged: 10 percent of the aggregate SES payroll. In all other respects, however, the regulations require agencies to completely rethink the way they manage executive salaries and bonus awards.

Performance-Based Pay in the Federal Government: An Historical Overview

by John Kamensky in *Pay for Performance: A Guide for Federal Managers* by Howard Risher

The federal government has experienced a series of fits and starts over the past quarter century in the use of performance-based pay. The following chronology reflects some of the challenges that have faced government-wide reformers: Should these efforts be government-wide or agency specific? Should all levels of employees be subjected at the same time, or should it be targeted to, or implemented by, segments (Senior Executive Service, managers, line staff)? Can such a system be cost neutral, or should additional funds be appropriated? Following are some of the steps taken along the way.

1978: The Civil Service Reform Act of 1978 (CSRA) held promises for performance-based pay for both executives and the managerial ranks. But in the succeeding years, Congress did not support the funding needed to support this initiative, which would have been on top of the existing cost-of-living adjustment and within-grade increases.

1980: CSRA authorized a series of "demonstration projects" to pilot new approaches in personnel management. The Naval Air Warfare Center Weapons Division in China Lake, California, conducted a wide-ranging pilot that centered on the use of performance pay. While not adopted government-wide, its success led to its permanent authorization at China Lake (CSRA demonstration projects were to have ended after five years). In addition, several other Department of Defense organizations have since adopted similar approaches. This demonstration showed both an increase in performance and an overall increase in salary spending.

1984–1993: Congress creates the Performance Management and Recognition System, tying pay increases for GS-13 through GS-15 employees to their performance ratings. Regulations were issued in 1986. Congress revised and extended the program twice, but after numerous implementation and funding problems, the program was terminated in 1993.

1993: In this year, several events revived the notion of pay for performance. First, the National Performance Review (NPR) recommended decentralizing the civil service system to each individual agency, within a framework of guiding principles, and allowing each agency to create its own incentive and bonus systems. Second, Congress adopted the Government Performance and Results Act (GPRA), requiring agencies to create strategic and performance plans, and to measure and report on their performance.

1996: While the administration and Congress took no action on NPR's proposed civil service reforms, the Results Act contributed to agencies more clearly defining and measuring their performance. Also in 1996, NPR recommended the creation of performance-based organizations (PBOs), patterned after British "Next Steps" agencies that created a performance contract between the chief executive of the agency and the home department. A share of the executive's pay was based on meeting performance targets; in exchange, the department delegated administrative flexibilities (in pay, personnel, procurement, etc.) to the executive in the operation of the agency.

1999–2000: By this time period, most agencies had clear missions, goals, and measures. This in turn created some political pressures for agencies to deliver on their goals, resulting in agency leaders creating better links with what their employees did to contribute to these goals. Some agencies had adopted elements of the PBO—the Internal Revenue Service, the Federal Aviation Administration, the Patent and Trademark Office, and the Office of Federal Student Aid—and they pioneered variations of pay-for-performance systems within the limits of existing law.

OPM abandoned government-wide civil service reform in favor of streamlined demonstration authority. But this made no progress either. The President's Management Council (PMC), composed of the chief operating officers of the major departments and agencies, commissioned a task force to examine other alternatives for dealing with poor performers and providing incentives for better performance. Based on the task force's findings, the PMC outlined an approach to improving performance that included elements of a pay-for-performance system.

2001: The President's Management Agenda set forth by the George W. Bush administration included an element that required agencies to link SES performance plans to the goals and performance of their agencies. The director of the Office of Personnel Management decried the trend whereby nearly all members of SES were rated at the top of the rating scale, calling for agencies to make "meaningful distinctions in performance" when rating their executives. In addition, the new leadership in OPM supported agency-by-agency personnel reforms within the bounds of broad performance-based criteria rather than holding out for government-wide reforms. As a consequence, various agencies pursued personnel reforms, including NASA and the Securities and Exchange Commission.

2002: The creation of the new Department of Homeland Security included a requirement for a performance-based personnel performance management system. The same legislation also lifted the government-wide cap on total SES compensation, with the proviso that agencies first create executive performance management systems that make "meaningful distinctions in performance."

2003: Congress authorized the Defense Department to overhaul its performance management system to be more performance based. The same legislation also eliminated government-wide pay levels and automatic cost-of-living adjustments within SES ranks. It also lifted the pay ceiling from Executive Schedule 3 to Executive Schedule 2, but with the condition that agencies first create performance management systems that make meaningful distinctions in performance among executives and that are certified by OPM before they can provide performance pay up to the new ceiling. The law also created an OPM Performance Fund.

2004: OPM put in place the SES pay-for-performance system. This included the creation of a new position for agencies, the "senior performance officer," who is responsible for approving performance goals at the beginning of the year and evaluating the performance of both the agency and its executives at the end of the year, in addition to pay decisions.

2006: OPM implemented the concept of "beta sites" in which agencies demonstrate, through an organizational unit within the agency, the linking of performance-related outcomes and accountability down through all levels of that unit. OPM helped 25 agencies establish operational beta sites. These sites provide agencies an opportunity to assess the success of the new performance management systems, as well as identify problems that need to be addressed before expansion. Each year, the beta site is to be expanded to include other parts of the agency.

Demonstration Projects Involving Pay for Performance

Department of Commerce
National Institute of Standards and Technology (made permanent in 1996)
Department of Commerce (implemented 1998)

Department of Defense
DoD Acquisition Workforce (phased implementation completed 1999)

Department of Defense, Department of the Air Force
Air Force Research Laboratory (implemented 1997)

Department of Defense, Department of the Army
Aviation Research, Development and Engineering Center (implemented 1997)
Engineer Research & Development Center (implemented 1998)
Medical Research and Material Command (implemented 1998)
Missile Research, Development and Engineering Center (implemented 1997)
Research Laboratory (implemented 1998)

Department of Defense, Department of the Navy
China Lake Research Laboratories (started 1980, made permanent in 1994)
Naval Research Laboratory (implemented 1999)
Naval Sea Systems Command Warfare Centers (implemented 1998)

PEOPLE

Nonstandard Work Arrangements

QUESTION: What are "nonstandard work arrangements" and should I use them in my organization?

ANSWER: You are entering government in a time of change. If you had entered government 10 or 20 years ago, you would have found that your organization consisted of nearly *all* full-time, permanent positions. This is changing and you now have more flexibility in how you staff your organization. In their report to the IBM Center, University of Illinois at Chicago's James Thompson and Sharon Mastracci state that the current employment model (full time, full-year, permanent) greatly impedes managerial flexibility when it comes to accommodating either rapid increases in demand requiring more staff or budget reductions requiring less staff.

To gain more flexibility and agility, several federal agencies (most notably the Office of Naval Research, the Transportation Security Administration, and the National Aeronautics and Space Administration) are increasingly moving toward nonstandard work arrangements (NSWAs), which are defined as work arrangements other than full-time, full-year, and permanent.

Thompson and Mastracci cite several advantages to moving toward nonstandard work arrangements:

- **To accommodate fluctuations in workflow.** Many agencies, such as the Internal Revenue Service and the Forest Service, have fluctuations due to changes in seasonal workload. Thus, IRS hires seasonal employees in April and May while the Forest Service brings on large numbers of seasonal employees in the summer.

- **To provide a family-friendly workplace and promote work/life balance.** A 2007 survey by the Pew Research Center reported that over 60 percent of employed mothers find part-time work highly appealing—but only 24 percent of them actually have part-time hours. In response to this trend, some agencies, such as the Environmental Protection Agency, are seeking to create more part-time opportunities.

- **To screen and recruit new talent.** The Forest Service has found that temporary seasonal employees serve as an excellent pool of candidates for permanent positions. In addition, nonstandard work arrangement positions can become a competitive advantage when seeking to recruit individuals who desire a nonstandard position.

- **To obtain skills on demand.** This is becoming increasingly important as government needs to obtain skilled talent who may not be interested in a permanent federal position but might consider a term appointment. In addition, the cumbersome federal personnel system is often too time-consuming when access to talent is needed quickly to facilitate mission accomplishment. The Department of Veterans Affairs is using nonstandard work arrangements to obtain skills that are in short supply and difficult to hire through normal hiring mechanisms.

- **To expand the labor pool by addressing demographic trends.** According to Thompson and Mastracci, "One reason for NSWAs is to access the talents and capabilities of populations who prefer such arrangements.... The most prominent groups in this category are retirees, students, and those with family obligations."

Based on their research, Thompson and Mastracci are very positive on the use of nonstandard work arrangements. They recommend that heads of organizations, like yourself, expand the availability of part-time work arrangements and use limited appointments as a means to bring in individuals from outside government to stimulate new thinking.

What Are Nonstandard Work Arrangements?

From *The Blended Workforce: Maximizing Agility Through Nonstandard Work Arrangements*
by James R. Thompson and Sharon H. Mastracci

We define a "nonstandard work arrangement" (NSWA) as any work arrangement other than full-time, full-year, and permanent, as well as those involving people whose services are acquired via a contractual arrangement with another organization. Examples of NSWAs include part-time, seasonal, and on-call workers, as well as temporary help agency and contract company personnel. A key source of data on NSWAs for the economy as a whole has been the Contingent Work Supplement (CWS), which was conducted biennially between 1995 and 2001 by the Bureau of Labor Statistics (BLS). In this survey, BLS identifies four nonstandard arrangements:

- **Independent contractors**—"workers who were identified as independent contractors, independent consultants, or freelance workers, whether they were self-employed or wage and salary workers"

- **On-call workers**—"workers who are called to work only as needed, although they can be scheduled to work for several days or weeks in a row"

- **Temporary help agency workers**—"workers who were paid by a temporary help agency, whether or not their job was temporary"

- **Contract company workers**—"workers who are employed by a company that provides them or their services to others under contract and who are usually assigned to only one customer and usually work at the customer's worksite"

Although these four types have been used in many studies, other studies define nonstandard arrangements somewhat differently. In her study of the flexible staffing arrangements used in the private sector, economist Susan Houseman uses the above categories plus "short-term hires" and "regular part-time workers." The U.S. Government Accountability Office (GAO) identifies a total of nine separate categories of nontraditional work arrangements: BLS's four types, plus "direct-hire temps," "day laborers," "self-employed workers," "standard part-time workers," and "leased workers." GAO finds that, depending upon the types of work arrangements included, estimates of NSWAs range from 5 to 30 percent of the workforce.

In this analysis, we use a blended definition that is informed by these past studies. Consistent with BLS, we include temporary help agency and contract company personnel in our definition of NSWAs. Consistent with GAO, we add part-time workers to our definition, and consistent with OPM, we include part-year or seasonal workers. We go further to identify separately "direct" and "indirect" nonstandard work arrangements. Direct arrangements include part-time, on-call, seasonal, and intermittent workers, and independent contractors, for whom the federal agency need not work through a third-party entity in order to hire. Indirect arrangements include temporary agency and contract company workers, whose services are acquired by the federal agency via an arrangement with a temporary employment service or contractor.

LABOR RELATIONS

QUESTION: Does government have unions and do I need to spend time on labor relations in my organization?

ANSWER: Yes, the federal government has unions and, yes, you should pay attention to the unions in your organization. After assuming your position, you will be briefed by your chief human capital officer. Your CHCO will tell you how many of your employees belong to unions and the "state" of agency relations with your unions. While the unions in the federal government sector are far different from their private sector counterparts and do not have collective bargaining authority regarding pay, the number of union members is growing in the public sector (including the federal government) and unions have become increasingly influential. The American Federation of Government Employees (AFGE) represents the largest number of federal employees, followed by the National Treasury Employees Union (NTEU).

The involvement of unions is essential if you plan to implement a performance management system in your organization. Laws governing federal bargaining are somewhat complex, but your CHCO will assist you in sorting out appropriate ways to engage your union members.

In local governments, there are many examples of innovative approaches to collaboration between unions and management. Collaborative management is a joint process where both employees and their employer share in managerial decision making. The essence of successful partnerships is the creation of a parallel structure to the traditional union-management structure for collective bargaining. Ideally, the parallel structure involves union and management representatives in collaborative decision making.

A well-known example of such a collaborative effort took place in Indianapolis, Indiana, in the 1990s that encouraged cooperation between the unions and management. Working in a collaborative mode, the city's Department of Public Works was able to lower its costs and win several public-private competitions. As a result, formal grievances declined significantly in number, which freed up both time and resources.

Labor Relations in the Federal Government

From *Labor-Management Partnerships: A New Approach to Collaborative Management*
by Barry Rubin and Richard Rubin

Key Events

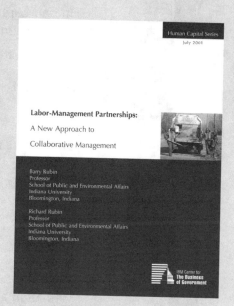

1962 Executive Order 10988 was signed by President John F. Kennedy. The E.O. recognized the rights of federal employees to join unions, granted recognition to those unions, and allowed limited bargaining rights.

1970 The Postal Reorganizations Act was passed allowing postal workers to come under the National Labor Relations Act (NLRA).

1978 The Civil Service Reform Act replaced previous executive orders concerning federal employee bargaining rights. Title VII of that act established the Federal Labor Relations Authority (FLRA) and modeled bargaining rights in the federal government after the NLRA.

1993 Executive Order 12871 was signed by President Bill Clinton as part of the reinvention initiative, creating a National Partnership Council to change the way management and unions relate in the public sector.

2001 Executive Order 13203 was signed by President George Bush, which dissolved the National Partnership Council.

2007 Legislation is introduced in Congress by Senator Daniel Akaka and Representative Danny Davis to create a new National Labor-Management Partnership Council.

Background

In 1962, President John F. Kennedy signed Executive Order 10988, which recognized the rights of federal employees to join or to refrain from joining labor organizations, granted recognition to those labor organizations, and detailed bargaining subjects. Before 1962, only 26 union or association units in the executive branch of the federal government had union shops, and they represented only 19,000 workers. Six years after the Kennedy order, there were 2,305 bargaining units, with a total membership of 1.4 million employees. A number of different unions represented federal workers, the largest being the American Federation of Government Employees.

Currently, federal employee labor relations are governed by the provisions of Title VII of the Civil Service Reform Act of 1978. Title VII, Federal Service Labor-Management Relations, is modeled after the National Labor Relations Act. Central authority was placed in a three-member panel, the Federal Labor Relations Authority.

The Federal Labor Relations Authority oversees creation of bargaining units, conducts elections, decides representation cases, determines unfair labor practices, and seeks enforcement of its decisions in the federal courts. The Federal Service Impasse Panel was continued by the act and provides assistance in resolving negotiation impasses. Unlike private sector labor laws, Title VII mandates inclusion of a grievance procedure with binding arbitration as a final step in all federal collective bargaining agreements.

Source: *Adapted from M. R. Carrell and C. Heavrin,* Labor Relations and Collective Bargaining *(6E), 2001. Upper Saddle River, NJ: Prentice Hall (pp. 34-37).*

For Additional Information on People

The Transformation of the Government Accountability Office: Using Human Capital to Drive Change (2005) by Jonathan Walters and Charles Thompson

The authors present a case study of the transformation of the GAO. The report discusses challenges faced and overcome, mistakes made, and lessons learned. The report describes how human capital management can be a driver for organizational transformation and what it can mean for the public sector as a whole.

Growing Leaders for Public Service (2004, 2nd ed.) by Ray Blunt

This report includes two Center reports *(Leaders Growing Leaders: Preparing the Next Generation of Public Service Executives* and *Organizations Growing Leaders: Best Practices and Principles of Public Service)* in one volume. Both reports address the crucial question of how well the federal government is developing its next generation of leaders.

Mediation at Work: Transforming Workplace Conflict at the United States Postal Service (2003) by Lisa B. Bingham

This report addresses the history, implementation, management, institutionalization, and evaluation of the world's largest employment mediation program, the United States Postal Service's REDRESS (Resolve Employment Disputes, Reach Equitable Solutions Swiftly) Program. Designed and implemented top-down as a form of alternative dispute resolution for complaints of discrimination, it served as a bottom-up method for changing how employees and supervisors handle conflict at work.

The Power of Frontline Workers in Transforming Government: The Upstate New York Veterans Healthcare Network (2003) by Timothy J. Hoff

This report describes and analyzes how one organization within the Veterans Health Administration (VHA) encouraged its workforce to become more entrepreneurial and independent in performing their responsibilities.

Human Capital Reform: 21st Century Requirements for the United States Agency for International Development (2003) by Anthony C. E. Quainton and Amanda M. Fulmer

The report presents 50 recommendations for reforming human capital in the U.S. Agency for International Development. The recommendations were developed at a Thought Leadership Forum hosted by the National Policy Association in October 2002 at the Belmont Conference Center in Elkridge, Maryland.

For Additional Information on People

The Defense Leadership and Management Program: Taking Career Development Seriously (2002) by Joseph A. Ferrara and Mark C. Rom

This project examines the implementation of the Defense Leadership Management Program (DLAMP) and draws conclusions about its strengths and weaknesses. DLAMP is an attempt by the federal government to provide a program of systematic career development for civilian employees.

The Influence of Organizational Commitment on Officer Retention: A 12-Year Study of U.S. Army Officers (2002) by Stephanie C. Payne, Ann H. Huffman, and Trueman R. Tremble, Jr.

This report examines employee retention rates within the public sector by examining the longitudinal influence of organizational commitment on turnover. By determining the length of time it takes for organizational commitment to develop, government will have a better understanding of when and how organizational commitment develops.

Life After Civil Service Reform: The Texas, Georgia, and Florida Experiences (2002) by Jonathan Walters

As with the federal government, states and local governments are examining alternatives to the traditional civil service system. This report examines civil service reform programs in Texas, Georgia, and Florida.

Toward a 21st Century Public Service: Reports from Four Forums (2001) by Mark A. Abramson

This report presents recommendations from four forums on the future of the civil service: Two Federal Leadership Summit Conferences; a Forum on "A New American Diplomacy: Requirements for the 21st Century," hosted by the National Policy Association; and a Forum on "People and Performance: Challenges from the Future of Public Service," hosted by the Maxwell School of Citizenship and Public Affairs, Syracuse University.

Winning the Best and Brightest: Increasing the Attraction of Public Service (2001) by Carol Chetkovich

This report examines the ways in which public policy programs at two universities shape the public service orientations of students in these programs. The study focuses on the important question of how the goals and aspirations of policy students interact with policy training to shape their career trajectories.

PEOPLE

For Additional Information on People

A Changing Workforce: Understanding Diversity Programs in the Federal Government (2001) by Katherine C. Naff and J. Edward Kellough

This report assesses the scope and effectiveness of diversity initiatives undertaken by federal agencies. The report identifies practices that have been effective in creating an equitable work environment.

A Weapon in the War for Talent: Using Special Authorities to Recruit Crucial Personnel (2001) by Hal G. Rainey

This report examines the impact of special authorities to hire people into government via streamlined procedures and at higher salaries. This report describes these special authorities and assesses their value to the agencies. The report presents conclusions about effective uses of special hiring authorities.

Using Virtual Teams to Manage Complex Projects: A Case Study of the Radioactive Waste Management Project (2000) by Samuel M. DeMarie

This report describes how technologies are reshaping the workplace. The project studies how the U.S. Department of Energy and its contractors and subcontractors used information and communication technologies to manage a highly complex Radioactive Waste Management Project at Yucca Mountain, Nevada. The Yucca Mountain project implemented "virtual teamwork" as a means to provide efficient and effective collaboration among employees.

Reflections on Mobility: Case Studies of Six Federal Executives (2000) by Michael D. Serlin

This report presents case studies of six former members of the Senior Executive Service, each of whom accomplished major changes in several different federal agencies. The study identifies common factors in their experiences that led to their interagency mobility.

A Learning-Based Approach to Leading Change (2000) by Barry Sugarman

This report examines the experiences of five federal agencies that undertook initiatives to apply the tools, principles, and perspectives of organizational learning. Based on the five case studies, the report describes the successes and failures of organizational learning and presents findings and recommendations.

For Additional Information on People

Managing Telecommuting in the Federal Government: An Interim Report (2000) by Gina Vega and Louis Brennan

This report analyzes and evaluates telecommuting in the public sector. It focuses on two federal agencies to describe the implementation and management of telecommuting. The report presents recommendations of best practices and suggestions for improvement for telecommuting in the public sector.

Profiles in Excellence: Conversations with the Best of America's Career Executive Service (1999) by Mark W. Huddleston

This report consists of a series of in-depth interviews with members of the Senior Executive Service who were identified as outstanding leaders. The report discusses the characteristics that have contributed to the success of these senior executives.

PEOPLE

Chapter Four: Money

Resources need to be invested and deployed strategically based on reliable, timely, high-quality information that helps policy makers and program officials make difficult choices in a highly complex environment.

IBM CENTER FOR THE BUSINESS OF GOVERNMENT
WASHINGTON, DC 20005

MEMORANDUM FOR THE HEADS OF EXECUTIVE DEPARTMENTS AND AGENCIES

SUBJECT: **Money**

In the federal government, the budget process is not simply a bean-counting game. The budget process shapes policy—and it inevitably reduces all decisions down to a dollar denomination. The process, including upfront strategic and long-range planning and performance targets, is where policy and strategic decisions are made in the federal government.

Obtain Resources in a Challenging Environment

Resources will be scarce, and the way in which they are allocated and used is crucial to you and your organization's overall effectiveness. The fiscal pressures on the U.S. government, particularly on discretionary spending, are unsustainable. The sources of revenue and range of options for funding new initiatives are becoming broader and more complex. A solid financial strategy can no longer be an afterthought, cobbled onto a policy proposal or developed as part of an after-the-fact business plan, if at all. Understanding costs and measuring program performance are critical to effective decision making and need to be part of the policy and program development process.

One of the secrets that only the initiated know is that budget numbers are the keys to the doors of everything. Spending for everything the government does—whether it is foreign aid, biomedical research, or education—and revenues from every source are all reflected, recorded, and battled over in numbers. And the sum of those numbers, and who gets how much, is fiscal and economic policy. If it matters, there are numbers that define it. For that reason, you need to understand the mechanics of the numbers process. And you have to give these resource numbers meaning—to put them in the proper context at the right time and know what every important player is trying to do to them or with them and the reasons for the different pressures.

Manage the Resources You Receive

Managing money in government is serious business. You can go to jail if you do not do it right. That said, managing resources means more than simply keeping the books straight and helping to ensure that funds are not misspent. Resources need to be invested and deployed strategically based on reliable, timely, high-quality information that helps policy makers and program officials make difficult choices in a highly complex environment. Understanding costs and measuring program performance are critical to effective decision making and need to be part of the policy and program development process.

By and large, starting with the Chief Financial Officers Act of 1990, financial management legislation has focused more on government-wide reform—particularly developing government financial standards, applying private sector financial standards and processes to the federal sector, aligning spending and performance, and reducing the size of government and competing federal functions that are commercial in nature. Consequently, federal financial management has been elevated to a more sophisticated platform.

While legislation has been put into place to strengthen the role of the federal chief financial officer (CFO), there is a lack of clarity for federal CFO roles and responsibilities. Oversight responsibilities for CFOs in the federal government vary from agency to agency. While CFOs are responsible for the financial management activities of their agency, not all CFOs are responsible for budgeting and planning. Similarly, some CFOs share responsibility for implementation of financial management systems with their agency chief information officer (CIO). Moreover, in some agencies, the CFO is responsible for many other agency activities, including human resources, asset management, procurement, facilities, bankcards, and general administration in addition to financial management. In some agencies, the CFO also reports to the CIO. In other words, there are no standard practices for federal CFO responsibilities.

Show Results from What You Spend

You and your organization will be under increasing pressure to produce—and to demonstrate—results in terms of your goals and mission. Integrating performance and results with decision making for budget resources has long been a goal of the U.S. federal government. During the past decade, Congress and the executive branch have increased their emphasis on improving management across all departments and agencies. A series of legislative proposals and changes to federal budget guidance have highlighted the presentation of performance and results information for the annual investment of public dollars. The Government Performance and Results Act (GPRA) of 1993 was first implemented on a government-wide basis in 1997 with the fiscal year 1999 budget. GPRA seeks to fundamentally change the focus of federal management and accountability from a preoccupation with inputs and processes to a greater emphasis on the outcomes and results that programs should be achieving. It brings together managers, workers, and stakeholders to focus on: (1) the purposes of programs; (2) the means to achieve them; and (3) progress toward achievement.

As noted in the *Memo on Performance*, you are coming into government at a time when much progress has been made on obtaining and using performance management information for government decision making. Initiatives have been launched to more effectively link budget and performance. George Washington University's Philip G. Joyce writes, "The federal government has never been in a better position to make its budget decisions more informed by considerations of performance."

A focus on results and outcomes can help enhance government's capacity to assess competing claims for budgetary resources by arming decision makers with better information both on the results of individual programs as well as on entire portfolios of policies and programs addressing common goals. The use of performance information is not an end in itself, but rather a means to support better decision making and lead to improved performance and accountability. While performance budgeting will never resolve the vexing resource trade-offs involving political choice, it does hold the promise of modifying and informing policy decisions and resource allocation by shifting the focus of debate from inputs to the program outcomes and results that are crucial to an organization's success and to the nation's security.

MONEY

LINKING RESOURCES TO RESULTS

QUESTION: Instead of making budget decisions based on past level of support, is there a way to inject performance information into the budget process?

ANSWER: The goal of "budget and performance integration" has received much attention in recent decades. Your challenge is to prepare a budget that includes performance information, which you forward to the Office of the Secretary in your department, which forwards it to the Office of Management and Budget (OMB). The budget preparation stage begins with the initial planning undertaken by your agency, which can start a year or more prior to the submission of the budget request to Congress. Instructions from OMB on budget preparation (OMB Circular A-11) state that the budget request should be informed by your judgment "regarding the scope, content, performance and quality of programs and activities proposed to meet the agency's mission, goals and objectives." In recent years, the expectation has increased that budget formulations within federal agencies are to be informed by performance considerations.

In his report to the IBM Center, George Washington University's Philip Joyce writes that agency heads can now use a variety of tools and measures to make their budget request more focused on performance. Joyce writes, "Making budget development more focused on performance normally requires that the agency budget office develop some framework for budget requests that clarifies the relationship between costs and performance." Joyce explains that these budget requests should include:

- **A strategic and performance context.** Since the enactment of the Government Performance and Results Act (see page 81), agencies are expected to have articulated some strategic vision. Joyce writes, "This means that budget requests should be presented in the context of their effects on the strategic priorities of the agency, normally established in the agency strategic plan." There should be a clear connection, states Joyce, between what the agency "does" on a day-to-day basis and its larger strategic and performance objectives.

- **Performance information.** As discussed in the section on Performance, agencies should have output and outcome measures that indicate the agency's success in meeting its objectives.

- **Cost information.** "The budget request should identify the true cost of providing services.... This will not be possible without some relatively sophisticated means of allocating overhead or indirect costs," contends Joyce. (For further discussion on developing cost information, see pages 80–81.)

Thus, the key to linking performance to your agency's budget is the availability and use of performance measures. According to Joyce, you can use this performance information to:

- Build your budget justification for submission to the department.

- Make trade-offs between your agency's programs to allocate funds strategically.

- Determine the productivity of your agency programs.

- Determine overlapping services within your agency.

- Determine in-house versus contractual production of services.

THE OPERATOR'S MANUAL FOR THE NEW ADMINISTRATION

Contrasts Between Traditional Views of Budgeting and Performance-Informed Budgeting

From *Linking Performance and Budgeting: Opportunities in the Federal Budget Process*
by Philip G. Joyce

Performance-informed budgeting exists in a context of more traditional input-focused efforts to allocate resources. This input focus has historically been less on results and more on incremental levels of funding. The first table below presents a contrast between traditional budgeting and performance-informed budgeting. It is important to keep in mind, however, that while performance-informed budgeting is probably unattainable, by the same token "traditional" budgeting, as described, is overly stylized. They are best viewed as ends on a continuum rather than discrete options.

The second table below presents the various stages in the budget process in which performance-informed budgeting can be applied.

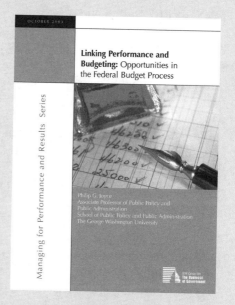

MONEY

Traditional vs. Performance-Informed Budgeting

Traditional Budgeting	Performance-Informed Budgeting
Inputs as ends in themselves	Relationship between inputs and results
Changes in inputs at the margin (for example, how many more dollars than last year)	Changes in inputs and results for the entire program (for example, how much more results for how much more money)
Divorced from planning and management in agencies	Budgeting integrated with planning and management
Budgeted resources	Costs

Stages of the Federal Budget Process

Stage of Budget Process	Description of Activities	End Product
Budget Preparation—Agency	Agency preparation of a budget for submission to OMB	Budget request
Budget Preparation—OMB	Analysis of agency budget request on behalf of the president; negotiation with agencies on budget allocation levels	President's budget
Budget Approval—Congress	The Congress makes overall fiscal policy, authorizes programs, and appropriates funds	Budget resolution, authorization bills, appropriation bills
Budget Approval—President	Action on congressional legislation affecting budget	Signature or veto
Budget Execution	Implementation of programs by federal agencies; allocation of dollars by agency subunit	Administration of programs
Audit and Evaluation	Review of tax and budget actions after the fact; recommendations made for changes	Audits and evaluations

ACCOUNTING FOR COSTS

QUESTION: My agency, like many other government agencies, is going to have to control its spending more tightly over the next several years. Do you have any suggestions on how we might better control our costs?

ANSWER: During one of your first conversations with your chief financial officer, you should probe the extent to which (or whether) your agency is able to measure the costs of its operations and programs. The truth of the matter is that very few federal agencies are able to capture and report the full costs of their major operations. In describing cost management in his report to the IBM Center, Louisiana State University's Lloyd Blanchard writes, "The cost management function of financial management systems is where costs are matched with activities and outputs. The level of sophistication of this function within the financial system is dependent on the operational nature of the programs involved, but ... four basic functions must be present: cost recognition, cost accumulation, cost distribution, and a working capital fund." The key here is linking costs to specific activities and outputs.

Based on his analysis of cost accounting practices in two federal agencies—the Small Business Administration and the National Aeronautics and Space Administration—Blanchard sets forth recommendations for agency heads who desire to improve their cost accounting policies and procedures:

- **Align performance, costs, and accounts.** In order to accomplish this, you will need to ask your agency to carefully align, or map, major program activities to one or more of the strategic goals of the agency. This will entail: (1) synchronizing program performance measures with mission and strategic goals; (2) synchronizing program costs with the program performance measures; and (3) negotiating with your appropriations committee to better align Congress's appropriation account structures to your agency's budget structure.

- **Build outcome-based measures for ideal cost-performance integration.** By developing effectiveness, cost, and efficiency measures, you and your management team will be able to understand more precisely the relationship between budget costs and performance.

- **Develop a cost allocation method that fits the organizational design.** Your organization will need to clearly identify: (1) programs that provide direct services; and (2) non-program activities that will be the basis for your indirect cost categories.

- **Supplement existing systems to support performance costing.** This will be a challenge, but is crucial to the ultimate success of this initiative. Blanchard writes, "Agencies should start modestly and improve budget-performance integration capacity over time. The biggest reason for such an approach is the cost of implementing new cost accounting systems to handle the tasks required of good cost management."

- **Create incentives to improve effectiveness and efficiency.** As an agency head, you can do this. Experience has shown that agency head involvement and support is one of the keys to successful implementation of performance budgeting. At NASA, the agency head gave program managers authority over the use of their personnel. Blanchard writes, "By making direct personnel costs the program's responsibility, and not a separate budgeting line item, NASA created an incentive for program managers to reveal their true need for personnel resources.... In general, full cost at NASA creates the incentives for program and support managers to behave more as market-based producers, revealing their true need for certain resources, and paying for what used to be 'free' from a budgetary standpoint."

Statutory Foundations of Cost Requirements

From *Performance Budgeting: How NASA and SBA Link Costs and Performance*
by Lloyd A. Blanchard

As described below in "Key Legislation," the modern statutory framework for costing performance budgets ... starts with the Chief Financial Officers (CFO) Act of 1990 and the Government Management Reform Act (GMRA) of 1994. While these laws established the CFO function and position in federal agencies, the CFO Act calls for the "development and reporting of cost information" and instructs the CFO to regularly review "fees, royalties, rents, and other charges" for services provided and "make recommendations on revising those charges to reflect costs incurred." Congress has long been concerned about the lack of sophisticated financial management practices in the federal government, stating the following as a rationale for the bill:

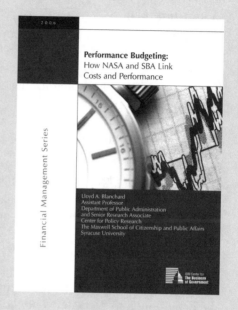

Current financial reporting practices of the federal government do not accurately disclose the current and probable future cost of operating and investment decisions, including the future need for cash or other resources, do not permit adequate comparison of actual costs among executive agencies, and do not provide the timely information required for efficient management of programs.

Key Legislation

Chief Financial Officers Act of 1990 (CFO Act)
Created the deputy director for management position and the Office of Federal Financial Management (with head as comptroller) at OMB, and established federal financial management and related system policies and requirements. Created agency CFO and deputy CFO in 24 agencies, and required them to develop and maintain integrated financial management systems; and direct, manage, and provide policy guidance and oversight of all agency financial management personnel and operations.

Government Performance and Results Act of 1993 (GPRA)
Required all agencies to set strategic goals, measure performance, and report on the degree to which goals were met. Required an annual performance plan that provides a direct linkage between the strategic goals and employees' daily activities. Required an annual report on program performance for the previous fiscal year, and in each report, the agency is to review and discuss its performance compared with the performance goals it established in its annual performance plan.

Government Management Reform Act of 1994 (GMRA)
Required all agencies covered by the CFO Act to have agency-wide audited financial statements, required a government-wide audited financial statement, allowed agencies to consolidate various financial and performance reporting requirements into a single report with a common reporting deadline, and extended the CFO Act to all agencies.

Federal Financial Management Improvement Act of 1996 (FFMIA)
Required agencies to implement and maintain financial management systems that comply substantially with federal financial management systems requirements, applicable accounting standards, and the United States Government Standard General Ledger at the transaction level.

Source: GAO. 1998. Managing for Results: The Statutory Framework for Performance-Based Management and Accountability. GAO/GGD/AIMD-98-52.

Creating a Culture of Cost Management

Question: I understand that moving from a "budget control" culture to a "cost management" culture is a major change. Can you tell me more about creating a "cost management" culture?

Answer: In their report to the IBM Center, Michael Barzelay and Fred Thompson present a case study of how General George T. Babbitt transformed the Air Force Materiel Command (AFMC) from an organization driven by "budget management" to one focused on "cost management." The goal of General Babbitt, according to Barzelay and Thompson, was to increase "the institution's capacity to manage costs, with potential benefit felt indefinitely if reinforced by his successors." Barzelay and Thompson describe the differences between the two cultures:

Budget Management Culture

- Focus on inputs
- Secure bigger budgets and more spending authority
- Spend everything (execute full obligational authority by the end of the fiscal year)
- Centralize budget decisions

Cost Management Culture

- Focus on accomplishments
- Cut budget/maximize productivity
- Understand costs (avoid expenses where possible)
- Decentralize decisions to those best situated to maximize productivity

General Babbitt concluded that in a time of declining resources for his command, it was necessary for the organization to get better control of its spending and costs. Barzelay and Thompson write, "He [Babbitt] foresaw the command increasingly losing control of its destiny as its overseers sought ways to reduce AFMC's resources in the name of paring infrastructure. His experience told him that the command had not developed the orientation, motivation, and tools to become more efficient, leaving AFMC extremely vulnerable to arbitrary budget cutting and mission failure over the medium and long run."

Based on their analysis of the experience of General Babbitt at the Air Force Materiel Command, Barzelay and Thompson conclude that there are six major steps involved in moving toward a cost culture:

- **Organizing participation in the intervention.** This step involves developing a broad-based commitment within the organization to manage costs.

- **Making sense of costs.** This is a crucial step in which managers develop ideas about what can be done to improve the relationship between benefits and costs within the organization.

- **Reordering relations with authorizing constituencies.** This step involves changes in the rules and procedures within the organization so that existing rules concerning expenditure planning and financial management are modified to permit more effective cost management.

- **Practicing performance planning.** This step involves managers within the organization gaining firsthand experience with cost management. The goal is to strengthen an organization's aspirations for achievement and willingness to correct organizational weaknesses as well.

- **Practicing execution control.** The essence of this step involves managers learning how to undertake corrective action as part of the delivery or execution process.

- **Stabilizing the practice.** This step is important because a serious practice of cost management is vulnerable to collapse, especially when institutional leadership passes from one individual to another. This step involves providing a secure footing for ideas, people, and organizational arrangements for the continuation of the cost control culture over time.

Developing the Capacity to Manage Costs

From *Efficiency Counts: Developing the Capacity to Manage Costs at Air Force Materiel Command* by Michael Barzelay and Fred Thompson

Cost management can be viewed in terms of the authority of managers to acquire assets and the kinds of financial targets that would align responsibility with authority:

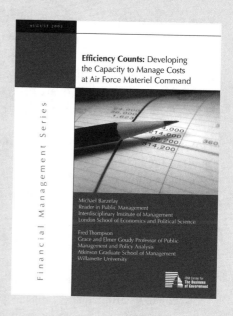

- *Discretionary expense center managers* are accountable for compliance with an asset acquisition plan (expense budget). They have no independent authority to acquire assets. Their superiors must authorize each acquisition. Managerial accountants generally believe that a unit should be set up as a discretionary expense center only when there is no satisfactory way to match its expenses to final cost objects. Most governmental organizations are discretionary cost centers.

- *Cost center managers* are responsible for producing a stated quantity and/or quality of output at the lowest feasible cost. Someone else within the organization determines the output of a cost center—usually including various quality attributes, especially delivery schedules. Cost center managers are free to acquire short-term assets (those that are wholly consumed within a performance measurement cycle), to hire temporary or contract personnel, and to manage inventories.

    1. In a standard cost center, output levels are determined by requests from other responsibility centers, and the manager's budget for each performance measurement cycle is determined by multiplying actual output by standard cost per unit. Performance is measured against this figure—the difference between actual costs and the standard.

    2. In a quasi profit center, performance is measured by the difference between the notational revenue earned by the center and its costs. For example, let's say a hospital's department of radiology performed 500 chest X-rays and 200 skull X-rays for the department of pediatrics. The notational revenue earned was $25 per chest X-ray (500) = $12,500 and $50 per skull X-ray (200) = $10,000, or $22,500 total. If the radiology department's costs were $18,000, it would earn a quasi-profit of $4,500 ($22,500 minus $18,000).

- *Profit center managers* are responsible for both revenues and costs. Profit is the difference between revenue and cost. Thus, profit center managers are evaluated in terms of both the revenues their centers earn and the costs they incur. In addition to the authority to acquire short-term assets, to hire temporary or contract personnel, and to manage inventories, profit center managers are usually given the authority to make long-term hires, set salary and promotion schedules (subject to organization-wide standards), organize their units, and acquire long-lived assets costing less than some specified amount.

- *Investment center managers* are responsible for both profit and the assets used in generating profit. Thus, an investment center adds more to a manager's scope of responsibility than does a profit center, just as a profit center involves more than a cost center. Investment center managers are typically evaluated in terms of return on assets (ROA), which is the ratio of profit to assets employed, where the former is expressed as a percentage of the latter. In recent years, many have turned to economic value added (EVA), net operating "profit" less an appropriate capital charge, which is a dollar amount rather than a ratio.

MANAGING RISK IN FEDERAL CREDIT PROGRAMS

QUESTION: I understand that my agency has a number of credit programs that provide loans and loan guarantees. What are some best practices regarding risk management that I should consider?

ANSWER: While the use of credit as a "tool" of government has expanded in recent years, the last decade has also brought an expansion of information technologies that can be used in assessing the risks involved in your agency's credit portfolio. In his report to the IBM Center (2005), Johns Hopkins University's Tom Stanton concludes that each stage of the credit management cycle—loan origination, servicing, monitoring of lenders or other private parties, loss mitigation, and default management—has benefited from the development of a broad array of approaches that are applied based on analysis of information databases.

Stanton concludes that these new technologies provide new opportunities for the federal government in regard to credit programs. He writes, "Opportunities occur as federal credit agencies increasingly develop risk management systems that might have been unavailable or unaffordable in the past. These risk management systems often are based on improved business processes as well as the application of new technologies to those processes."

In his report, Stanton recommends that you:

- **Develop a process to analyze pertinent information about the nature and dimensions of risks of each of your loan programs.** The first step in effective risk management, according to Stanton, is to be able to assess program risks systematically and on a continuing basis. This requires development of an ongoing process to gather, quantify, and evaluate information about risks.

- **Create a risk management office responsible for creating and overseeing effective risk management systems and for reporting important risk issues to top agency management.** Such an office will assist you in effective risk detection and assessment. The major task of this office will be to ensure that you always have a clear picture of the risks inherent in the programs you manage.

- **Require that your risk management office prepare regular and special reports concerning significant risk factors and the state of your agency's program and portfolio.**

- **Establish a credit committee, or a similar body, which you will chair to review risk-related information regularly.** This committee will grapple with the trade-offs that must be made between program development, on the one hand, and protection of the program from unacceptable risks and surprises, on the other.

- **Review the ability of your agency to address major forms of risk that potentially could emerge and determine if you need additional tools or regulations.** Based on this review, you might conclude that additional enforcement tools may be needed to address program partners that create unacceptable risks. You might also conclude that it is necessary to issue new regulations or amend guaranty agreements with lenders or take other steps to improve the agency's position in the event serious risk problems do emerge.

The Size and Scope of Federal Credit Programs

From *Federal Credit Programs: Managing Risk in the Information Age* by Thomas H. Stanton

The federal government provides loans or loan guarantees as a way to encourage funding for borrowers or activities that are considered important. Credit is one of a range of tools that government may use to achieve public purposes. As with the other tools of government, credit programs must be carefully matched with the public purposes that they are supposed to serve. The U.S. government extends credit for a broad range of purposes, from overseas activities to the needs of people caught in a disaster. In appropriate circumstances, it can be extremely effective to extend government credit to borrowers who are capable of using the funds and then repaying their debt obligations; by contrast, provision of credit to borrowers who are not creditworthy can be costly both to the government that must take the losses on the defaulted loans and to the borrowers themselves.

The federal government borrows money to fund direct loans and provides loan guarantees that are backed by the full faith and credit of the U.S. Treasury. Given the financial strength of the U.S. government, the federal government thus can maintain very large direct loan and loan guarantee programs.

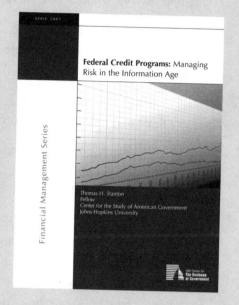

Financial Management Series

Federal Credit Programs: Managing Risk in the Information Age

Thomas H. Stanton
Fellow
Center for the Study of American Government
Johns Hopkins University

The figure below shows the volume of federal direct loans and loan guarantees outstanding in recent decades. Over the past 20 to 30 years, the volume of federal loan guarantees has grown significantly, while the volume of direct loans outstanding has remained at a more constant level.

The figure captures several trends. First, starting in the late 1960s, the government greatly expanded federal credit programs. The federal government responded to urban unrest with new Federal Housing Administration mortgage insurance programs, both for single-family homes and for apartment buildings. Many of these programs involved heavily subsidized interest rates, as a way of helping to lower housing costs for low-income home buyers and renters. The government created the guaranteed student loan program in 1965 and greatly expanded its coverage in subsequent years. Credit programs of the Farmers Home Administration (now succeeded by the Rural Housing Service) multiplied sixfold in outstanding volume between 1973 and 1984, to $61 billion. This resulted from more generous loan terms and also from an expansion of the types of loan program that the agency offered.

For federal credit programs, budget constraints caused a shift to loan guarantees rather than a constriction in the actual volume of credit outstanding.

Face Value of Federal Credit Outstanding (FY 1970 to FY 2005)

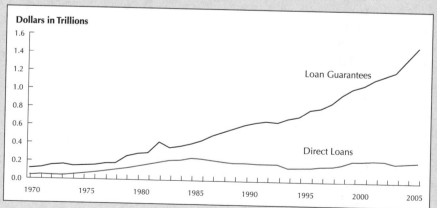

Source: Budget of the United States Government: Analytical Perspectives, Fiscal Year 2006, Chart 7-2, p. 108 (February 2005).

MONEY

MANAGING FEDERAL ASSETS

QUESTION: I understand that my agency owns some buildings and might have other assets. What can I do to improve my agency's asset management activities?

ANSWER: The first step is to understand exactly how many assets your agency is now holding. Assets include real property (buildings), financial assets, personal property, and fleet assets. The federal government, as a whole, now owns over 440,000 buildings. Financial assets include accounts receivable, such as tax debts, defaulted federal loans, and outstanding direct loans.

There are three major actions that you can take to improve asset management in your organization:

- **Adopt a portfolio strategy.** The current problem is that many agencies, perhaps your own, treat their federal assets on an individual basis rather than addressing the whole portfolio of assets and managing them through a comprehensive strategy. In the area of financial assets, Tom Stanton found, as noted in his report to the IBM Center (2003), that the Small Business Administration "took a comprehensive look at its business loan guarantee program and determined that sales of nonperforming loan assets could save considerable resources that the agency then could use more productively to further its mission of supporting small businesses."

  The Public Building Services (PBS) of the General Services Administration developed a portfolio strategy to respond to the problem of scarce resources for property maintenance. The goal of the strategy was to restructure its portfolio to consist primarily of strong income-producing properties. According to Stanton, this enabled PBS to limit expenditures on marginal assets, concentrate resources on performing assets, and improve the quality of its space.

- **Adopt a life-cycle approach to managing federal assets.** By using this approach, federal agencies plan for the operations, support, and disposal costs associated with government assets, starting before asset acquisition and continuing through the life of the asset. Stanton observes, "It is not unusual for maintenance costs of an asset to far exceed the initial acquisition costs or for unanticipated servicing costs to exceed the value of the asset." In the area of loans, it is much less expensive to take early actions to forestall loan defaults than it is to try to restructure or foreclose on poorly originated or serviced loans when borrowers fail to make the payments.

  A key element of an asset life-cycle approach is to develop a specific plan for each stage. For example, the first stage is the development of an Asset Strategy, which includes the overall direction of the asset base—whether to outsource, or to dispose of the assets or to increase the asset base, or to improve reliability. From the Asset Strategy, an Asset Plan is developed to execute the strategy and requires having a good accounting and status of the existing asset base. Other stages include the Evaluate/Design phase, the Acquire/Construct phase, the Operate/Maintain phase, the Modify phase, and finally the Disposal phase. In each phase, the asset has different characteristics or requirements which necessitate different asset management strategies, processes, and technology solutions.

- **Outsource the asset management function to the private sector.** In some cases, it may be more efficient to transfer an agency's assets to a private entity that would then take over the asset management function. In this case, the agency establishes performance metrics on the manager of the portfolio and rules on how the portfolio is to be managed. The agency does not manage the assets in the portfolio, although it can direct how those assets are to be managed. For example, a portfolio of loans might be sold to a financial institution that might be able to manage the portfolio more efficiently than the government. The terms and conditions of the loans would not be changed.

Management of Federal Assets Today

From *Understanding Federal Asset Management: An Agenda for Reform* by Thomas H. Stanton

Management of many federal assets today is characterized by (1) disinvestment of government, (2) a growing discrepancy between the nature of assets in an agency's portfolio and the needs of that agency's mission, (3) acquisition of federal assets without consideration of the costs and effort to maintain and eventually dispose of the assets, and (4) statutory requirements that impede effective asset management.

Disinvestment results when the government fails to invest adequate amounts of money in the staff, systems, and facilities that agencies require to manage their programs well. Budget and staff cuts have reduced the management capabilities of many agencies. One agency after another faces an increasing disconnect between growing duties and mostly static resources.

For asset management, this means that many federal agencies may lack the capacity that is needed to manage assets in the most cost-effective manner. For buildings and real property, this means that federal agencies often lack the kinds of information needed to make sound decisions about their asset portfolios. For financial assets, the government may lack the capacity to originate, service, and collect on loans, especially where improvements might require the installation of the types of systems that support comparable private sector activities. Another consequence of disinvestment is the cost of neglected maintenance and modernization, especially of real and personal property and fleets. When an agency faces budget constraints, property maintenance too often seems easy to defer, compared to the pressures of supporting current operations. Assets such as information systems may become obsolete if they are not regularly modernized, and this too has its costs.

The second issue facing government assets is an increasing divergence between the needs of an agency's mission and the nature of the assets it holds. Again, buildings and real property provide the most striking examples. When an agency's mission changes, it may require quite different assets than it needed before. The case study of Rocky Flats illustrates the asset management problems that confront the Department of Energy now that nuclear weapons production has gone from being a national priority to becoming the focus of mutual reductions with the former Soviet Union. Other agencies find that downsizing or the consolidation of offices can leave them with unused or underutilized assets. Especially after September 11, with increasingly costly security requirements for federal facilities, excess or partially used buildings can be expensive for an agency to maintain.

The third issue relates to statutory and other constraints that impede effective asset management. Federal budget scoring rules are a particular problem. Past reforms, such as the institution of credit budgeting in the 1990s and the creation of the Federal Buildings Fund in the 1970s, brought progress to federal asset management. Now, however, the world has changed. To keep up, the budget scoring rules need to be reviewed once again to address critical deficiencies such as their impact on acquisition of buildings and real estate assets and on asset sales.

Managing Grants

Question: As a major provider of grants, what are the key challenges I will face?

Answer: Grants are an effective tool of government when used and managed well. While the use of grants dates back to the 1800s, they are still important today and their use is increasing. In his report to the IBM Center, George Mason University's Tim Conlan writes that grants are "typically designed to support or augment an existing service or activity that is already being carried out by the recipient, or to encourage the provision of new services or activities."

They do, however, provide management challenges for you and your organization. Conlan presents four challenges regarding grants:

- **Achieving accountability.** The government has long had a fiduciary responsibility to ensure that grant funds are not diverted to corrupt or illegal purposes, spent in racially or other discriminatory ways, or wasted on inappropriate or excessive expenditures. The current challenge is moving beyond legal and financial accountability to performance accountability.

- **Assessing performance.** In order to achieve greater performance accountability, the government will need to develop new ways to assess the performance of grantees. Conlan writes, "The focus on assessing and enhancing the performance of federal grant programs—and federal program activities generally—has grown in recent years." There is now, according to Conlan, an increased demand for higher standards of performance in federal programs, including grant programs.

- **Providing adequate grantee flexibility.** As a manager of grant programs, you will face the challenge of determining how much flexibility is needed (or is not needed) to accomplish the performance objectives of a grant. On the one hand, overly restrictive rules and conditions can be counterproductive to successful implementation and can obstruct innovation and experimentation. On the other hand, too much flexibility might move the project away from its original federal program objectives.

- **Overcoming complexity.** Like much of what we have discussed in this volume, government can get very complicated. There are now over 1,300 individual grant programs, many of which overlap and intersect with each other. There has been some progress in recent years to standardize grants management rules through OMB circulars. Another effective response has been the use of e-grant reforms, including the Grants.gov web portal.

How can you best respond to these challenges? Based on analysis of improvements in the grants arena in recent years, there are two promising innovations which you should consider:

- **Continue movement to the web.** The Grants.gov initiative appears to be heading in the right direction. Additional work can be done to expand this capability to include post-award related activities, as well as simplifying and standardizing report and accountability processes. You should be cautioned *not* to create your own website or another unique database. When possible, you should always strive to align your systems with those of other agencies and not duplicate capabilities that already exist.

- **Use performance partnerships.** A promising practice has been the use of performance partnerships, which are agreements between states and the federal government intended to develop measurable performance goals and standards in the implementation of federal programs in return for greater state flexibility in achieving these objectives. The performance partnership model has been used effectively by the Environmental Protection Agency.

Rationales for Federal Grants-in-Aid

From *Grants Management in the 21st Century: Three Innovative Policy Responses*
by Timothy J. Conlan

There are several reasons for the early use and lasting popularity of the federal grant tool. From a legal and historical perspective, grants-in-aid long were viewed as the most constitutionally permissible means of federal involvement in traditional spheres of state and local responsibility in the early Republic. The scope of the federal government's enumerated powers was one of the most important and contentious political issues in the early Republic. While this issue played out most dramatically in debates over the constitutionality of the Bank of the United States, issues such as the permissible scope of federal involvement in transportation projects and other forms of "internal improvements" were one of the chief causes of conflict between the early political parties.

Grants-in-aid provided a means of finessing this constitutional debate. Grants, first of land and later of cash, could be viewed as constitutionally permissible means of executing accepted federal powers, such as establishing post roads, disposing of and regulating the territories, or spending to promote the general welfare. Although the use of grants in this way remained controversial, the grant tool was clearly less invasive than direct federal administration. As the tool became more and more widely used, grants became a key feature of the shift from "dual federalism," with its sharply demarcated lines of authority between the national government and the states, and the 20th century development of broadly overlapping roles and "cooperative federalism."

Grants also enjoy support for economic reasons. They can, for example, provide an effective way to redress fiscal imbalances in the intergovernmental system. For most of our nation's history, the federal government has enjoyed significant resource advantages vis-à-vis states and localities. In addition, it has historically derived revenues from comparatively productive and efficient forms of taxation. This was particularly evident after enactment of the federal income tax in 1913.

Another economic argument on behalf of grants-in-aid involves the efficiency advantages that grants make possible. Conceptually, grants can allow a closer coincidence between the delivery of public goods and payment for them. In economic theory, public goods and services should be underproduced when those who pay for them do not capture all of the benefits, and they should be overproduced if those who benefit and control production can avoid paying all of the costs for them. One solution to this problem is to provide interjurisdictional grants-in-aid designed to compensate for this fiscal mismatch. An example of this concept was provided by an influential U.S. Treasury Department study in the 1980s: "If 20 percent of the benefits of local police services provided by a city is realized by commuters and visitors to the city from throughout the state, a state matching grant paying 20 percent of the city's total outlays for those services would ensure an appropriate level of provision." Although the empirical evidence that most grants are actually adopted and implemented to serve this function is rather weak, the potential for efficiency gains with grants remains an important rationale for their use.

MONEY

For Additional Information on Money

Strengthening Homeland Security: Reforming Planning and Resource Allocation (2008) by Cindy Williams

This report presents findings about the organizational structure, processes, and tools that surround planning and resource allocation for homeland security in the executive branch and Congress. The report offers recommendations for consideration by the White House and Congress to improving planning and resource allocation to help leaders establish control over priorities by strengthening the links between strategies and budgets.

Transforming Federal Property Management: A Case for Public-Private Partnerships (2007) by Judith Grant Long

This report examines the potential of public-private partnerships as a response to federal property management issues. This report focuses on the major property-related issues and assesses how public-private partnerships might be used to resolve property management problems, such as excess and underutilized property, deteriorating facilities, and reliance on costly leasing. The report presents a series of recommendations to successfully implement PPPs in the federal government.

Government Garage Sales: Online Auctions as Tools for Asset Management (2004) by David C. Wyld

This report presents examples of how government agencies are succeeding at selling both everyday items and high-end goods via online auctions. Five case studies of online auctioning are presented. The report presents lessons learned and recommendations for government executives to use in making decisions about the management of surplus, seized, or forfeited assets in the public sector via online auctions.

Audited Financial Statements: Getting and Sustaining "Clean" Opinions (2001) by Douglas A. Brook

This report examines the organizational factors and management strategies that affect the ability of federal agencies to generate reliable information for financial statements and achieve unqualified audit opinions. By identifying successful management strategies, the report offers recommendations about how agencies can effectively meet recurring requirements to produce annual audited financial statements.

An Introduction to Financial Risk Management in Government (2001) by Richard J. Buttimer, Jr.

This report examines the role of financial risk management techniques in government. The report discusses which private sector financial risk management techniques are best suited for government adoption. The report examines successful financial risk management practices now being used in government and contains a series of recommendations for their future use.

For Additional Information on Money

Using Activity-Based Costing to Manage More Effectively (2000)
by Michael H. Granof, David H. Platt, and Igor Vaysman

This report examines the value of activity-based costing (ABC) for decision making in the public sector. The study shows how activity-based costing can be applied to public sector organizations. The report discusses the feasibility and benefits of applying ABC, as well as the obstacles and limitations in the application of ABC.

Credit Scoring and Loan Scoring: Tools for Improved Management of Federal Credit Programs (1999) by Thomas H. Stanton

This report examines the potential of credit scoring and loan scoring techniques in the federal government. These techniques can be used by federal credit agencies to devise scoring-based database management systems for a broad range of purposes. The federal government currently administers loan and loan guarantee programs that amount to about $1 trillion of credit outstanding. When applied to federal direct loans and guarantees, scoring may help federal credit agencies improve their credit management practices.

MONEY

Chapter Five: Contracting

Your first step should be to take a strategic look at contracting and align your agency's use of contracting and contractors to support your agency's goals and objectives.

IBM CENTER FOR THE BUSINESS OF GOVERNMENT
WASHINGTON, DC 20005

MEMORANDUM FOR THE HEADS OF EXECUTIVE DEPARTMENTS AND AGENCIES

SUBJECT: **Contracting**

In addition to managing your own workforce, you will be responsible for managing a large contingent of contractors. You will need to ensure that contractor performance is high and that contractors are meeting and hopefully exceeding your agency's expectations, as set forth in your contracts.

Government today depends more on contractors than at any time in its history. This increase stems from several factors: limits on the number of government employees, a difficult process to hire government workers, and the need for government to frequently ramp up quickly to solve immediate problems. Given this history, you will likely find that your agency now has a large contingent of contractors working to support your agency's operations and mission.

As a consequence, you will face a series of challenges.

Align Contracting Practices with Your Agency Goals and Objectives

For the past decade, government has increasingly contracted out many government operations with little or no overall contracting strategy for the entire organization. Your first step should be to take a strategic look at contracting and align your agency's use of contracting and contractors to support your agency's goals and objectives.

An effective and efficient government requires a strong cadre of government workers supported by a strong cadre of contractors, each in an appropriate role. As part of your strategic assessment of your organization, you will have to work to align roles and responsibilities for both your government employees and your government contractors.

Align Contracting with the Appropriate Number of Government Staff

At the same time that government contracts have gotten more complex and the number of contracts and contractors has grown, the number of government employees to manage contractors has decreased. The government now spends less to manage its contracts (on a percentage basis) than at any point in history. In some cases, this has created poor contract oversight, which has resulted in ineffective and costly contracts.

There is now agreement that government is severely understaffed in the contracting arena. Legislation is pending to create a government-wide acquisition intern program for contract specialists and to increase funds devoted to workforce development and the hiring of contract specialists. The shortage of contracting specialists is due to the downsizing of those positions in the 1990s and to the increasing rate of retirement of "baby boom" contract specialists. You should devote your personal attention to the unique issues and problems facing the acquisition profession. This will include program experts and contracting professionals.

There are specific actions that you can take to strengthen the acquisition cadre in your organization:

- Establish sound career ladders for acquisition professionals so that your agency can retain qualified individuals by providing them with career progression.

- Get direct hire authority for your agency so it can recruit and acquire staff in a timely fashion.

- Put in place intern, mentoring, and coaching programs to increase the capability of your acquisition cadre.

- Design recruiting programs to bring in mid-career acquisition specialists from outside of government.

- Offer joint program and contracting staff training programs to promote a collaborative working environment.

- Establish effective succession planning to respond to impending retirements.

Align Contracting with Industry Best Practices

There is little doubt that government will continue to contract many activities in the future and will continue to work closely with contractors and their staffs. Because of this, you must align your contracting activities with industry best practices. The work of government contractors has substantially changed in recent years, as well as the relationship between government and contractors. These changes are, in part, responsible for some of the recent challenges. Government and contractors are moving into new terrain, and both will need to learn how to deal with changing expectations and new relationships.

In recent years, three major shifts have occurred in the government contracting arena. Shifts one and two are clearly related. The "buying" of services (shift one) will require a new partnership relationship (shift two). Shift three reflects technology as an enabler to provide faster, more cost-effective services.

- **From buying goods to buying services.** While government will continue to buy goods (although it may do it differently, such as purchasing goods via an electronic catalogue), the driving force behind the procurement revolution has been government's increasing need to buy services. When buying services, it is not easy to specify the height or weight of the desired product or deliverable. There is now increasing recognition that the role of government is changing—from the *purchaser of goods* to the *manager of the providers of goods and services*.

- **From a "command and control" relationship to a partnership relationship.** Buying services is a more complex and uncertain activity than buying goods. While buying goods can indeed be complex, there are many more unknowns when buying services. Complexity and uncertainty will determine the type of relationship and interactions required in managing large contracts in the 21st century. The concept of operating as partners is indeed revolutionary for government. It was not part of the traditional model.

- **From a paper-based procurement system to electronic procurement.** The third shift is just as profound and significant as the first two. This shift will also significantly alter the way procurement officials operate. While the first two shifts centered on the impact of the shift from buying goods to buying services, electronic procurement will likely have an important impact on government's ability to buy goods more quickly and efficiently at a reduced cost.

Align Your Expectations with Contracting Realities

Finally, it will be crucial for you to align your expectations in this area. While all the areas discussed in this book will be challenging, contracting presents special challenges. Specifically, challenges include:

- **Dealing with a cumbersome, process-bound system.** For legitimate reasons, there are no "shortcuts" in the world of contracting. You will have to be patient and rely heavily on the advice of your contracting experts. Their job will be to keep your agency procurements moving along while in full compliance with the rules of the system.

- **Dealing in a highly contentious area.** Over the past decade, the pendulum has continued to swing back and forth from flexibility-driven to rule-tightening contracting reforms. You can expect the pendulum to continue to swing; in recent years, it has been moving toward rule-tightening reforms.

CONTRACTING

ALTERNATIVE STRATEGIES FOR DELIVERING SERVICES

QUESTION: What are alternative sourcing strategies? I thought my only two alternatives were either to outsource via contract or to continue to perform activities in-house with government employees.

ANSWER: Today, your job has become more complex than in the days when government performed its activities primarily with government employees. Contracts were primarily used to either support government employees or to buy goods and materials. Your job is now to determine how best to accomplish your mission and what sourcing strategies can best fulfill the mission of your organization.

Moreover, your job is to accomplish your mission in the most cost-effective and efficient manner possible. Over the past two decades, government has found that the introduction of some form of competition will likely produce both performance gains and cost reductions. In your review of how best to accomplish your mission, you and your team will consider the following options:

- **Insourcing.** This is when your own employees provide the services. When creating the Transportation Security Administration (TSA), it was decided that TSA employees would be federal civil servants and not "contractors" provided by private sector firms.

- **Competitive sourcing.** This is a public sector–private sector competition to see who can do the job at a lower cost and with better performance. At the Internal Revenue Service (IRS), competitive sourcing was used to rethink its functions and modernize its business processes, which resulted in substantial improvements in service delivery. In two competitive sourcing initiatives, government employees at IRS won both competitions; however, this still resulted in reductions in the number of federal employees in both instances.

- **Outsourcing.** Outsourcing differs from competitive sourcing in that the decision to move work out of the government has already been made. Private sector firms compete to provide greater efficiency, higher performance, and greater costs savings. In recent years, the National Aeronautics and Space Administration outsourced its desktop computing (hardware, software, and support) to a private sector firm, which resulted in significant cost savings.

- **Public-private partnerships.** In selecting a public-private partnership approach, you decide to share the costs, risks, benefits, and profits with a private sector firm. One example of this approach is the Defense Logistics Agency, which selected a "Virtual Prime Vendor" to provide parts and consumables for C-130 aircraft propeller assembly.

In their report to the IBM Center (2004), University of Maryland's Jacques Gansler and William Lucyshyn provide specific recommendations on how you can best accomplish your examination of alternative sourcing strategies in your organization:

- **Leadership.** Your personal involvement is crucial in obtaining and maintaining organizational support for examining alternative sourcing strategies.

- **Planning.** You must ensure that there is adequate planning in order to reap the maximum benefits of alternative sourcing strategies.

- **Change management.** You must recognize that alternative sourcing strategies will drive major changes in your organization, and you must develop approaches and incentives to manage the selected strategy.

- **Communication.** You must develop and maintain comprehensive communication with all stakeholders.

- **Follow-up.** You must follow up to ensure that all contracts and agreements are executed as proposed.

Understanding Alternative Sourcing Strategies

From *Implementing Alternative Sourcing Strategies: Four Case Studies*
edited by Jacques S. Gansler and William Lucyshyn

Competitive Sourcing

The competitive sourcing bidding process determines whether the public or the private sector can do the job faster, at lower cost, and with better performance. Competitive sourcing is a method of introducing competition into government services, replacing the government's traditional monopoly with much greater incentive for improved operational efficiency at significantly lower costs. Jobs that are deemed "not inherently governmental" (i.e., "commercial") are put into bid packages, with the private and public sectors competing for the contract. In cases where the government agency wins the competition, however, there is not a formal "contract award." This occurs only when the private sector bidder wins.

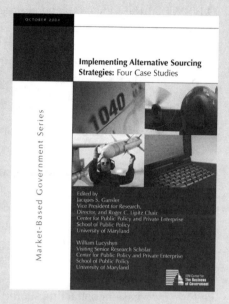

These competitions are held under guidelines established by the federal Office of Management and Budget (OMB). The guidelines are referred to as "A-76 competitions" after the federal circular in which they are published. The private sector bids, along with the proposal from the government organization, are evaluated, and the lowest cost provider (in some cases A-76 allows best-value criteria to be used) is selected to provide the desired services.

Outsourcing

Outsourcing differs from competitive sourcing in several ways. Under outsourcing, the government agency concludes, in advance, that the best way to achieve greater efficiency, higher performance, and substantial cost savings is to contract out the work to a private vendor. There is no competition between the government agency and the private vendor for the work to be performed. The "competition" is among the private vendors bidding for the contract to perform the work or provide the service. Outsourcing has become an increasingly common practice in federal, state, and local agencies.

The private sector has made increasing use of outsourcing over the past decade. Recent press accounts indicate that many private sector companies have moved non-core operations to (mostly) third-world countries, which offer substantially lower salaries to workers in repetitive or low-grade occupations such as order taking, service inquiries, software programming, and telemarketing.

Public-Private Partnerships

Another category of government acquisition is public-private partnerships; these allow the public and private sectors to share the costs, risks, benefits, and profits. Public-private partnerships can take many forms where production work, facilities management, and the investment of capital are functions that can be shared between public and private entities to obtain efficiency and cost savings. Public-private partnership must operate in a competitive environment to be truly effective; otherwise, there are no incentives for improving performance.

One type of public-private partnership that the government has established is known as "prime vendor." This concept originated in the private sector, with the creation and fostering of close working relationships between companies and their suppliers.

CONTRACTING

PERFORMANCE-BASED CONTRACTING

QUESTION: What is performance-based contracting? What has been the experience of other public sector organizations in using it?

ANSWER: The Office of Federal Procurement Policy (OFPP) has defined performance-based contracting as containing four key elements:

- **Performance requirements** that define, in measurable terms, the work to be accomplished or the service to be provided

- **Performance standards** that define the "acceptable quality level" of performance

- **A quality assurance plan** that specifies the means by which contractor performance will be determined and documented

- **Positive and negative incentives** that are tied to the quality assurance plan

Over the past decade, the use of performance-based contracting has increased in the federal government and there continues to be interest in further increasing the use of such contracts. In recent years, the Office of Federal Procurement Policy has set a goal that at least 40 percent of eligible contracts awarded are performance-based contracts.

Performance-based contracting should be viewed as part of the increasing movement toward a greater performance orientation in government, as discussed in the section on Performance. The success of performance-based contracting will depend, in great part, on how effectively your organization can describe the desired outcomes of the performance-based contract. The goal is to focus on the intended results of the project, not the process. Performance-based contracting includes the use of shared incentives to permit greater innovation and cost-effectiveness.

The use of performance-based contracts is closely related to the procurement partnership model described on pages 100–101. In performance-based contracts, the government specifies the desired outcome of the project, as opposed to methods to be used. The challenge facing governments in developing performance-based contracts is to clearly define the expected "performance" of a contract consisting of contract outputs, quality, outcomes, and various combinations of the three. The goal is also to provide contractors with more agility and flexibility in determining their approach to achieving the desired outcomes.

In his report to the IBM Center (2002), University of Central Florida's Lawrence L. Martin examined the experience of state and local governments with performance-based contracting. He found that state and local governments were experimenting with various approaches to performance-based contracts, including innovations such as share-in-savings contracting, revenue enhancement contracting, and milestone contracting. Overall, Martin found that state and local governments were ahead of the federal government in performance contracting as they had adopted a wider variety of policies, practices, techniques, approaches, and tools all designed to change the behavior of contractors to focus more on performance.

As noted in the *Memo on Contracting*, reform in the procurement process is being driven, in part, by the movement toward contracting for services rather than the traditional contracting for goods. Martin writes, "The transition to service contracting constitutes a fundamental paradigm shift for federal procurement. Federal procurement must find new ways of conducting the federal government's business including the development of new policies, procedures, concepts, and tools to deal with a new service reality."

Examples of Performance-Based Contracting (PBC)

From *Making Performance-Based Contracting Perform: What the Federal Government Can Learn from State and Local Governments*
by Lawrence L. Martin

In his report to the IBM Center (2002), Lawrence Martin found numerous examples of performance-based contracting at the state and local level across the United States. The table below describes how state and local governments are designing contracts to place increased emphasis on performance and to reward or penalize contractors based on that performance.

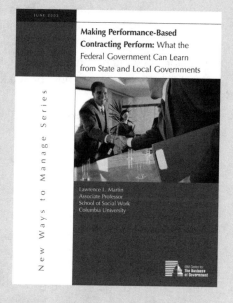

Examples of Approaches to Performance-Based Contracting in the United States and Canada

Case Example	Description
1. Metropolitan Government of Nashville & Davidson County, Tennessee: PBC for Share-in Savings with Partnering	PBC for change management services using share-in-savings and partnering whereby the contractor and public employees share in the cost savings
2. Arizona Department of Economic Security: PBC with Indefinite Performance	PBC for job training and placement services with indefinite performance where the contractor's compensation and performance standards are tied to the performance benchmarks of another provider
3. City of Charlotte, North Carolina: PBC with Step-Up/Step-Down Incentives and Penalties	PBC for help desk and desk side support services with incentives and penalties that step-up/step-down from the performance standards or acceptable quality levels (AQLs)
4. Oklahoma Department of Rehabilitative Services: PBC for Individual Client Milestones	PBC for employment services using a milestone approach where each person served is treated as an individual project with a start point, end point, and major milestones
5. Pinellas County, Florida: PBC with Penalties for Incomplete Service Data	PBC for ambulance services with penalties for data integrity problems
6. Illinois Department of Children & Families: PBC by Manipulating Contractor Workload	PBC for child permanency placements (family reunification, adoptions, and subsidized guardianship) using workload manipulation to increase contractor performance
7. Ontario (Canada) Realty Corporation: PBC with "Floating" Incentives and Penalties	PBC for multi-year property management services using "floating" incentives and penalties tied to 112 performance requirements

THE PROCUREMENT PARTNERSHIP MODEL

QUESTION: What is the procurement partnership model? How does it differ from the traditional procurement model?

ANSWER: As you will quickly find out, much of the work of your agency is done via contracts with other organizations (both private sector firms and nonprofit organizations). In fact, you will probably find contractors sitting in offices throughout your building. Without looking closely at their identification badges, you might not even be able to tell the difference between which individuals work for you and which work for a contractor. They often sit right next to each other. Contractors are likely to be assisting in your information technology (IT) offices and directly working with your program staff in delivering services to citizens.

In the past, government contracts were used to buy things (such as the proverbial widget) that were built to government specifications in factories spread across the United States. While the government still does buy many things, the dramatic shift over the past 20 years has been toward the purchase of professional services. Buying services has turned out to be far different from buying commodities. As a consequence, a different relationship is now necessary to best accomplish the goals of government contracts.

In her report to the IBM Center, University of Delaware's Kathryn Denhardt concluded that a new relationship is now required between the government and its contract workforce. Successful contracts, according to Denhardt, now require arrangements and relationships that have been adapted to a results-driven, resource-constrained government. Denhardt defines four desirable changes from the traditional procurement model to the new partnership procurement model:

- **Moving from low trust to high trust.** Because of the complexity of many government contracts, unexpected problems are likely to occur and developing solutions to these problems will require "a close partnership between the government and the contractor in order to share information, brainstorm ideas, and find mutually agreeable ways to move forward." Trust is required when problem solving is necessary.

- **Moving from a diffusion of leadership to executive leadership.** During interviews for her IBM Center report, Denhardt was told that successful contracts were characterized by having a single executive on both the contractor and government side who was fully committed to making the project successful and who has sufficient authority to make necessary decisions along the way.

- **Moving from stovepipe organizations to team-based approaches.** Because of the increasing complexity of projects as noted above, "integrated solutions" teams are now required. These teams pull together expertise from various parts of your organization: contract staff, program staff, IT staff, financial staff, and other appropriate staff members.

- **Moving from "accountability to rules and audits" to "accountability for results."** This is a major change in the evolution of contracting. Today, performance-based service contracts are increasingly being written to contain clear standards for performance and results.

In his report to the IBM Center, University of Central Florida's Wendell Lawther identified the need for longer-term commitments and relationships as key factors in a successful partnership model. Given the increasing complexity of projects, Lawther found that additional flexibility will be needed to revise projects based on unanticipated problems and evolving knowledge and new technologies.

Understanding New Contracting Vehicles

From *The Procurement Partnership Model: Moving to a Team-Based Approach*
by Kathryn G. Denhardt

The variety of contracting vehicles available to government has expanded. With the right people involved, these vehicles can incorporate both a performance-based management orientation and a partnership approach.

Share-in-savings contracts can be used when contracting for the reengineering of a business process that will substantially reduce costs for the government over time. In some cases, the vendor makes the up-front capital investment and realizes return on investment over a one- to three-year period following the reengineering. The agency pays the vendor through savings from what the agency would have spent under the old system and keeps a share of the savings itself.

Commercial item purchase or service contracts are used for the purchase of items or services available on the commercial market rather than specially developed for the government. Such contracts are appropriate in order to reap the price benefits of competition among multiple providers and to allow immediate purchase of widely accessible products and services. Purchasing commercial items avoids the problematic issue of intellectual property rights that arises when vendors develop solutions for government that also have a commercial value to the vendor. These intellectual property issues present a significant barrier to successful partnerships between government and the vendor, and may be avoided by using commercial items and services. Purchasing commercial items usually results in more timely delivery as well.

Government-wide acquisition contracts (GWAC) are contracts intended for multi-agency use. A program manager might utilize a GWAC to access services without going through a new procurement process. Program managers who do not have successful relationships with their own agency's procurement office have been known to utilize GWAC vehicles from another agency.

Fixed-price contracts are appropriate for services that can be objectively defined in the Request for Proposal and for which there is a track record of what such services cost. With fixed-price contracts the vendor maximizes profit by providing the service in the quickest possible fashion, so it is essential to have good performance and quality measures in the contract, or it will be difficult for the project manager to hold the contractor accountable for quality and outcomes.

Cost-reimbursement contracts are necessary when it is impossible to clearly define in advance what will be required of the vendor. In those cases government might enter into cost-reimbursement contracts in which vendors are reimbursed for the actual costs of performing the service. The incentive for the contractor is to have the project take longer in order to maximize profit. Thus, services that have been previously acquired under cost-reimbursement contracts should use that previous experience to convert to a fixed-price contract.

Fixed base price plus performance incentive contracts are appropriate when periodic measures of performance such as target completion dates or levels of quality can be determined and rewarded (or sanctioned) based on actual performance during the contract period.

CONTRACTING

PUBLIC-PRIVATE PARTNERSHIPS

QUESTION: What are public-private partnerships? Should I consider them for my organization?

ANSWER: Public-private partnerships (PPPs) have been defined as an arrangement of roles and relationships in which two or more public and private entities work together to achieve a common objective. PPPs usually have various public-private cost-sharing arrangements, which potentially provide additional investment dollars for public projects that might otherwise not be available. In the Collaboration section, we discuss the advantages and disadvantages of government participating in partnerships (see page 144). It is clear that it must be in the self-interest of government organizations to participate in such partnerships.

Given the prospect of tight budgets for both civilian and military agencies across the federal government in the years ahead, interest in public-private partnerships is likely to increase. Thus, it might be highly worthwhile for your organization to consider whether a public-private partnership approach is appropriate for the types of activities for which you are responsible. Governments across the world are now exploring new types of public-private partnerships, including partnerships in areas such as health, education, and real estate.

Traditionally, PPPs have been used predominantly for public sector infrastructure projects, such as highway construction. The building of privately financed toll roads across the United States is a prime example of such PPPs. PPPs have been used extensively across the world. Many nations now have much greater experience with PPPs than the United States. Over the last 20 years, the United Kingdom has used its Private Finance Initiative (PFI) to increase the flow of capital projects during a period of restraints on public spending.

In his report to the IBM Center, Rutgers University's Trefor Williams concludes that the federal government should consider options other than the current procurement model in which government traditionally procures and funds separate services via distinct contracts, such as construction, design, or operating services. According to Williams, PPPs allow for "greater efficiency and cost savings by bringing private sector discipline to new areas of project construction, operation, and financing." Williams also emphasizes that PPPs "attract new private investment.... Projects where no government funding may have been available are allowed to move forward due to private sector investment."

As noted above, the challenge for government leaders like you is to begin to consider new applications of the PPP model to various public sector activities beyond the transportation sector, which has been the dominant user of PPPs. In her report to the IBM Center, Harvard University's Judith Grant Long argues that PPPs could be a powerful means to leverage public buildings and real property to generate investment and long-term revenues for the government. Since federal managers are likely to be facing a critical and ongoing shortage of public funds, Long states, "it is imperative to consider creative financing solutions, such as public-private partnerships that can attract private capital for public property purposes." In the property management arena, PPPs are also a potential response to the government's current heavy reliance on costly leasing.

It should be pointed out that receiving "approval" to create a public-private partnership will be a challenge for you. In some cases, legislation will be required to undertake a public-private partnership. You will also confront an outdated, complicated set of budget rules which does not easily accommodate itself to public-private partnerships. Even though it is difficult, you might conclude that it is worthwhile and cost-effective for your agency to explore the possibility of public-private partnerships.

Types of Public-Private Partnerships

From *Moving to Public-Private Partnerships: Learning from Experience Around the World*
by Trefor P. Williams

Range of Public-Private Partnerships

Fully Public ←					→ Fully Private
Design Build	Design Build Finance Operate	Build Transfer Operate	Build Operate Transfer	Build Own Operate Transfer	Build Own Operate

Moving to Public-Private
Partnerships: Learning from
Experience around the World

New Ways to Manage Series

Trefor P. Williams
Associate Professor of Civil Engineering
Rutgers University

Models of Public-Private Partnerships

Design-Build	When one entity makes a contract with the owner to provide both architectural/engineering design services and construction services.
Design-Build-Finance-Operate	A constructor is responsible for the design, construction, maintenance, and financing. The constructor is compensated by specific service payments from government during the life of the project.
Build-Transfer-Operate	A private developer finances and builds a facility and, upon completion, transfers legal ownership to the sponsoring government agency. The agency then leases the facility back to the developer under a long-term lease. During the lease, the developer operates the facility and earns a reasonable return from user charges.
Build-Operate-Transfer	A concession is granted to a constructor to design, finance, maintain, and operate a facility for a period of time. The constructor recoups the cost of the project by collecting tolls during the life of the concession period.
Build-Own-Operate-Transfer	Ownership of the facility rests with the constructor until the end of the concession period, at which point ownership and operating rights are transferred to the host government.
Build-Own-Operate	Resembles outright privatization. Projects of this type are often let with no provision for the return of ownership to government.
Build-Lease-Transfer-Maintain	In this type of arrangement, a facility is typically designed, financed, and constructed by the private sector and is then leased back to government for some predetermined period of time at a pre-agreed rental.
Lease-Renovate-Operate-Transfer	This model is for facilities that need to be modernized. The private sector constructor pays a rental to government and agrees to renovate the facility. In exchange, the constructor is granted a concession to operate the facility for a fixed period of time and to charge a fee for the service.

CONTRACTING

COMPETITIVE SOURCING

QUESTION: I understand that competitive sourcing is very controversial. What exactly is it? If I undertake competitive sourcing, what is likely to happen?

ANSWER: In brief, the competitive sourcing bidding process determines whether the public or private sector can undertake a set of activities currently done by the government and do the job faster, at lower costs, and with better performance. The public sector–private sector competitions are held under guidelines set forth by the Office of Management and Budget in its A-76 circular. In competitive sourcing, the private sector "bids" against a government unit that has put together a "most efficient organization" (MEO) staffing plan. It should be emphasized that these competitions are about whether specific government functions (or activities) can most efficiently be conducted in-house or by those outside of the organization.

In their report to the IBM Center (2004), Jacques S. Gansler and William Lucyshyn examined over 1,200 public-private competitions conducted by the Department of Defense (DoD) over a 10-year period from 1994 to 2004. DoD was selected for analysis because the department had conducted more competitions than the rest of government and had collected data on each of the 1,200 competitions. Based on their analysis of the data, Gansler and Lucyshyn found:

- **Competition results in savings.** This finding has been consistent in all studies of competitive bidding. Regardless of who wins the competition (the public sector organization or the private sector contractor), savings result. Competitions resulted in an average estimated savings of 44 percent of baseline costs (with either improved performance or no decrease in performance).

- **Involuntary separations are few.** Counter to common perceptions, few federal employees actually lose their jobs as a result of competition. Data showed that only 5 percent of DoD job competitions resulted in involuntary separation. Most employees were transferred to other positions in government as a result of competitions. In addition, a variety of tools have been developed to provide "soft landings" for employees who have been separated.

- **The government's "most efficient organizations" are winning most of the competitions.** Again counter to common perceptions, an analysis of data showed that since 2003, the government has actually won twice as many competitions as have contractors.

Over the past decade, the government has created several "soft landing" programs for cases in which the private sector wins a competition. It has become a best practice for the winning private sector firm to provide job offers to federal employees displaced by the competition.

Based on their analysis, Gansler and Lucyshyn set forth the following recommendations to agency leaders, like yourself, on how best to conduct competitive sourcing:

- Work toward **minimizing the potential impact** on employees when planning for competitive sourcing competitions.

- **Know and use all of the available tools, alternatives, and techniques** to minimize any negative impact on separating employees.

- **Look for innovative ways** to offer employees a smooth transition in the event of involuntary separation.

- Continually **communicate** with both employees and external stakeholders during a competition.

Notwithstanding the positive conclusions of Gansler and Lucyshyn, you should be aware that competitive sourcing has become politically contentious and will require a substantial amount of your time and political capital if you choose to use this approach.

Glossary of Key Terms About Competitive Sourcing

From *Competitive Sourcing: What Happens to Federal Employees?*
by Jacques S. Gansler and William Lucyshyn

Activity. A specific task or grouping of tasks that provides a specialized capability, service, or product based on a recurring government requirement. Depending on the grouping of tasks, an activity may be an entire function or may be a part of a function. An activity may be inherently governmental or commercial in nature.

Commercial Activity. A recurring service that could be performed by the private sector. This recurring service is an agency requirement that is funded and controlled through a contract, fee-for-service agreement, or performance by government personnel. Commercial activities may be found within, or throughout, organizations that perform inherently governmental activities or classified work.

Competition. A formal evaluation of sources to provide a commercial activity that uses preestablished rules (e.g., the Federal Acquisition Regulation [FAR], OMB Circular A-76). Competitions between private sector sources are performed in accordance with the FAR. Competitions between agency, private sector, and public reimbursable sources are performed in accordance with the FAR and A-76. The term "competition" as used in A-76 includes streamlined and standard competitions performed in accordance with A-76 and FAR-based competitions for agency-performed activities, contracted services, new requirements, expansions of existing work, and activities performed under fee-for-service agreement. The term also includes cost comparisons, streamlined cost comparisons, and direct conversions performed under previous versions of OMB Circular A-76.

Inherently Governmental Activities. An activity that is so intimately related to the public interest as to mandate performance by government personnel as provided by OMB Circular A-76 Attachment A.

Most Efficient Organization (MEO). The staffing plan of the agency tender, developed to represent the agency's most efficient and cost-effective organization. An MEO is required for a standard competition and may include a mix of government personnel and MEO subcontracts.

Performance Work Statement (PWS). A statement in the solicitation that identifies the technical, functional, and performance characteristics of the agency's requirements. The PWS is performance based and describes the agency's needs (the "what"), not specific methods for meeting those needs (the "how"). The PWS identifies essential outcomes to be achieved, specifies the agency's required performance standards, and specifies the location, units, quality, and timeliness of the work.

Privatization. A federal agency decision to change a government-owned and government-operated commercial activity or enterprise to private sector control and ownership. When privatizing, the agency eliminates associated assets and resources (manpower for and funding of the requirement). Since there is no government ownership and control, no service contract or fee-for-service agreement exists between the agency and the private sector after an agency privatizes a commercial activity or enterprise. Moving work from agency performance with government personnel to private sector performance where the agency still funds the activity is not privatization.

CONTRACTING

For Additional Information on Contracting

Effectively Managing Professional Services Contracts: 12 Best Practices (2006) by Sandra L. Fisher, Michael E. Wasserman, and Paige P. Wolf

This report is targeted to the growing number of government managers who are responsible for managing professional services contracts. The report presents a dozen best practices, based on real-world experience, currently used by successful managers across the government.

International Experience Using Outsourcing, Public-Private Partnerships, and Vouchers (2005) by Jón R. Blöndal

This report is based on research conducted by the Organization for Economic Cooperation and Development (OECD), including site visits, interviews, and two major OECD conferences. The report focuses on key design and implementation issues for three principal market-type mechanisms used to provide public services in OECD countries: (1) outsourcing, (2) public-private partnerships, and (3) vouchers.

Transborder Service Systems: Pathways for Innovation or Threats to Accountability? (2004) by Alasdair Roberts

This report describes the emergence of new transborder service systems that constitute a radical change in the administrative structure of government. Service delivery organizations that were previously independent and geographically dispersed are being integrated into border-spanning corporate structures. Three trends have encouraged the rapid expansion of these systems: an increased international emphasis on outsourcing and privatization, an increase in the scope and complexity of government outsourcing, and the elimination of barriers to entry to national markets for the provision of public services.

IT Outsourcing: A Primer for Public Managers (2003) by Yu-Che Chen and James L. Perry

This report assesses the potential of using application service providers (ASPs) for improving the efficiency and effectiveness of public information and service delivery. Renting application services allows government to use the most advanced applications and technology at an affordable rate. ASPs address e-government challenges, such as lack of technology-trained staff, capital investment, implementation and maintenance, and uncertainty associated with fast-paced technological changes.

Moving Toward Market-Based Government: The Changing Role of Government as the Provider (2003) by Jacques S. Gansler

This reports examines competitive sourcing, a major shift in the way government does its business. This report defines competitive sourcing and outsourcing, discusses in which situations it is appropriate to use one or the other, and lists steps for successful implementation.

For Additional Information on Contracting

Franchise Funds in the Federal Government: Ending the Monopoly in Service Provision (2002) by John J. Callahan

This report provides an evaluation of the franchise funds authorized in 1994 under the Government Management Reform Act. The report includes a case study of the Office of Federal Occupational Health (OFOH) in the Department of Health and Human Services. The report evaluates the successes and failures of franchise funds and the competition they face from the private sector and other government service providers.

A Vision of the Government as a World-Class Buyer: Major Procurement Issues for the Coming Decade (2002) by Jacques S. Gansler

This report analyses the key issues facing government procurement and the steps that should be taken to address these key issues. The report presents a "vision" of the government's procurement process for the next decade and describes how government can efficiently and effectively transition to this new vision.

Contracting for the 21st Century: A Partnership Model (2002) by Wendell C. Lawther

This report examines federal agencies that have contracted out large-scale programs and evaluates their effectiveness. Outsourcing of services formerly provided in-house has become a strategy used by an increasing number of local and state governments to lower service delivery costs and/or improve service quality.

Managing for Outcomes: Milestone Contracting in Oklahoma (2001) by Peter Frumkin

This report documents examples of milestone contracting between public agencies and social service nonprofit agencies, with a particular focus on an innovation in Oklahoma's way of managing its contracts with nonprofit organizations. Oklahoma's milestone contracting specifies a series of distinct and critical achievements and confers payment for a set of collaboratively defined programmatic results.

Determining a Level Playing Field for Public-Private Competition (1999) by Lawrence L. Martin

This report provides an analysis of the theoretical and practical issues involved in creating a level playing field for public-private competitions. The notion of a level playing field is that governments should create a set of policies and procedures governing public-private competitions such that neither government nor the private sector has a competitive advantage. The study assesses the challenges involved in attempting to create a level playing field.

CONTRACTING

Chapter Six: Technology

IT can be a tool to change the way your agency does business, to redesign work processes, and to eliminate inefficient ways of working.

IBM CENTER FOR THE BUSINESS OF GOVERNMENT
WASHINGTON, DC 20005

MEMORANDUM FOR THE HEADS OF EXECUTIVE DEPARTMENTS AND AGENCIES

SUBJECT: **Technology**

While you may not have come to Washington to manage information technology (IT), you should pay attention to it for two reasons. First, if you leverage IT effectively, it will help you achieve your goals. Second, if IT is managed poorly in your agency, it has the potential to thwart your agenda, tarnish your legacy, become a major distraction, and take up a large amount of your time and energy.

While IT is an area which is subject to hype, over-promises, and significant risks, it also has great potential. You have more flexibility with technology than in changing the amount of funds your agency now has. IT can be a tool to change the way your agency does business, to redesign work processes, and to eliminate inefficient ways of working. Technology also increases economies of scale.

There are five elements to successfully managing information technology in your organization:

Begin with your policy and program objectives. Begin with what you want to accomplish. Then, and only then, bring in the technology experts to assess how technology can help you reach those goals. Get them to frame the technology agenda in terms of the mission to be achieved or the customers to be served. The technology agenda might include better service delivery, lower costs, or more transparency. The technology agenda linked to your mission is *not* faster processors, more bandwidth, or infrastructure.

A large number of big government IT projects involve upgrading infrastructure or various support systems, such as financial management systems. Though important, this is not where the big payoffs are. Infrastructure and financial systems should be viewed as means to an end. Make sure someone is watching them, but put your energy in the efforts to enhance what your agency actually does. Make sure those projects are driven by the mission, not your IT or financial folks.

Technology can be the enabler of new ways of doing business or can be used to make your existing business model more effective or efficient. Your vision can embrace either or both. If you embrace it as the enabler, consider getting other organizations to do some of the work and even to support your mission. Plan on significant changes to what work needs to be done. Look to similar organizations for lessons on how best to pursue this strategy. If you focus on improving the current business model, plan on fewer and more formally managed operations supporting multiple programs. These will replace the multiple program-specific applications that are typical in the government.

Get a handle on your ongoing IT projects before there is a crisis. Large IT projects often fail. In the federal government they fail publicly. It is a near certainty that your agency has projects under way that have been going on for years, with past or planned expenditures in the hundreds of millions of dollars. It is important for you to get a handle on these projects early in your tenure. You should consider bringing in outside experts to do a quick independent review of the projects and give you a sense of the risks the projects face. You should act on their recommendations.

You should also ensure that your chief information officer (CIO) has a process for reviewing progress on an ongoing basis. You should request that projects provide incremental deliverables every few months.

Make sure that the deliverables are used, user satisfaction is measured, and the results are factored into later phases. Even given all this, be prepared for a crisis involving a system development effort getting into trouble. Have a contingency plan.

Make sure you have a capable, qualified, and effective chief information officer. An effective CIO will be critical to your success and must be able to deal effectively with both technology and the agency mission it supports. Your CIO must have strong program, technical, management, and people skills, and will be the person who translates mission needs into technology solutions. This is a difficult job and those with the needed skills are in short supply. A key component of the CIO job will be to work closely with the Office of Management and Budget to secure resources and to respond to its oversight of your agency's projects.

Most agencies are limited by legacy IT systems that barely get the work done, cost a fortune to maintain, are inflexible, and lock operations into outmoded approaches. Technically savvy in-house staff is in short supply and much of the work is done by contractors. More modern technology that would give you needed flexibility is difficult to develop and requires a discipline across organizational lines that is rare in government agencies. Your CIO will be critical to making it all work.

Empower your CIO but have a process for reconciling IT and other imperatives. Making programs work depends on combining money, people, technology, and contracts. Effective technical solutions cross organizational lines and require that representatives of the different disciplines work together as a team. Solutions require reconciling various interests. The CIO must have the power to enforce technology decisions. You also will need to ensure that you have a process that reconciles the interests of key players in your department, such as your chief financial officer, and have mechanisms for balancing the very real issues that will arise.

Do not get engaged in the debate over who among the key players in your department is in charge, who is more important, or who reports to whom. Instead, empower the CIO to ensure that information technology issues are properly addressed. Your CIO will almost certainly be turning off obsolete systems, forcing the buying of different software than others want, and directing the migration of existing users to new systems. These moves, though necessary to meeting program or customer needs, will clash with existing ways of operating. Expect conflict, but ensure there is a process for resolving it.

Make sure security and privacy concerns are a priority for program managers. The trends in technology are to connect everyone to everything. Privacy and security problems that were minor with 20 participants are horrendous if millions of people might be involved. It is a near certainty that during your tenure, your agency will lose a laptop full of sensitive information, have a security breach that affects service delivery, or have some other public crisis involving security.

Previous crises mean your agency is already spending millions on compliance reviews and certifications. Your inspector general (IG) is doing reviews as well. Make sure that your senior managers take security and privacy seriously as an operational matter. Your program managers should be regularly testing security and using the results to improve it. They should not be depending solely on IG audits.

You should support these efforts. There is more to security than getting the paperwork right. Have a contingency plan for a possible incident. In short, security should be viewed as part of your program management responsibilities.

STARTING A PROJECT

QUESTION: What questions should I ask at the start of an IT project?

ANSWER: Asking a series of simple questions will usually lead to more insight than volumes of written justifications and PowerPoint presentations. This is particularly true when asking questions about large IT programs that develop their own momentum.

- **How does this project help my agency achieve its mission?** Any project that comes to your attention will be significant. The program manager needs to be able to explain why it is important in mission or customer terms. Don't accept justifications like the need for the latest technology, compliance with a regulatory mandate, or a previously made decision. Of course these factors can be important, but they must be tied to how they help achieve the mission. The justification should be framed in mission terms.

- **Who is the customer and what does that customer want from the project?** Meeting a need means there should be a customer who will say whether it was successful. Make sure that the customer is engaged and looking forward to the results, and that there is a process that balances customer desires with technical realities.

- **Does the project management team have the wherewithal to deliver, and is there a management framework to give them a fighting chance?** Any technology that matters will cross organizational lines in your agency and perhaps with other agencies. Success requires that you have a strong project manager and that there is a project management framework in place to work together effectively between those different organizations.

  Your agency should have a systematic approach to project management including a standard methodology. Project managers should be full-time, have formal project management certifications, be accountable for project success, and have authority over project budgets. Are they, and do they have the necessary experience, given the size of the project?

  - Projects should have deliverables in the short run (a few months) that are real and can be used by customers. Do they?

  - There needs to be a formal process for raising and resolving issues that cross organizational lines. Is there?

  - Important projects need regular and real executive involvement. Who is that executive and how is he or she engaged?

  Projects tend to take on a life of their own once started. No one wants to take responsibility for stopping them if they start to fail. The temptation is to wait a while longer, hope for the best, and at worst give the problem to a successor. Projects need formal go/no-go "gates" at the end of each key phase. What are those gates and are they real?

- **Does the IT strategy make sense?** It may seem the height of arrogance to second-guess the technology judgment of experts in the field. Nonetheless, there are some basics that you ignore at your peril. They involve architecture, proprietary versus standard solutions, and what others are doing.

  New technology may solve a business problem but may be proprietary and lock you into a single or very few vendors. If the approach is proprietary, why is it and what is the strategy to avoid being locked in?

  What are similar organizations doing? If your agency is doing something different, why? Has anyone else done this? Did it work?

  Finally, and most important, if the project fails, what is the fallback strategy?

MONITORING PROJECTS

QUESTION: How do I monitor ongoing IT projects?

ANSWER: Projects significant enough to warrant your attention will be tracked in your agency by project tracking systems and almost certainly will be tracked by the Office of Management and Budget (OMB) as well. Typically, these tracking systems will identify programs as green (everything working well), yellow (project in jeopardy), or red (project in real trouble). Deviations from schedule or budget by more than 10 percent usually trigger significant concern and a yellow flag. These tracking systems will be used by your CIO to track IT projects and intervene as appropriate. You will want to know why projects are yellow or red and what is being done to address this.

Don't rely solely on these tracking systems. Tracking systems do not always give a clear picture, and projects rated green can end up wasting hundreds of millions of dollars. Make sure that what is being tracked is meaningful. Projects have their own momentum. Milestones can become irrelevant as needs change. Ask what the milestones mean and why they are still relevant.

Conversely, some projects are always updating milestones to meet changing needs. This can lead to a vicious cycle that leads to nothing being accomplished while millions are spent. If milestones are changing, find out why.

Your CIO should establish systems that go beyond project tracking to address these issues, but while you are waiting, here are some additional factors you should consider. These draw on the insights of Gopal K. Kapur from the Center for Project Management, but other project management frameworks would have similar questions.

- **What is the total cost of the project to date?** The longer a project has been going and the more that has been spent, the harder it is to kill. No one wants the responsibility for ending a project, so the incentives are to interpret optimistically and pass problems to the next manager.

- **Is the project still in alignment with the agency's strategy?** It would be silly to continue a project to improve a system that is now scheduled to be replaced, but it happens. Ask whether the same strategy would be followed if starting today.

- **Is there an engaged executive sponsor with the necessary clout?** Is the executive sponsor engaged? Projects usually need an executive sponsor to remove roadblocks and keep the project focused on the business problem. Executive sponsors in name only are an indication that the project is going south.

- **Are the contractors you are depending on (and it will almost certainly be contractors) still viable?** Technology and markets change quickly. Ask if the contractors are still a good fit.

- **Do you still have customer buy-in?** Every project needs a customer. That customer needs to still want the results. It does not count that two years ago the customer wanted it. What do they want today? Ask the customer. Don't depend on the sponsor or the project manager to speak for the customer.

- **What are the unresolved issues with the project?** Any important project will raise issues that need to be resolved in order for progress to continue. Bureaucracies tend to be poor at raising and resolving issues. If there are more issues than milestones, expect trouble.

- **What are the risks and how are they being addressed?** No project is risk free. This holds doubly true for big projects. Ask what the risks are and what is being done to mitigate them. If your people tell you there are no risks, find someone more honest, more knowledgeable, or both.

- **Finally, what is the mitigation strategy should the project fail?**

TECHNOLOGY

TERMINATING A PROJECT

QUESTION: What are the factors to consider in ending a project?

ANSWER: The previous two questions covered what you should do to keep projects on track. Hopefully, problems will be identified while they still can be fixed. Unfortunately, hopes do not always become reality and you may need to shut down some projects. This will be harder to do the longer you wait. When you first come into your agency, you may even find projects that have been on hold, waiting for the "coup de grace" to fall on someone else's (your) watch. Expect that the longer a project has been going and the more that has been spent, the harder it will be to kill.

Candidates for termination are:

- Projects that are in deep trouble according to basic project tracking criteria, such as milestones and budget being missed by more than 10 percent, substantial changes to scope or redefinition of milestones, and the absence of engagement of key stakeholders.

- Projects that are no longer in alignment with the business strategy of the agency.

- Projects that customers no longer value. Even a project that looks great in terms of milestones and budget should be canceled if the customers no longer need or want it.

- Projects that depend on issues being resolved but for which no resolution is in sight.

Skills of the project management team or engagement of the executive sponsor may also be a reason to terminate a project, but it is also quite likely that new staff can be brought in or the priorities of the executive sponsor adjusted. This may be much less costly than project termination.

However, what may be most important is what to do after the project is terminated. There may be practical and legal issues if one terminates a project. Find out what they are and then develop a strategy to address these issues. Terminating a project also requires an alternate strategy to meet the need that the project was to meet. Expect to consult with OMB, potentially Congress, and other stakeholders both before and after the decision. You may find many stakeholders eager to "help" you make a decision of this sort.

You should require your staff to develop the alternative strategy and have them assure you that it will not lead to the problems that led to the termination. It is also important to keep in mind that a decision to terminate is likely to attract attention from outside your agency. How you explain the decision will be an important part of the mitigation strategy.

ENSURING SECURITY AND PRIVACY

QUESTION: What do I need to do to address security and privacy concerns?

ANSWER: It is a near certainty that you will face a major security breach during your tenure. It could be a simple theft of a laptop, private information being released to the public, a compromise of your systems that prevents your agency from conducting its business, or one of a range of other possibilities too long to list. Any of these could lead to loss of trust in your agency, severely impact its operations, or cost millions to mitigate.

You will find that your agency is already spending substantial sums on security. These include operational expenditures as well as systems of certification and reporting. You have a chief information security officer and a chief privacy officer to oversee this, and your inspector general will be evaluating them. A briefing on the status of these efforts will give you a sense of where your agency is, but you should go beyond this.

You should ask: What are our risks and vulnerabilities? What are we doing about them? Who is in charge? How much is enough? How can I tell?

Vulnerabilities from a security or privacy standpoint need to be balanced with the need to get the job done. There is no such thing as perfect security, but you can ensure that the right trade-offs are made as you perform your mission.

Key additional questions to ask include:

- **Who is accountable for security?** How can I be confident that person has the wherewithal to protect my agency?

- **What do our systems tell us about how safe we are?** Standard reports that cover all your systems go regularly to OMB. Find out the concerns they flag and how they are being addressed.

- **What are the threats?** What is their likelihood, our vulnerability, and how do we know? Look strategically, not system by system. Your people should put priority on the most likely threats that can do the most harm.

- **What is the operational impact of addressing the threats?** Find out the operational impact of security procedures from the operational people, not the security people. Security procedures with high operational impacts lead to workarounds. The two groups need to work together. Make sure they do.

- **Do we regularly test our systems to ensure that the process of certification is more than a paperwork exercise?** This should be done by program managers as part of their duties. Don't leave this key program management function to the inspector general.

- **What is the plan should something go wrong?** The plan should have been tested and include communicating to those affected as well as other stakeholders.

- **What don't we know? What are we doing about it?** The rate of technological change makes it hard to keep up with the threats. A bit of time spent anticipating surprises can be useful even if you get a different one. To quote President Eisenhower, "Plans are nothing; planning is everything."

TECHNOLOGY

Using Shared Services

QUESTION: How can shared services help me achieve my mission?

ANSWER: Supporting you and your agency's mission are many administrative processes that can suck away the time and attention of you and your senior staff. Shared services offer a way out of this morass.

What are shared services? In shared services, one consolidates support operations around an optimized business process, establishes accountability and metrics for both the suppliers of a service and its users, and benchmarks the operations against alternatives. Properly managed, it can substantially reduce your costs while increasing customer satisfaction and speeding up your agency's reaction time.

Effective use of shared services does not simply mean consolidating support operations. It also requires that those consolidated and optimized operations be accountable to customers for both customer satisfaction and cost as compared to external benchmarks. By the same token, it requires customers to be accountable for their responsible use of the shared service.

There need to be metrics for both suppliers and customers and a means of resolving disputes. Your staff may be conflicted on the approach. Internal service providers tend to resist being held accountable to customers and the customers don't want to depend on others. Without careful attention to these dimensions, shared services will fail.

Shared services are typically found in such areas as human resources, financial management, and information technology, as well as functions such as billing and call centers. Relevant services are transitioned into a single delivery organization, either supported by in-house resources or outsourced to an independent organization. Your agency may be a service provider, may obtain service from another agency, or both.

Businesses have moved to shared services in part to address problems in earlier rounds of consolidation that achieved savings from economies of scale, but often at the price of abysmal customer service.

Based on past experience, it has been found that successful use of shared services requires four key conditions:

- Roles and responsibilities of both suppliers and users of services must be explicitly addressed.

- Metrics for both must be developed, measured, and agreed to.

- A framework for resolving performance, customer service, and cost issues must be implemented.

- Shared service performance must be regularly benchmarked.

When considering shared services, you should ask the following questions of your IT team:

- Who is the service provider and why should I have faith in the provider's ability to deliver both the cost and quality of the service?

- Who are the other customers of the service provider? How can I be confident that those other customers are pleased with the service?

- How are we measuring cost and customer satisfaction?

- What happens if something goes wrong? How will disputes be resolved? What are our alternatives should the relationship not be salvageable?

- How are we benchmarking the service? How does the service compare to the benchmarks?

Understanding Shared Services

From Sharing an Understanding of Shared Services, A Brief Snapshot of What FM and HR Service Providers Are Offering Federal Agencies by Amit Magdieli and Jonathan Breul
(*The Business of Government*, Fall 2006)

Momentum has been building in the federal government to align many of government's administrative functions with designated shared service providers in several "lines of business." To match the interest and need of current and potential clients, a group of shared service providers has been designated by the Office of Management and Budget. OMB has been working to ensure that the "offerings" of these service providers are robust and distinguishable enough to attract a large number of clients and provide them with a high degree of service over the long term.

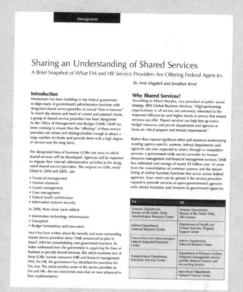

The designated lines of business (LOBs) are areas in which shared services will be developed. Agencies will be expected to migrate their internal administrative activities to the designated shared service providers. The original six LOBs, established in 2004 and 2005, are:

- Financial management
- Human resources
- Grants management
- Case management
- Federal health architecture
- Information systems security

In 2006, three more were added:

- Information technology infrastructure
- Geospatial
- Budget formulation and execution

Much has been written about the benefits and issues surrounding shared service providers since OMB announced its plan in March 2004 for consolidating core government functions.

Rather than expend significant effort and resources modernizing existing agency-specific systems, federal departments and agencies are now expected to select, through a competitive process, a government-wide service provider for human resources management and financial management services. OMB has estimated cost savings of nearly $5 billion over 10 years from the consolidation of common systems and the streamlining of similar business functions that occur across federal agencies. Even more can be gained if the service providers expand to provide services to quasi-governmental agencies with similar functions and missions to government agencies.

Financial Management

- Treasury Department, Bureau of the Public Debt, Administrative Resource Center
- Interior Department, National Business Center
- General Services Administration, Federal Integrated Solutions Center
- Transportation Department, Enterprise Services Center

Human Resources

- Treasury Department, Bureau of the Public Debt, HR Connect
- Department of Health and Human Services, Program Support Center
- Interior Department, National Business Center
- Department of Defense: Civilian Personnel Management Service and the Defense Finance and Accounting Service
- Agriculture Department, National Finance Center

TECHNOLOGY

For Additional Information on Technology

Ramping Up Large, Non-Routine Projects: Lessons for Federal Managers from the Successful 2000 Census (2005) by Nancy A. Potok and William G. Barron, Jr.

The report examines the management challenges, including procurement issues, faced by the 2000 Census. The report discusses how the Census Bureau met these challenges and looks ahead to the 2010 Census and how the Bureau might best respond to future challenges.

Understanding Electronic Signatures: The Key to E-Government (2004) by Stephen H. Holden

The report describes the Internal Revenue Service's (IRS) use of electronic signatures for its electronic filing program for individual tax returns. The case study describes how IRS approached the need for electronic authentication solutions. Since its launch, the number of returns signed electronically has increased. Resolving the challenge of electronic signatures is a key element in expanding the use of technology in government.

Government Management of Information Mega-Technology: Lessons from the Internal Revenue Service's Tax Systems Modernization (2002) by Barry Bozeman

This report provides a history of computer modernization efforts by the Internal Revenue Service, beginning with the initial Tax Systems Modernization project. The study reviews the many hurdles faced by the IRS, highlighting those obstacles related to legislative constraints, bureaucratic entanglements, political complexities, civil service restrictions, and contracting and procurement requirements.

Public-Sector Information Security: A Call to Action for Public-Sector CIOs (2002, 2nd ed.) by Don Heiman

This report expands upon the themes and issues raised at a forum on Security and Critical Infrastructure Protection sponsored by the National Association of State Chief Information Officers (NASCIO). Conference participants identified a series of actions designed to combat emerging cyber-threats to security and critical infrastructure. The report includes recommendations for improving public-sector information security in three areas: management, technology, and homeland security.

Privacy Strategies for Electronic Government (2001) by Janine S. Hiller and France Bélanger

This report provides a framework for understanding the implications of privacy and security in the public sector, the challenges of the increased use of the Internet to deliver government services and information, and the lessons that can be learned from the private sector in dealing with privacy and security issues and experiences.

Chapter Seven: Innovation

Recognize that employees, especially those who are on the front line of your organization and who regularly deal with your agency's customers, often are the source of innovative services that can benefit your customers. Getting them engaged is key.

IBM CENTER FOR THE BUSINESS OF GOVERNMENT
WASHINGTON, DC 20005

MEMORANDUM FOR THE HEADS OF EXECUTIVE DEPARTMENTS AND AGENCIES

SUBJECT: **Innovation**

Innovation is a hot topic. While not usually viewed as a tool, innovation can assist you in improving performance and achieving your goals. Many organizations in the public, nonprofit, and private sectors are devoting much time and effort to developing new approaches to innovation. In *Expanding the Innovation Horizon: The Global CEO Study 2006*, IBM developed a typology to characterize different types of innovation:

- **Business model innovation** that changes the structure and/or financial model of agencies or organizations that provide programs, deliver services, or support operations. In government, business model innovation is more about the "what" rather than the "how" of government.

- **Operations innovation** that improves effectiveness and efficiency at the tactical or core process/function level.

- **Products/services innovation** that creates new programs or services, or citizen-facing activities.

In his new book, *The Future of Management* (Boston: Harvard Business School Press, 2007), Gary Hamel adds a fourth type of innovation:

- **Management innovation** that "substantially alters the way in which the work of management is carried out, or significantly modifies customary organizational forms, and by so doing, advances organizational goals."

Your challenge is to foster the right mix of the four types of innovation in your organization.

Foster Business Model Innovation

You should challenge your management team to examine your current agency-wide business models. For example, in the case of the Internal Revenue Service's (IRS) *e-file*, IRS moved toward the adoption of electronic filing. Your team should ask themselves: (1) Are we sufficiently challenging the way our agency conducts its business? and (2) How can we better measure and manage our agency's performance in achieving objectives?

Changing a business model in government will not be easy. Business model innovation frequently creates anxiety and fear within agencies. It is thus crucial that you target your business model changes wisely, communicate effectively, implement the changes quickly, and make adjustments as necessary over time.

Foster Operations Innovation

For the development of innovations in business operations, you will need to create "safe spaces" for mid-level management entrepreneurs to pilot new ways of doing business. For example, in the case of shared services, this approach was piloted a decade ago in selected agencies, with great trepidation by both oversight bodies as well as by the providers (who thought their previously mandated customers would go elsewhere). After several years of successful operation, this concept was expanded government-wide.

For the implementation of innovations in operations, you will need to champion things that work and expand them beyond the pilot phase. For example, as the pilots begin to demonstrate promise, you should export them to other parts of agencies and begin to share them as best or promising practices so that they can be developed in other parts of government.

Foster Products/Services Innovation

To foster innovation in products and services delivered by your organization, there is much that you can do. First, recognize that employees, especially those who are on the front line of your organization and who regularly deal with your agency's customers, often are the source of innovative services that can benefit your customers. Getting them engaged is key. You can do this by creating an atmosphere that encourages individuals to be entrepreneurial in proposing and advocating for innovations. This goes beyond the traditional "suggestion box" to allowing them to try new ways of doing things and recognizing them for their efforts.

Second, the success of most innovations involves effective collaborative approaches—whether it is within your organization, across agencies, across levels of government, or across public-private-nonprofit sectors. Recognizing that this is both an opportunity and a challenge is important when endorsing efforts to pilot or implement innovative products or services.

Foster Management Innovation

In *The Future of Management*, Hamel sets forth a three-prong approach to fostering management innovation in your organization:

- **Challenge long-standing management "orthodoxies" in the organization.** In short, Hamel recommends that you should go to "war" with precedent. If you are going to undertake innovation in the above three areas (business model, operations, and products/services), you will also have to undertake management innovation by developing new approaches to management "systems" in your organization.

- **Develop new principles that will encourage new approaches which will "reinvent" the "management genome" in your organizations.** Hamel recommends that you bring together your management team to examine specific processes within your organization to ask questions such as:

  - Who "owns" this process and who has the power to change it?

  - Who are the "customers" of this process?

- **Find insights from what Hamel calls "positive deviants"—those individuals or organizations with management practices that are eccentric yet effective.**

Be Engaged

In its 2006 survey of 765 CEOs, business executives, and public sector leaders, IBM found that a crucial element in the success of innovation is the following:

- **Innovation requires your personal engagement.** This is where you come in. The survey found that CEOs believe that the major obstacles to innovation reside in their own organization: Culture, budget, people, and process were cited as the most significant hurdles. The federal government is no different. You can change these.

Innovation does not happen in isolation to all of your other activities and initiatives. Innovation can become a key ingredient on actions related to all the tools discussed in this volume. The test of the success of innovation in your agency will be whether it has contributed to improving performance and achieving your goals.

INNOVATION

Undertaking Innovation

QUESTION: Why do leaders undertake innovation?

ANSWER: First, we need to define innovation. In the *Memo on Innovation*, we discuss four types of innovation. There is no shortage of definitions of innovation. While there are many nuances in the various definitions, there appears to be general agreement that an innovation is new, usually novel, and aspires to change the way an organization (or part of an organization) operates and delivers service to the public.

In his report to the IBM Center (2001), Jonathan Walters analyzed the first 15 years of award winners in the Innovations in American Government Awards program. He found six major reasons why leaders like you undertake innovation within their organization:

- **Being frustrated with the status quo.** Simply put, you may not like some of the answers you are getting from members of your organization. Many leaders find that the organization is taking too long to get things done. Impatience quickly sets in and leaders begin to push for change and improvement. In many cases, the organization is ready for change and responsive to leaders pushing to reexamine current practices and develop new approaches.

- **Responding to crisis.** In this case, it isn't just frustration but an acute event which demonstrates that part of the organization isn't working. After a crisis, leaders have a strong case for change to take to their organization. A crisis often enables a leader to propose major change, not just incremental change at the margins. It's been estimated that 30 percent of innovations are crisis inspired.

- **Focusing on prevention.** In contrast to responding to a crisis where government is reactive, leaders often take a proactive approach to nipping a problem in the bud. Leaders often build a case for investing money to improve a program before it "breaks" and problems arise. Walters concludes that "applying a little inventiveness to treating the problem at the front end is ultimately much cheaper and much more effective than treating it at the back end."

- **Emphasizing results.** As seen throughout this volume, there is an increased emphasis now being placed on "results." Innovations have often been characterized by a leader's desire to move to results-oriented outcomes, rather than the traditional emphasis on process within government. An innovation enables leaders to have results-focused discussions and to design performance monitoring and measurement systems up front, at the start of a new initiative.

- **Adapting technology.** While technological innovations have been a characteristic of many innovations in recent years, there continue to be new opportunities for government to apply the latest technologies in new ways. The next frontier of technological innovations appears to be in the social networking arena, where government can find new ways to engage citizens via the use of these new tools.

- **Doing the right thing.** In his analysis of innovations, Walters found that there were a series of innovations that were "hard to explain in any other way than that they are flat out about doing the right thing." Some of these innovations might have been politically controversial, but leaders decided to pursue them because they felt the activity was needed and could make a difference in a specific policy arena.

There are additional practical reasons for implementing innovation. In IBM's *Global CEO Study 2006*, the CEOs report that a desire for cost reductions and increases in flexibility and organizational responsiveness were prime drivers in seeking increased innovation in their organizations.

Personal Observations on Chronicling Innovators

From *Understanding Innovation: What Inspires It? What Makes It Successful?* by Jonathan Walters

For all the millions of words written about innovation in government (and the private sector), and for all the long-winded attempts to analyze the alchemy of change management in government, innovation, at the end of the day, is a pretty straightforward proposition: It's a people-driven business. And the people behind innovation are a fascinating group.

It's easy to attach to them all the typical adjectives: creative, persistent, even courageous. But those words are used so often they've lost a lot of their punch, as accurate as they might be. Besides, what I've noticed about those who have been identified through the Innovations awards is something a little subtler: They are restless.

When it comes to how public jobs get done, there's a group of people (many, to be sure, who have never been recognized by any awards program and who never will be) who just seem, like the mythical Prince Valiant, to be perennially dissatisfied. Which is why no change-management recipe book in the world is ever going to capture the magic of innovation in the form of some immutable quasi-political or social-scientific math equation. In the end it's actually more of a nurture-nature question best left to psychologists—who, by the way, don't really have any answers, either.

Still, "experts" have been analyzing innovation in the public (and private) sector for eons. Whether it's Borins, Osborne, Light, Peters, or Walters, dozens have gone through the exercise of putting innovative organizations and programs under the microscope in hopes of finding that magic bit of genetic material that will allow innovation to be cloned.

It's not an easy thing to do. Yes, organizations can be structured in a way that will encourage innovation. And certainly it helps to understand the inspiration behind certain types of innovation so that when opportunity visits it can be turned to action. Characteristics of sustainable and replicable programs are worth identifying so that once-and-future innovators at least have the benefit of knowing some tricks of the trade as they embark on the frequently frustrating adventure of pushing change.

But if innovation were a matter of organizational dynamic or just the right opportunity, it would hardly ever happen in the public sector, or probably anywhere else, for that matter. It is people who push it, people often working in dysfunctional organizations under miserable circumstances, and in spite of that, they try to change things.

Very few of the programs recognized have been pushed by high-level, well-known public sector all-stars. For the most part, the programs are the product of inside and outside stakeholders who are simply tired of doing something one way when they suspect—or know—there's a better way; who are tired of chronic mediocrity (or outright failure) when they know government should and could do better.

If pressed to come up with my own formula for how all this should work, and to borrow from the contemporary political lexicon, maybe we need to institute some sort of "two strikes" rule for innovation based on the following observation: If some policy or program is not humane and it's not therapeutic (or, more broadly, if it's not morally defensible and it's not working), then it's a signal to everyone that it's time for change. Or maybe it ought to be a "one strike" rule. But either way, it's going to be people who decide that.

INNOVATION

INNOVATION TYPE ONE: BUSINESS MODEL

QUESTION: Can you define business model innovation and give some examples of this type of innovation?

ANSWER: A business model is a summary of how an organization intends to serve its citizens, customers, and employees. It involves both what an organization intends to do as well as how the organization will carry out its plans. In short, business model innovation is a successful change in the elements of the business model that substantially enhances the organization's ongoing performance in delivering benefits versus the current or other available alternatives. It entails innovation in the structure and/or financial model of an organization, regardless of whether it delivers programs, provides services, or supports other operations.

One way to think of business model innovation in government is to think of an organization as a set of processes that turn inputs into outputs, which lead to outcomes. These processes turn labor and capital into services and products. It is these business processes that govern workflow. They include such things as logistics systems, order processing, call centers, customer support, and program operations. Surrounding the work of transforming inputs into outputs, however, is everything the managers do: pulling resources together, developing policy, setting priorities, building teams, nurturing relationships, and forming partnerships.

Business model innovation entails constructing different relationships between users and services, new relationships between institutions, new funding arrangements, major alterations in governance and accountability, and, not infrequently, a redistribution of rights and responsibilities among the public, other stakeholders, managers, and professionals.

Here are two examples from government:

- **Service Canada.** The Canadian government recognized it must introduce new and better ways to serve its citizens to help them adjust to the realities of the modern labor market. In 2006, the government consolidated two departments, with the goal of ensuring integrated policy development as well as improved delivery of programs and services through "Service Canada."

  Service Canada is the government of Canada's new, easy-to-access, one-stop service delivery network that brings the range of federal services together to meet the individual needs of Canadians wherever they live. No matter what government of Canada service citizens are looking for, their one stop is Service Canada: at any of the 320 Service Centers across Canada, online at servicecanada.gc.ca, or by phone at 1 800 O-Canada.

- **IRS *e-file* Program.** In 1998, Congress told the Internal Revenue Service that by 2007 it wanted 80 percent of all tax returns, over 120 million annually, to be filed electronically. IRS realized that it needed a new business model if it stood a chance of meeting the congressional deadline. IRS then speeded up its efforts to increase the *e-file* adoption rate, which had already been under way for several years. The strategy was simple. Rather than continue to try to encourage taxpayers to file directly through the IRS or other government sites, IRS turned to software companies, national tax preparation firms, and tax accountants. "It was a no-brainer," explained Terry Lutes, the career IRS employee who ran *e-file*. "We needed to work with the private sector to accomplish our goals." (For a fuller discussion of this innovation, see page 125.)

IRS e-*file* History

From *A Model for Increasing Innovation Adoption: Lessons Learned from the IRS* e-file *Program*
by Stephen H. Holden

Since the program's inception in 1985, the IRS has made a variety of changes to the *e-file* program, its organizational support, and the technology it relies on. Some changes seem as simple as changing the name from electronic filing or "ELF" to IRS *e-file*; others are as fundamental as changing how the IRS relates to its private sector partners. The nature of these changes has significance for other federal agencies seeking to replicate the success of IRS *e-file* in increasing e-government adoption.

- It's one of the longest-standing e-government programs, dating back to 1987 and predating popular notions of e-government. As a result, there are nearly 20 years of history and documentation to explore, in addition to a myriad of changes.

- IRS *e-file* is faced with conditions that most e-government programs would find insurmountable barriers to adoption:

  - There is no legal or regulatory mandate for individual taxpayers to e-file their tax returns

  - Paper filing is essentially free, and electronic filing often costs taxpayers money for software or services.

  - Private sector firms intermediate the vast majority of electronic transactions.

- Despite its slow start, IRS *e-file* is generally considered to be a success. The IRS announced that it received 70 million e-filed individual returns at the end of the 2006 filing season, more than filed on paper. The Government Accountability Office (GAO) found that of the 24 initiatives identified in the federal government's original strategic plan for e-government, the IRS *e-file* initiative was one of two initiatives that substantially met its originally stated objectives.

Part of what makes studying IRS *e-file* so compelling is its relative and absolute success of adoption in an area of innovation (i.e., information technology and e-government) where there is little visible success on a larger scale. While the IRS *e-file* program has experienced significant growth, especially in the last several years, the IRS was under significant pressure in the mid to late 1980s to more rapidly increase the proportion of electronically filed returns. External stakeholder groups, most notably GAO on behalf of Congress, issued a report saying the IRS was not doing enough to increase electronic filing rates. Within the executive branch, the Office of Management and Budget (OMB) and the Treasury Department were also reported to be pushing the IRS to increase electronic filing as a means to reduce paper submission processing costs. Even private sector partners in the IRS *e-file* program, such as professional groups like the Council for Electronic Revenue Communication Advancement (CERCA) and the National Association of Computerized Tax Processors (NACTP), argued that the IRS was still not doing enough to enable and promote electronic filing. Prior to 1998, though, there was no real coordinated legal or policy initiative from the legislative or executive branch to boost electronic filing volumes.

At the same time as the external pressure for electronic filing was growing, albeit somewhat disjointedly, there was also some internal impetus as the IRS hoped to decrease its reliance on the expensive and error-prone paper submission processing it had been using since the 1960s.

INNOVATION

INNOVATION TYPE TWO: OPERATIONS

QUESTION: Can you define operations innovation and give some examples of this type of innovation?

ANSWER: Operations innovation is an underlying enabler that leads to improved efficiency or effectiveness in program operations at the tactical, or core process, levels. The impact of business operations innovations tends to be internal to an organization, something that the customer might not see but would benefit from.

The source of business operations innovation is a matter of practical necessity, and it often stems from organizational entrepreneurs in mid-management trying to solve a real problem.

In recent years, there have been the following examples in government:

- **Shared services.** Shared services represent an organizational form in which common functions across a number of departments/agencies are consolidated and undertaken by a specialized agency/service delivery center. The federal government hopes to save more than $5 billion over the next 10 years by moving to a shared services model for financial management and human resources. Most of the current arguments favoring increased use of shared services by governments have centered on achieving cost efficiencies, improved customer service, and enhanced process efficiencies.

  The concept of shared services is not new to the federal government. Since the early 1980s federal entities have provided payroll and financial services to other federal entities ("cross-servicing"). In the early 1990s the Department of Defense formed the Defense Finance and Accounting Service (DFAS) to consolidate 338 offices (now down to 26 offices) into a single organization providing financial services to the military and other defense entities. Numerous other federal departments have consolidated financial management operations to form internal shared service organizations, particularly when implementing new financial management software.

- **Air Force's cost management initiative.** The commanding general of the U.S. Air Force Materiel Command (AFMC) in the late 1990s, General Bruce Babbitt, wanted to improve his command's efficiency by shifting from a budget to a cost management culture. AFMC's internal customers in the Air Force felt AFMC worked fairly well but its services cost too much. Instead of the traditional emphasis on short-term cost-cutting or productivity-improvement approaches, General Babbitt decided to pursue a longer-term effort. His goal was to change the command's capacity to manage costs by systematically improving the command's sophistication with cost measurement and analysis. When taken together, the operational innovations General Babbitt introduced into AFMC had their intended effect. As AFMC developed its fiscal year 2000 budget, it reduced its budget request by $2.7 billion over what had been previously estimated, and it stopped losing money in its working capital funds. (For further discussion of the Air Force Material Command, see pages 82–83.)

- **SeaPort:** In the late 1990s, the Naval Sea Systems Command (NAVSEA) had to reduce its spending on professional services. While there was agreement that spending needed to be cut, NAVSEA was unable to determine exactly how much it was then actually spending on professional services. As a consequence of the need to save money, better control spending, and speed up the procurement process, NAVSEA created SeaPort. SeaPort became the first federal e-marketplace for the acquisition of professional services. It was an innovative application of e-business practices to the naval procurement system. Navy Captain K. R. Wheelock describes SeaPort: "Simply put, SeaPort-e (SeaPort Enhanced) provides a faster, better, and more cost-effective means of contracting for professional services."

SeaPort: An Innovation in Navy Procurement

From SeaPort: Charting a New Course for Professional Services Acquisition for America's Navy
by David C. Wyld

Headquartered in the historic Washington Navy Yard, the Naval Sea Systems Command is the arm of the Navy responsible for designing, acquiring, and maintaining the Navy's 300+ ship fleet and its shipboard and combat weapons systems. NAVSEA's origins can be traced back to 1794. Today, NAVSEA is the largest of the Navy's five systems commands. NAVSEA has an annual budget of nearly $20 billion—accounting for almost a fifth of the Navy's total budget. Through its approximately 50,000 employees, NAVSEA manages more than 130 acquisition programs. It also administers over 1,400 sales contracts to approximately 80 foreign militaries, amounting to more than $16 billion annually. NAVSEA's operations encompass all phases of the life cycles of the Navy's ships—which now can reach 40 to 50 years—and its weapon systems.

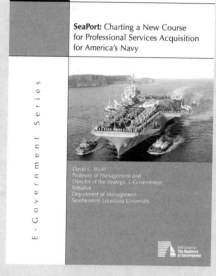

SeaPort was established by NAVSEA to be the first e-marketplace for services acquisition in the federal government. SeaPort has become an e-business portal through which NAVSEA acquires a significant portion of the over half a billion dollars worth of professional support services (PSS) necessary to support the Navy's mission around the world. The total value of the SeaPort multiple award contracts (MACs) is placed at $14.5 billion over the potential 15-year duration of the indefinite delivery/indefinite quantity (ID/IQ) contracts. It was initiated by NAVSEA to streamline the services contracting model:

- To achieve $250 million in savings

- To enable the Navy to meet the secretary of defense's mandate that performance-based contracting be used in 50 percent of professional services contracting by 2005

Through its use of ID/IQ contracts of up to 15 years, issued to 20 MAC holders (with fully one-third being small businesses), SeaPort has many innovative measures, including:

- Built-in, guaranteed cost reductions

- Award-term and performance-based contracting provisions

- Totally electronic order process

- Real-time monitoring of contractor performance and quality

- Alternative dispute resolution procedures

The SeaPort website, shown at right and accessible at www. seaport.navy.mil, is a constantly updated "community of practice."

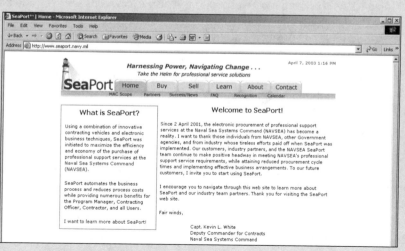

INNOVATION

INNOVATION TYPE THREE: PRODUCTS AND SERVICES

QUESTION: Can you define product and service innovation and give some examples of this type of innovation?

ANSWER: Product and service innovations are mission- or citizen-focused in their effects. They result in a substantially different approach to products or services, or are an entirely new product or service. These types of innovations can result in three effects:

- They can empower customers to serve themselves rather than having to depend on government employees or middlemen to provide a service.

- They can offer new products or services that have not been previously available to customers.

- They can enable the integration of existing services that benefit the citizen in a way that provides new convenience or value.

Interestingly, oftentimes the genesis of new products or services in the public sector stem from initiatives by career mid-level managers who are entrepreneurial in spirit. They are often inspired by something they've seen in the private sector or in other governments. Frequently, these innovations come about because of a certain level of technological maturity that allows an innovation to flourish and take root. For example, the use of wikis to develop country profiles by State Department employees and the new "Diplopedia" initiative would have been unthinkable just five years ago, even though such a collaborative tool was needed.

In recent years, there have been the following examples in government:

- **USA.gov.** How do you find out anything in the federal government? A decade ago, you looked in the Blue Pages of your telephone directory and started to call around. If you were lucky, you found someone to answer. If you were really lucky, that person knew the answer to your question. Other times, you were on your own. For example, one Baltimore Blue Page entry was a phone number for Building 203, listed under the heading for the U.S. Customs Service. That was then. Today, you can find out more helpful information yourself by going on the Internet. By starting at www.usa.gov, you can find out virtually anything the federal government does and, in some cases, what state and local governments do, as well.

  While the idea for an innovative service—a one-stop government-wide web portal—evolved organically, it took root and grew because of the dedication and passion of a small core of staff at the mid-level of an agency, with strong top-level support. It also evolved its services and value in ways not anticipated by the original sponsors—such as the collaborative network of web masters. In addition, external validation strengthened its position and helped protect it from political forces. These characteristics seem to be the case in many other service innovations.

- **ClinicalTrials.gov.** If you have a life-threatening illness, you are likely to be willing to try anything to recover, including volunteering for experimental clinical trials for drugs or therapies that may not be effective, or if effective, not commonly available for years. The federal government allows public and private researchers and companies to conduct hundreds of clinical trials every year. But how do you find out if there are any that could benefit you?

  ClinicalTrials.gov, administered by the U.S. Department of Health and Human Services, is a pioneering online health care resource serving patients and families facing life-threatening illnesses with vital information related to clinical trials. The system has its roots in law: The Food and Drug Administration (FDA) Modernization Act of 1997 mandated a registry of both federally and privately funded clinical trials "of experimental treatments for serious or life-threatening diseases or conditions."

The law required that the registry be easily accessible and understandable by the public. Prior to this point in time, clinical trial information was neither. Previous attempts to create such a "one stop shopping" for clinical trial information was targeted to researchers, not patients. The innovation was making it "customer-centric" with the patient, not the researcher, being seen as the customer.

- **Electronic health records at the Department of Veterans Affairs (VA).** How many times have you gone to one doctor but he or she needed to see your medical history kept by another doctor? Or you were visited by multiple doctors in a hospital setting, but your health records, kept by different doctors, were not readily accessible? Or your doctor could not find your files? Even scarier—every year, an estimated 48,000–98,000 patients die unnecessarily in hospitals because of a preventable medical error. Though these errors can occur at any point in the health care delivery system, the root causes of many of these errors are often linked to faulty human judgment and a lack of standard protocols. Health care providers that use electronic medical records along with related technology have dramatically reduced errors. The VA's Veterans Health Administration (VHA) has been a leader in introducing these kinds of service innovations.

  Now, imagine an electronic health record (EHR) system that can pull it all together. The VA's electronic health record system integrates all elements of a veteran's health history, medications, lab work, X-rays, scans, EKGs, medical diagnoses, and more, in one place. Through VA's remote access capability, the patient's entire record is available at all VA health care sites nationwide. In fact, when Hurricane Katrina wiped out the VA hospital in New Orleans, veterans' records were not affected. VHA calls this system "VistA"—its Veterans Health Information Systems and Technology Architecture.

- **OSHA's compliance advisors.** Small business owners, for the most part, want to provide safe and healthy workplaces for their employees. But knowing how to do this, and knowing the government rules that apply, can be complicated. Also, how do you find workplace hazards that you don't even know you have? Complying with complex rules oftentimes means hiring consultants to conduct an assessment and providing advice. This, however, can be costly for business owners. Is there a way to do what's right, but not have to pay a third party to provide that assurance?

  In the mid-1990s, the federal Occupational Safety and Health Administration (OSHA) piloted a service innovation to attempt to do this. OSHA is responsible for protecting the health and safety of American workers. To do this, it creates regulations that define safe workplace behavior from offices to construction sites. It then conducts inspections to ensure employers are complying with the rules. Business owners often see OSHA much as they see the IRS—a place to avoid contact as much as possible.

  So, while OSHA wants to help businesses comply, they are not the first place business owners turn to for help. OSHA's Ed Stern became an advocate for electronic tools and "expert" systems to assist small business owners comply with complex OSHA requirements by allowing anonymous self-assessments. As a proponent of this innovative approach, he developed several pilots that were well received by the business community. These interactive "Expert Advisors" use artificial intelligence software to identify and solve problems in layman's terms. OSHA notes that it provides confidential, free guidance, 24 hours a day, with consistent and reliable answers.

  As a result of its success as a pilot program, OSHA's Expert Advisor system has been expanded to nearly a dozen different business scenarios. For example, a business owner might start with the general "Hazard Awareness" advisor. According to OSHA, the advisor guides the owner through a series of questions about activities, practices, equipment, materials, conditions, and policies at the workplace. Based on what it learns from the user, there are follow-up questions that then result in customized reports ranging from four to 30 pages. Unlike a typical Internet search, the artificial intelligence built into each Expert Advisor program can "continue asking the user questions until it can devise a reasonable answer," notes Advisor champion Stern. "It's like the difference between a medical librarian and a medical doctor. The librarian will help you get a lot of information to read. But if you need expert help, you talk to the doctor."

INNOVATION

INNOVATION TYPE FOUR: MANAGEMENT INNOVATION

QUESTION: What is management innovation?

ANSWER: In his book *The Future of Management*, Gary Hamel defines management innovation as "anything that substantially alters the way in which the work of management is carried out, or significantly modifies customary organizational forms, and by so doing, advances organizational goals." The goal of management innovation, according to Hamel, is to change the way managers do what they do and to do so in a way that enhances organizational performance.

The goal of management innovation is to improve the performance of your organization by focusing on its management practices. The three other types of innovation (business model, operations, and products/ services) discussed in this section focus on specific programs or activities of a government organization. In contrast, management innovation focuses on the systems and processes now being used in your organization to "manage" itself. Management innovation targets a company's management processes. Hamel includes the following types of *management* processes that are common in all organizations: strategic planning, capital budgeting, project management, hiring and promotion, training and development, internal communications, knowledge management, and employee assessment and compensation. We discuss many of these systems and processes in other parts of this volume.

Hamel writes that management innovation can improve your organization's performance when one or more of the following conditions are met:

- The innovation is based on a *novel management principle* that challenges some long-standing orthodoxy.

- The innovation is *systemic*, encompassing a range of processes and methods.

- The innovation is part of an *ongoing program* of rapid-fire invention where progress compounds over time.

There are two keys in implementing management innovation in government. The first is not to assume that all the management processes you find in your organization are written in stone and cannot be changed. There have been studies that found that about 80 percent of these rules and regulations were "self-imposed" by the organization itself and not mandated by either legislation or executive branch circulars. You will likely find that these processes were put in place to combat a specific problem or a one-time abuse and the rule or process might have now outlived its usefulness.

The second key is to create an organizational environment in which individuals in your organization feel comfortable in raising management reforms. You must communicate to them your belief that your agency's rules and processes can be changed and improved when there is a clear business case to be made for such change. Management innovation should be encouraged throughout the organization and not limited to just those currently "in charge" of specific processes.

In his book, Hamel proposes several challenges related to creating an organizational environment supportive of management innovation:

- The challenge of enrolling every individual within your organization in the work of innovation and equipping each one with creativity-boosting tools

- The challenge of ensuring that the agency's top leadership doesn't straitjacket innovation and gives new ideas a chance to prove their worth

- The challenge of creating the time and space for grassroots innovation

Forging Management Innovation

From *The Future of Management* by Gary Hamel (with Bill Breen)
Boston: Harvard Business School Press, 2007

The Courage to Lead

… you have the guts to tackle problems that others are too timid or too shortsighted to take on.

To build a capacity for relentless management innovation, you must be willing to ask, "What new management challenge, if mastered, would give us a unique performance advantage?"

An Inescapable Conversation

What you need is a steady breeze that will help the flames of management innovation to spread. You need to get people … talking about the opportunity to reinvent the technology of management. You need to get them thinking about how they can turn management itself into a competitive advantage.

A Focus on Causes, Not Symptoms

To cure a crippling disease, drug researchers have to uncover the genetic flaws or disease mechanisms that cause the malady. The same is true for organizational "diseases"—the incapacities that stem from inherited management beliefs. Here, too, a painstaking analysis of first causes is essential to inventing a cure.

Accountability

One suggestion: have senior staffers meet quarterly to review one another's innovation performance. Questions to consider should include:

- Are we generating a robust flow of new management ideas and experiments?

- Are we experimenting broadly enough? Are there any innovation "black spots"? Are there management processes, or sub-processes, where there are few if any ongoing experiments?

- Are our experiments bold enough?

- Which experiments should we scale up now, which should we abandon, and which need to go through another round or two of development?

Permission to Hack

Perhaps the most important thing you can do to help … is to give "ordinary" employees and lower-level managers the opportunity to "hack" those processes. No, this doesn't mean letting the janitorial staff tear up the employee handbook. What it does imply is creating a forum in which anyone … is free to suggest alternatives to the management status quo.

INNOVATION

Increasing Your Chances of Success in Innovation

Question: Are there specific actions I can take to increase the chances of a successful innovation?

Answer: There is now much experience with innovation. It has been a "growth" industry over the past 20 or so years. In addition to studying the Innovations in American Government Awards program (see Jonathan Walters on page 135), University of Toronto's Sandford Borins in his report to the IBM Center also examined innovation award winners identified by the Institute of Public Administration of Canada (IPAC) and the Commonwealth Association for Public Administration and Management (CAPAM). In his study, Borins examined nearly 400 award winners.

Based on his analysis of award-winning innovations, Borins developed a series of recommendations for executives like you who are interested in pursuing innovations within their organization:

- **When attempting to implement an innovation, anticipate a wide variety of obstacles.** A list of such obstacles is presented on page 133. Borins is optimistic, however, that many of these obstacles can be overcome once identified. The most frequent obstacle, not surprisingly, is resources. As noted in the Money section, you will need to work closely with your finance and budget staff to find resources. Borins also emphasizes that there is most likely a much larger group of potential supporters for innovation than you might anticipate: innovators within your own organization, within the larger government, and among your clients in the private and nonprofit sector, as well as in state and local level government. Your job will be to mobilize this support.

- **Clearly demonstrate your support.** There is wide agreement that your support is crucial. You can show your support and encouragement for innovation in the following ways: making innovation a priority within your organization, providing support and recognition to those who undertake innovation, and encouraging innovations to bubble up through the organization.

- **Reward those who undertake innovations.** Rewards are a key tool you can use to encourage the types of behavior (and resulting culture) you wish to see in your organization. Many types of rewards are at your disposal: financial compensation (such as bonuses for members of the Senior Executive Service) and the creation of "gain-sharing" programs. When financial compensation is constrained, Borins reports, non-financial awards and recognition are powerful substitutes.

- **Consider creating an "innovation fund" for your organization.** There are many examples of such funds being used in the public sector, including the federal government. Since it is often hard for innovators to find additional funds within their specific programs, it is very effective to have an agency-wide "pool" of funds to which innovators can apply for funding. Creation of such a fund is also a clear signal of your support for innovation. But a word of caution should be added. As with many "special" funds in government, be careful to ensure that the fund cannot be labeled a "slush" fund. Keep it small, have clear procedures for allocating the money, and create metrics to track the benefits.

- **Consider collaborating with client organizations within the private and nonprofit sectors, as well as state and local government.** One of the greatest challenges facing your organization is to create new partnerships and collaborations with appropriate client groups (see the section on Collaboration). Innovation will allow you the flexibility of experimenting with new approaches to the delivery of services.

One final note: You must be careful to manage expectations regarding innovation. While the concept of innovation implies that not all initiatives will be successful, government does not like any initiatives to so-called "fail." Your overall innovation strategy will only be successful if you and your organization accept that a reasonable amount of failure is part of the process, and you are prepared to explain and defend this approach.

Identifying Obstacles to Innovation

From *The Challenge of Innovating in Government* by Sandford Borins

Identifying obstacles enables you to formulate questions to ask when designing an implementation strategy.

- How much will this program cost? Can the money be found through public sector appropriations? Will user fees be possible? Are private sector donations a possible funding source?

- Will the program require any changes in current regulations or laws? If so, what is the process involved and whose support will be required?

- Which organizations will be involved in delivering the program? If multiple organizations will be involved, what are their ongoing relationships? Are they organizations that rarely deal with one another, or do they have a history of rivalry, for example, turf battles? Will they fight for control of the program or fight to avoid involvement?

- If the innovation involves the application of a new technology, will it encounter incompatible legacy systems being used by different organizational participants? Will the technology lead to job losses, especially in unionized positions? Will users of the new technology require special training?

- Who will be the key participants in delivering the innovation? Will they be expected to go beyond what is normally expected of them in their current positions? If so, how will they be motivated?

- Will public sector unions oppose the innovation because it threatens job losses or affects the working conditions of union members?

- Will middle managers oppose the innovation because it devolves responsibility to frontline staff and weakens their supervisory authority?

- Will the innovation be opposed by central agencies, for example, because it reduces their control over financial or human resource decisions?

- Will the innovation face political opposition because it is inconsistent with some politicians' values? Will it face political opposition because it will reduce their ability to allocate resources to their constituents?

- Will there be public doubt or skepticism about whether the program can work?

- Will there be public opposition to the program, for example, an application of information technology that is considered by some to be an invasion of their privacy?

- Will the program face opposition from the public because it allows public servants to operate in ways or receive compensation (for example, performance-related pay) considered to be more appropriate to the private sector than the public sector?

This list of questions—formidable as it might seem—is not intended to dissuade potential public management innovators, but is designed to alert them to the challenges faced by those who have preceded them on the road to change. While all of these questions are worth asking, only certain obstacles may be encountered in a given case.

INNOVATION

SUCCEEDING WITH INNOVATION

QUESTION: What can be learned from successful innovations?

ANSWER: One of the most successful innovations in recent years has been the *e-file* program at the Internal Revenue Service. The *e-file* story is an excellent example of innovation which started back in the late 1980s and overcame many obstacles in the ensuing two decades. In 2006, nearly 60 percent of all taxpayers filed electronically and that figure is expected to continue to rise dramatically in the years ahead.

In his 2006 report to the IBM Center, Stephen Holden sets forth five lessons you can learn from the IRS *e-file* experience:

- **When an innovation matures, consider creating an organizational location for the innovation.** This is a common problem facing many innovators in government—where is the best organizational location to nurture the innovation after it matures? While "skunk works" facilities can work well to design an innovation, they frequently are not the right place from which to launch an initiative. ("Skunk works" refers to "off line" R&D facilities common among military contractors in the 1950s.) In the IRS case, a pivotal event in the ultimate success of the initiative was the creation of the Electronic Tax Administration (ETA) office. Holden writes, "Prior to the creation of ETA in 1998, the IRS had seemingly been ambivalent about electronic filing, with responsibility spread among various offices and a resulting lack of a singular voice within and outside the organization."

- **Develop collaborative partnerships with stakeholders.** The *e-file* program is an excellent example of Sandford Borins' advice to partner with client organizations in undertaking innovations (see page 132). It became clear to IRS that they could not undertake this innovation by themselves. They would need the cooperation of all IRS stakeholders, including the private sector. The controversies surrounding IRS in the mid-1990s also created an atmosphere for the IRS leadership to reach out to stakeholders. Holden writes, "By working effectively with external stakeholders, the ETA was able to create a powerful 'innovation directive' for *e-file*."

- **Invest in innovation.** Innovations are seldom "free." They do require some investments, such as the creation of innovation funds recommended by Borins. In the IRS case, the organization made investments in knowledge building at the outset of the program by creating an R&D project and fielding it as a prototype and then as an operational program.

- **Shift from a "field of dreams" mentality of marketing to proactive outreach.** A common challenge facing all innovations is that while many will agree that the new innovation is a "good idea," that does not mean that it will be self-executing and quickly become widely accepted and adopted. Holden describes the change of attitude at IRS as movement away from "the old 'inform and educate' mind-set to that of a product-oriented organization that created brand identity and promoted the benefits of the *e-file* brand and associated product over the alternative (paper)."

- **Use program performance data to drive decisions.** A key investment made by IRS was in developing a variety of program measures. IRS had traditionally had a rich collection of output and outcome data. What is unique is that IRS used the data to provide product enhancement decisions and to evaluate marketing efforts. The collection and analysis of this data provided the analytical basis for IRS's marketing efforts, which distinguished *e-file* from paper filing and highlighted the benefits of e-filing to users.

Additional Insights into What Makes Innovation Successful

From *Understanding Innovation: What Inspires It? What Makes It Successful?* by Jonathan Walters

Keep It Simple in Concept

Innovations in American Government award winners can be divided into two categories: the ones that are easy to explain and the ones that are hard to explain. There are far more in the former than the latter category, to be sure. But it's clear from looking at those programs that have caught on and those that haven't, that the more straightforward the concept, the better a program's chances of sticking around and being adopted by other jurisdictions.

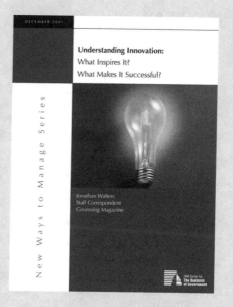

Make It Easy to Execute

Programs that seem to have natural powers of survival and replication don't require major legislation or huge administrative rule changes to create or implement, nor do they force participation. That is, stakeholders can choose to be part of a new way of doing business of their own free will.

Shoot for Quick Results

Many of the Innovations in American Government award winners that have gone on to be widely copied have another thing in common: They yield measurable results in a very short period of time. David Osborne puts it another way: "They have a good story to tell." And in the innovations business, a good story revolving around quick, easily communicated results is priceless.

Be Frugal

As many have noted, one of the organizational imperatives damping down innovation in the public sector is a general disinclination to spend new money on untested ideas, even ones ginned up by seasoned veterans who might know what they're up to. This rule holds even for programs that extensive research indicate are probably going to be a worthwhile investment—eventually.

… it's actually hard to find many Innovations award winners that involve huge investments of money. This holds true even for the high-ticket world of health care. Indeed, many of the health-related programs identified by the Innovations award program have been picked specifically for the fact that they extended health care to some previously uncovered population and did it without significantly increasing a jurisdiction's costs.

Make It Appealing to the Widest Possible Constituency

One of the really interesting features of the Innovations award program is that it clearly doesn't tend toward political pandering. Of course, it shouldn't. But still, what easier way to recognize replicable programs than to stick one's finger in the air, see which way the political winds are blowing, and then choose an early "three strikes and you're out" initiative knowing that 49 of them are bound to follow in rapid succession. In fact, the awards program tends to attract—and reward—those who buck conventional political "wisdom" and eschews the quick fix of the day.

INNOVATION

COLLABORATIVE INNOVATION

QUESTION: What is collaborative innovation and can I use this approach in my agency?

ANSWER: Much of the discussion in the previous Q&As was focused on innovation by employees within your organization to transform your business model, operations, products/services, or management practices.

In his report to the IBM Center, Rensselaer Polytechnic Institute's Satish Nambisan sets forth a model of collaborative innovation in which government agencies partner with a variety of external networks and communities to drive innovation. In other words, government agencies do not have to "do it all" themselves in regard to developing innovative ideas and programs. By deploying a collaborative approach to innovation, government gains the benefits of the knowledge and experience of those outside of government.

You and your agency can play four distinct roles in seeking innovative ideas and solutions from organizations external to government:

- **Innovation integrator:** In this role, you are dealing with a defined problem or issue and you have decided that you want to take the lead in developing an innovative solution or new program. Within government, the Department of Defense has traditionally played this role with government contractors in developing innovations where the innovation desired could be defined and government takes the lead.

- **Innovation seeker:** In this role, you are dealing with a much less defined problem and you decide that your agency will take the lead in "seeking" a solution. A portion of the research supported by the National Institutes of Health (NIH) fits this model. Frequently, NIH requests researchers to submit proposals in response to general descriptions of problems for which NIH and the scientific community is seeking solutions.

- **Innovation champion:** In this role, you are dealing with an "ill-defined" problem for which the community at large has the leadership role. You become a "cheerleader" in this situation and must develop ways in which you can encourage the development of innovation on public problems in the private and nonprofit sectors. Your agency might become a member, but not leader, of a consortium of organizations seeking innovations. An example is the All Hazards Consortium, an initiative consisting of federal, state, and local government organizations and the private sector.

- **Innovation catalyst:** In this role, the community at large has the major leadership role with a more defined problem to be solved. As described by Nambisan, innovations in this arena usually focus around existing programs or services which can be provided by the community, such as volunteer initiatives.

As we discussed in the previous answers, you can take specific actions to enhance your organization's capabilities. In order to foster an innovative collaborative organization, Nambisan concludes, you must:

- Create a culture of openness in which your organization is willing to work closely with those outside of government to seek new solutions.

- Find the "right" organizational structure from which your agency can play the desired innovation role.

- Develop appropriate leadership and relationship skills needed to foster both collaboration and innovation.

- Adopt a portfolio of success metrics.

Four Roles for the Government in Collaborative Innovation

From *Transforming Government Through Collaborative Innovation* by Satish Nambisan

Two important dimensions structure the landscape of collaborative innovation and problem solving in government. The first dimension relates to the nature of the innovation or problem—that is, how well the problem is defined and how the innovative idea evolves. The second dimension relates to the nature of the collaboration arrangement or network leadership—that is, how the innovation activities are coordinated and how the network partners share in the decision making.

Consider the first dimension: the nature of *innovation*. The innovation or problem space can be conceptualized as a continuum that has "defined" problems at one end and "emergent" or ill-defined problems at the other end. At the defined end of the continuum, the problem space is framed or defined by existing government services and programs or technology infrastructure and systems; for example, innovations that improve the delivery of existing social welfare programs or technological infrastructure innovations that enhance the effectiveness of tax collection. At the other end of the continuum, the problem space may be less well defined or more emergent in nature; for example, innovations that involve creating new mechanisms and systems for disaster management or those that address emerging public sector issues such as global warming. Although the broad contours of the problem might be known—for example, the target population for a new government service or program—bringing more clarity to the problem might require acquiring inputs from diverse stakeholders.

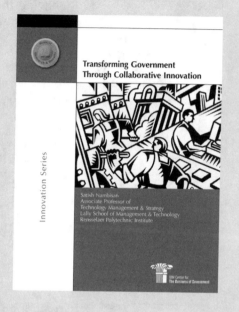

The second dimension, the nature of the *network leadership*, reflects the organization or structure of the network. Network leadership can be conceptualized as a continuum of centralization, ranging from government-led or highly centralized to community-led or diffused. At the centralized end of the continuum, the relevant government agency assumes the role of the dominant partner and leads the network. For example, in most defense-related innovation projects, the lead agency plays such a leadership role. Note that leadership can be exercised in different ways—envisioning and establishing the innovation goals, selecting the network members, and making the critical decisions that affect or shape the nature or process of innovation. At the diffused end of the continuum, the leadership tends to be loosely distributed among the members of the network or community, with the government agency playing a non-dominant role. A good illustration of this in the non-governmental context is the case of open-source software projects, which often have a leadership structure wherein the community members share in the decision-making powers.

These two dimensions define four different roles that government agencies can play in network-based collaborative innovation and problem solving.

Innovation Space	Network Leadership	
	Government-Led (centralized; formal structure/linkages)	**Community-Led** (diffused; informal structure/linkages)
Emergent (new services/programs; unstructured problem space)	Government as Innovation Seeker	Government as Innovation Champion
Defined (existing services/programs; structured problem space)	Government as Innovation Integrator	Government as Innovation Catalyst

INNOVATION

For Additional Information on Innovation

Managing the New Multipurpose, Multidiscipline University Research Centers: Institutional Innovation in the Academic Community (2003) by Barry Bozeman and P. Craig Boardman

This report describes the shift from funding individual projects to funding science centers. This study includes historical analysis of the evolution of science centers, focusing on new science and technology centers, and explores the management imperatives resulting from this new mode of organizing scientific research.

Advancing High End Computing: Linking to National Goals (2003) by Juan D. Rogers and Barry Bozeman

The report discusses the critical importance of high end computing (HEC) to science, engineering, and the overall research and development system of the nation, as well as the role of policy makers in ensuring HEC's continued advancement. The report addresses the importance of high end computing as a tool for achieving national goals and the application needs of the scientific, research, and business community.

Creating a Culture of Innovation: 10 Lessons from America's Best Run Cities (2001) by Janet Vinzant Denhardt and Robert B. Denhardt

Through a comprehensive case study of Phoenix, Arizona, this report explores how managers create a culture of innovation. Based on interviews with Phoenix's mayor, city manager, and department heads, themes are developed on creating a culture of change, encouraging responsible risk-taking, and undertaking public entrepreneurship. The study provides recommendations for managers who are focused on change and innovation within their organization.

San Diego County's Innovation Program: Using Competition and a Whole Lot More to Improve Public Services (2000) by William B. Eimicke

This report focuses on lessons learned in San Diego County, California, from the various innovations undertaken by the county. The lessons learned from San Diego are used to make recommendations for other jurisdictions to consider when introducing innovation in the public sector.

Entrepreneurial Government: Bureaucrats as Businesspeople (2000) by Anne Laurent

This report examines the story of a group of civil servants who moved away from stovepiped, red-tape-ridden bureaucracies to create new businesses within government. These programs—an amalgam of franchise operations, revolving fund reimbursable services, multi-agency contract operators, and fee-based service providers—offer lessons for implementing innovations in government.

For Additional Information on Innovation

Innovation in the Administration of Public Airports (2000)
by Scott E. Tarry

This report examines the innovative approaches taken by five publicly owned and operated airports to adjust to the evolution of America's air transport system. The study provides examples of how to make public enterprises more efficient and innovative.

Business Improvement Districts and Innovative Delivery (1999)
by Jerry Mitchell

This report focuses on providing a better understanding of Business Improvement Districts (BIDs), a significant innovation in local service delivery. BIDs are self-help ventures organized by property owners and local governments to identify and develop areas of cities where a more successful and profitable business climate is needed.

INNOVATION

Chapter Eight: Collaboration

Few national problems can be met exclusively by the federal government alone. Instead, government is now at the center of forming partnerships and networks to collaborate on any given national problem.

IBM CENTER FOR THE BUSINESS OF GOVERNMENT
WASHINGTON, DC 20005

MEMORANDUM FOR THE HEADS OF EXECUTIVE DEPARTMENTS AND AGENCIES

SUBJECT: **Collaboration**

Fostering collaboration will be a key component of your job. The need for improved and enhanced collaboration within and between agencies in the federal government, with state and local governments, as well as with nonprofits and businesses, is now clearly needed. The federal government's ineffective collaboration with other government organizations was clearly apparent and widely criticized during Hurricane Katrina in 2005.

Collaborate to Solve National Problems

Why is collaboration rising in importance? In short, the federal government's role in responding to national problems is dramatically evolving. Few national problems can be met exclusively by the federal government alone. Instead, government is now at the center of forming partnerships and networks to collaborate on any given national problem. University of Pennsylvania's Don Kettl aptly describes this new phenomenon: "Effective 21st century governments work to ensure seamless service delivery in which governments structure their service delivery systems according to the problems to be solved, not by focusing on the organizations charged with solving them."

The traditional model of government agencies administering hundreds of programs by themselves is giving way to one-stop services and cross-agency results. This transition implies collaboration—within agencies, among agencies, between levels of government, and between the public, private, and nonprofit sectors. Applying collaboration in diverse policy arenas, such as law enforcement, social services, transportation, homeland security, and the environment, is expanding. As networks and partnerships take on many new shapes, organizations are shifting their focus from "within" to "between."

Use Networks and Partnerships

While the reliance on networks and partnerships is increasing, there are still many challenges in effectively using these new tools. For example, as networks and partnerships grow, how do you fund them? As agency lines blur, who gets the credit, or when things go wrong, who is held accountable and for what? As networks go beyond the traditional approaches of cooperation and coordination between hierarchical agencies, how are they held accountable in the context of the traditional "rule of law" paradigm?

Collaboration occurs when people from different organizations produce something together through joint effort, resources, and decision making, and share ownership of the final product or service. The focus is often on producing or implementing something. Collaboration, however, can mean using one or a mix of tools on a continuum that ranges from the traditional approaches of coordination and cooperation to the creation of new networks, some of which may contain formal partnership agreements.

- **Using networks.** Because of their informal nature, networks tend to be time-consuming to develop and fragile to maintain. The decision on whether to use this approach depends on an initial assessment of whether the right dynamics exist and whether they reflect the characteristics of a successful network. Key dynamics include factors such as the styles of leaders, the types of measures of success, the use of technology, and the various approaches to accountability. Successful networks share five characteristics: shared vision and trust, independent members, voluntary links, multiple leaders, and clearly defined roles. Conducting a hard-headed assessment up front as to the probability of a network approach working effectively and succeeding will save many headaches later.

Even given the difficulty of creating networks, networks possess attributes that cannot be easily created by other vehicles. Networks provide a boundary-spanning mechanism, increase the capacity of participating organizations to combine capabilities, and spur innovation and adaptation to local conditions.

- **Using partnerships.** Much like networks, there are different types of partnerships. While partnerships tend to be more defined than networks, they may as a result face more difficulties in getting established. Partnerships do have some distinct advantages. First, a partnership tends to be more resilient when there is a transition in leadership among its members. Since networks are based largely on interpersonal relationships rooted in trust among members, networks are more vulnerable to falling apart when there is substantial turnover of membership or sponsorship. Second, because partnerships involve a more formal set of relationships, it is easier for them to leverage the resources of others. Key determining factors in your decision as to whether to join or create a partnership is whether you conclude that your interests are in alignment with your potential partners' and whether the benefits of the partnership outweigh the potential costs to you and your organization.

As the government moves forward in the decades ahead to meet challenges in many diverse arenas, collaborative networks and partnerships are approaches that can provide you with greater leverage to achieve national goals than the traditional "stovepipe" approach to individual federal programs. We recommend their increased use.

Build New Management Skills

As the use of collaboration increases, you and your management team will be challenged in new ways because you and your team will have to behave far differently than in the past. One part of this shift is a change from the traditional bureaucratic approach focused on individual programs run by separate agencies to an approach that places increased emphasis on services and results. The new model implies organizing around customers and outcomes, not the traditional agency and programs. The Government Accountability Office (GAO) noted in a January 2003 report that "national goals are achieved through the use of a variety of tools and, increasingly, through the participation of many organizations that are beyond the direct control of the federal government." In other words, government is now turning increasingly to networks and partnerships to achieve many national objectives.

The value of collaboration as a new approach or tool for government managers is receiving increasing appreciation and notice throughout the federal government. GAO notes, "Promoting effective partnerships with third parties in the formulation and design of complex national initiatives will prove increasingly vital to achieving key outcomes...." The Office of Personnel Management's list of the core competencies for the federal senior executive of the future now includes not only the ability to work in a team environment, but also the ability to develop alliances with external groups (e.g., other agencies or firms, state and local governments, Congress, and clientele groups), and to be able to engage in cross-functional activities, as well as find common ground with a widening range of stakeholders.

Benefits of Participating in Collaborative Partnerships

Question: I'm not sure I know the answer to the "What's in it for me and my institution" question regarding participating in a collaborative partnership. How will I benefit from a collaborative partnership?

Answer: This is a perfectly reasonable question. In their report to the IBM Center, Robert Klitgaard and Greg Treverton answer that question from the point of view of a public executive who would ask, "What are the advantages and risks to us and our mission from various kinds of partnerships, structured how, managed how?"

In short, your job is to assess the pros and cons of potential collaborative partnerships and to determine whether the benefits outweigh the costs. On the benefit side, a nonprofit or private sector organization can potentially bring the following to the table:

- **Bring down costs.** In the case of nonprofits, one visible cost advantage is usually their access to volunteer labor, as well as potentially having innovative service delivery mechanisms.

- **Bring up quality.** According to Klitgaard and Treverton, there is some evidence that nonprofits deliver high-quality services because of their organizational ethos, which may be "more caring" and "mission-oriented" than other organizations.

- **Access hard-to-reach target populations.** Some nonprofits have earned the trust of hard-to-reach populations and thus provide access to such communities.

- **Provide complementary capabilities.** This is often a compelling reason for collaborative partnerships. The private sector can provide technical know-how to government, as well as additional resources via public-private partnerships (see page 102 for further discussion of public-private partnerships.)

- **Reallocate resources and gain economies of scale.** Partnerships provide the opportunity to reallocate resources among partners and potentially reap increased efficiencies by tapping the specialized capability of each partner. There also might be resulting economies of scale for various functions, such as planning, research, and capital equipment.

On the cost side, you should consider risks as well. A major negative is the so-called "hassle factor," which will be recognizable to anyone who has ever tried to coordinate activities among government agencies, let alone coordinate across sectors. Anecdotal evidence suggests that "no one likes to be coordinated."

There is also the danger that the costs of a partnership will be higher than anticipated. Klitgaard and Treverton write, "Some of these costs can be measured directly in currency, but others involve reduced effectiveness because of drains on managers or staffs. Creating a new partnership, organization, committee, staff, or council costs time and money. So do training a multipurpose worker, sharing data and reports and impressions, and designing and implementing joint incentive and evaluation systems."

There is no magic algorithm, according to Klitgaard and Treverton, which can add up all the considerations in creating a partnership and tell you whether a particular partnership is worthwhile. You face two challenges. The first is to seek out collaborative partnership opportunities for your agency to consider as an alternative way to provide services or to increase the impact of your agency on national problems. The second challenge is to weigh the costs and benefits of each collaborative partnership opportunity. You should expect to see an increased interest in collaborative partnerships over the next decade and to be confronted with an increasing number of such opportunities. Klitgaard and Treverton write, "… we are entering the era of hybrid governance. More and more issues raise the desirability not just of changing the boundaries of who does what … but of considering something more: real partnerships."

About Partnerships

From *Assessing Partnerships: New Forms of Collaboration*
by Robert Klitgaard and Gregory F. Treverton

Partnerships are emerging in many areas of public life, and they pose challenging questions for potential partners as well as for policy makers. For example:

MARCH 2003

Assessing Partnerships:
New Forms of Collaboration

New Ways to Manage Series

Robert Klitgaard
Dean and Ford Distinguished Professor of International Development and Security
RAND Graduate School

Gregory F. Treverton
Associate Dean and Senior Policy Analyst
RAND Graduate School

IBM Center for
The Business
of Government

- *Better schools* are being forged through partnerships of communities and education providers, including public schools but also the private sector. Results-oriented education demands excellent evaluation, including better measures of quality, the design of incentive systems, and the design and management of public-sector/citizen/private-sector interactions. But how might we assess the many kinds of partnerships that have been formed between businesses, the schools, and parents' groups?

- *Health care* will become fairer and more efficient by becoming more client driven, more sensitive to competition, and more accountable for results. Again, it becomes crucial to forge and manage effective partnerships among the public, private, and non-profit sectors, and the consumers of health care. But how might we assess the various kinds of institutional hybrids and overlaps that have arisen in our health care systems?

- From roads to water supply, from electrification to environmental projects, *infrastructure* increasingly involves partnerships of the public and private sectors in their design, finance, and management. Communities also play a key role in deciding what is done and how, and in monitoring progress. How should such partnerships be assessed?

- *International security* involves increasing sophistication in the ways of the private sector and in the management of military-business relationships such as privatization and outsourcing. "Operations other than war" involve the military in new kinds of relationships with civil society, government, international organizations, and business. Moreover, defense policy requires greater understanding of public-private collaboration to deal with terrorism, organized crime, and the vulnerability of the information infrastructure. What kinds of partnerships between businesses, communities, and government seem most promising for what kinds of security risks? What are the dangers and costs of such partnerships?

What's Driving the Rise of Partnerships

The rise of hybrid governance can be traced to several sources. One predominant driver is technology, including the communications revolution, which enables partnerships within and across borders. While much has been written about the role of technology as a driver of change, another factor is equally critical—societal power is increasingly passing from government to the private sector, leading to a "market state."

The circumstances of the market state are transforming the role of government—and the roles of business and civil society as well. The government of a traditional territorial state was a doer; students of public administration and public policy learned that government's choice was "make, buy, or regulate." For tomorrow's public managers, the triad will be "cajole, induce, or facilitate" (or "carrots, sticks, or sermons"). Of course, all three may be involved simultaneously. To these emerging partnerships, government will provide its power to convene, its infrastructure, its legitimacy, and its information or intelligence. But it will often rely on business and civil society to provide public goods and services. The shift in mind-set this will require of government can hardly be overstated. It will not come easily to governments that they must work with, and indeed sometimes for, CARE and Amnesty International, not to mention Shell and Loral.

COLLABORATION

SUCCESS FACTORS FOR COLLABORATION WITH OTHER ORGANIZATIONS

QUESTION: What has been learned about successful collaboration between organizations to accomplish large inter-organizational outcomes?

ANSWER: There is a growing literature on this topic. The bottom line is that projects can succeed if there is an "absolute unquestionable shared commitment to the goal." In his report to the IBM Center (2003), Lambright writes, "When the goal is clear and worthwhile, coordination becomes possible. Although some turf battles may occur, the mission often overrides turf concerns."

Lambright's conclusion is based on his study of four large-scale research and development programs: climate control, nanotechnology, the International Space Station, and the Human Genome Project. While each of these programs was somewhat unique and scientific in nature, they all faced the challenge of coordination across several federal departments and agencies. In the case of the space station, international coordination was required as well. While your agency's initiatives might not approach the scale of these projects, Lambright found that the lessons learned regarding working across boundaries are applicable to all organizations requiring the cooperation of others:

- **Set a clear and focused goal.** A key lesson is that ambiguous goals exacerbate confusion and conflict.

- **Emphasize common interests.** Agencies clearly need a positive incentive to cooperate. In an era of declining resources across government, additional resources are likely to be a key incentive. To get resources that can be appropriately shared across agencies and put to use, organizations must cooperate.

- **Attract political support.** This relates to the first lesson: A clear and focused goal will make it more likely to attract political support.

- **Enlist the White House and its support agencies.** In most instances, the support of the White House and the Office of Management and Budget (OMB) will be essential. OMB will be key in approving funds that can be used for interagency activities.

- **Employ strong but diplomatic leadership.** You must realize that separate agencies (like separate nations) have their own power bases, independent of any would-be coordinator like yourself. You are more likely to get joint action through consensual tactics rather than "strong arm" tactics.

- **Retain staff support.** You will not only need the support of the heads of your "partner" organizations, you will also need the support of staff who will be devoted to facilitating the joint activity, such as meetings and the preparation of interagency documents.

- **Use an external threat to foster internal cohesion.** The threat can often be domestic (as in the Human Genome Project and nanotechnology initiatives) or international (the space station), where competition was used to bring an interagency enterprise together. An effective leader stresses strength in unity and potential defeat in division.

- **Keep the end in sight, but be flexible to the means.** None of this will be easy and it is likely to be undertaken over a multi-year time period. Lambright observes, "The leader helps the enterprise to adapt while keeping the end in sight. The successful leader has a strategy, but is flexible as to tactics."

Implications of the Human Genome Project on Collaboration in Government

From *Managing "Big Science": A Case Study of the Human Genome Project*
by W. Henry Lambright

Most observers of the Human Genome Project's (HGP) history concentrate on the contest between HGP and Celera. The record of HGP also shows the importance of partnership as instrumental in bringing about a capability to unravel the human genomic blueprint.

What HGP's approach suggests is that where very challenging objectives are involved, and talent is distributed widely, it may be necessary and desirable to link institutions into vast research consortia. More than one-third of HGP's budget came from sponsors other than the National Institutes of Health (NIH). Performers included national laboratories, universities, and researchers in six countries. Such partnerships have advantages and disadvantages. The negatives are obvious—the partners have wills of their own and may defeat or slow down the achievement of system-wide goals. There has to be a leadership structure of some kind to provide coherence, direction, and pace. The HGP model entailed a "lead agency" approach with NIH fulfilling that role by virtue of dominant funding, political support, and technical competence. While an agency may seek to lead, others may not necessarily follow. Partnerships require leadership of one kind or another, and sometimes a form that works at one point in a project's history may not at another. A mix of stability and change are essential in keeping partners together. Hence, the HGP model is one about which observers who prefer neat organizational lines, strong hierarchical management, and predictable strategy may find fault. There can be inefficiencies in partnership arrangements as consensus takes time to be forged. Nor are performers of R&D in universities or other entities always willing to go along with central decisions. Leadership often comes down to the power to persuade.

HGP seems to be a forerunner for what is to come. It reveals a type of large-scale "network" or "system" in which the leader (an organization or person) has power that is limited, but can be enhanced. It is not "power over," but "power with." Bargaining, negotiation, prodding, cheering, complaining, charming, coercing—all are techniques of management in partnership relations.

Looking forward, what great projects lie in the 21st century for which HGP is a possible model? One can imagine projects such as: the search for a new disease cure; a way to mitigate global warming, while still having energy to develop economically; a mission to Mars or one to divert oncoming asteroids; a technological front against terrorism; and others. Whatever lies ahead—and the unexpected is to be expected—HGP's lessons show that diverse institutions can be brought together in pursuit of bold goals that stretch beyond a decade. Partnership takes scientific vision and political will. But it also requires administrative leadership to get multiple, independent partners to adhere. It also helps if there is an urgency born of external competition and threat.

COLLABORATION

SETTING GROUND RULES FOR COLLABORATIVE NETWORKS

QUESTION: Since networks don't "belong" to any one organization, how do I come to agreement with my network colleagues on governance issues to ensure successful outcomes?

ANSWER: The governance question is one of the great challenges confronting network managers. A key step is the management of the design of these networks. In their report to the IBM Center, Rosemary O'Leary and Lisa Blomgren Bingham describe the steps that network managers must undertake in negotiating agreement on the governance of networks:

- **Identify network members whose agreement is necessary.** O'Leary and Bingham note that in some cases, legislation or another formal document might define the composition of the network. More frequently, however, network managers must convene and attract members to the network.

- **Identify the scope and jurisdiction of the network.** In this step, the network manager must resolve questions regarding the authority, goals, and objectives of the network. The result of this step is often embodied in the network's mission statement.

- **Address issues of the network's legitimacy to do its work.** As emphasized by Milward and Provan (see page 150), this is a key responsibility of network managers. If the network does not derive its legitimacy from a legal mandate, it must build its legitimacy through the effectiveness and quality of its work. Transparency also assists in building legitimacy.

- **Negotiate the ground rules for future discussions.** Ground rules might include such issues as how the agenda will be set, how information will be shared, and how the network will work with the press and the public.

- **Negotiate the process governing exchanging views within a network.** Network managers must decide how they will engage each other, how frequently, and through which mediums. In addition to face-to-face meetings, networks can now use collaborative technology tools (such as online discussion forums) to do the work of the network.

- **Discuss administration and allocation of responsibilities.** All networks require some administration. This set of decisions will be guided, in part, by which governance option is selected by the network: self-governance, the lead organization approach, or the network administrative organization. This set of negotiations will discuss the issues of staff, space, computing resources, and cost allocation.

- **Negotiate the decision rules for bringing discussion on an issue to closure.** There are a variety of techniques to reach agreement on how the network will handle problems and conflicts as they arise during a project or initiative.

- **If some form of unanimity or consensus decision is chosen, identify a system for resolving impasse and deadlock in discussions.** It is important to also reach agreement—in advance—on how impasses will be resolved. A common technique is the use of knowledgeable third parties.

- **Identify a decision process or event for determining when the work of the network is complete and it is time to close it down.** Again, it is best to resolve such issues in advance if possible. O'Leary and Bingham write, "In the initial discussions on governance, it may be wise to address this question up front, and to identify an event objective that would represent the logical ending point for the network, if one exists."

The Complex Nature of Network Conflict
From *A Manager's Guide to Resolving Conflicts in Collaborative Networks*
by Rosemary O'Leary and Lisa Blomgren Bingham

Managing and resolving conflicts in networks is no small task. Networks by definition are complex conglomerations of diverse organizations and individuals. The characteristics that add to the complexity of network disputes are numerous.

There are multiple members. Network disputes typically involve many individuals and organizations. Each member brings his or her own interests that must be met. If interests are not met, members may leave the network.

Network members bring both different and common missions. There must be some commonality of purpose to provide incentive for becoming a member of a network. Yet each organization also has its own unique mission that must be followed. These can at times clash with the mission of the network.

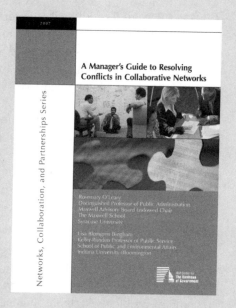

Network organizations have different organization cultures. Culture is to the organization what character is to the individual. Just as each individual is unique, so is each organization culture. Diversity among network organizations' cultures may present conflict management challenges within the network itself.

Network organizations have different methods of operation. They will differ in degrees of hierarchy. They will differ in degrees of management control. These and other differences may affect what a network can and cannot accomplish and the speed at which it is accomplished.

Network members have different stakeholder groups and different funders. To satisfy their diverse constituencies, network members will have different perspectives on appropriate direction and activities. Some of these preferences will overlap, some will not.

Network members have different degrees of power. Not all members of a network are created equal. Despite network rules that may give an equal vote to each member, some are typically more powerful than others. For example, in emergency management networks, oftentimes federal organizations are the beneficiaries of legislation that allows them to preempt local and state actions.

There are often multiple issues. Networks typically are formed to address complex problems that are not easily solved by one organization. Complex problems bring with them multiple issues and sub-issues. Multiple issues and sub-issues typically yield multiple challenges for conflict management.

There are multiple forums for decision making. Public decisions may be made by networks. At the same time, the same public issue may be debated and dealt with in the legislature, in the courts, or in the offices of career public servants. Whether and how a decision is made by a network can be a source of conflict.

Networks are both inter-organizational and interpersonal. The networks studied in the management literature typically are spider webs of organizations. But each organization typically is represented in the network by one or more agents of that organization. Just as networked organizations may clash, so too may networked individuals.

COLLABORATION

ROLES OF MANAGERS IN COLLABORATIVE NETWORKS

QUESTION: If my managers and I decide that our agency should use networks to accomplish its mission, what are the tasks to be performed in "managing" the network we create?

ANSWER: Your first task will be to determine the type of network that can best assist you in accomplishing your agency's mission. In their report to the IBM Center, University of Arizona's H. Brinton Milward and Keith G. Provan describe four types of networks: service implementation networks, information diffusion networks, problem solving networks, and community capacity building networks. For a description of these networks, see the table on page 151.

The second task of your team will be to undertake the five key management responsibilities described by Milward and Provan associated with running public networks:

- **Management of accountability.** This is clearly an important step and is more difficult to accomplish than in a hierarchical organization where you have clear lines of authority and responsibility. In networks, this task involves negotiating who is "responsible" for which outcomes and who will "reward and reinforce" network goals.

- **Management of legitimacy.** Because networks are usually "external" to the traditional government hierarchy, Milward and Provan maintain that managers must gain legitimacy by convincing "outside groups that the network itself is a viable entity that can and will be effective in addressing and resolving complex problems." Establishing legitimacy also involves attracting members to the network, generating good publicity, and securing needed resources.

- **Management of conflict.** Given that networks are usually voluntary, there will inevitably be some conflict and disagreement among members. Thus, a needed skill for 21st century managers is the management of conflict. In their report to the IBM Center, Rosemary O'Leary and Lisa Blomgren Bingham conclude that the most important skills for managers today are negotiation, bargaining, collaborative problem solving, conflict management, and conflict resolution.

- **Management of design.** This key responsibility involves determining which structural governance forms would be most appropriate for network success. This is a task on which many networks fail because a clear governance structure was never clearly articulated and agreed upon. Governance options for networks include self-governance, the lead organization approach, and the network administrative organization (where a distinct administrative entity is created).

- **Management of commitment.** This task involves making sure that the level of commitment is sufficiently high to ensure that network-level goals can be obtained.

You should caution your managers that they will need to change their management style when participating in networks. They must shift their role as a "hierarchical" manager to their role as a "collaborative" member of the network. When undertaking the above tasks, they must do so in a "collaborative" style rather than the traditional "command and control" style of bureaucracies.

The above responsibilities fit well with the advice for network managers provided by Robert Agranoff in his report to the IBM Center: Be a representative of your agency and the network; take a share of the administrative burden; operate by agenda orchestration; recognize shared expertise-based authority; stay within the decision bounds of your network; accommodate and adjust while maintaining purpose; be as creative as possible; be patient and use interpersonal skills; recruit constantly; and emphasize incentives.

Types of Public Management Networks

From *A Manager's Guide to Choosing and Using Collaborative Networks*
by H. Brinton Milward and Keith G. Provan

Network Type	Key Characteristics
Service Implementation Networks	• Government funds the service under contract but doesn't directly provide it (frequently health and human services). • Services are jointly produced by two or more organizations. • Collaboration is often between programs of larger organizations. • Horizontal management of service providers is a key task. These can be firms, nonprofits, or government agencies. • A fiscal agent acts as the sole buyer of services. • Key management tasks include encouraging cooperation, negotiating contracts, planning network expansion, etc.
Information Diffusion Networks	• Horizontal and vertical ties between interdependent government agencies. • Primary focus is sharing information across departmental boundaries. • Commonly used for disaster preparedness and other "high uncertainty" problems. • Key network goal is to shape government's response to problems through better communication and collaboration. • May be either designed or emergent.
Problem Solving Networks	• Primary purpose is to help organizational managers set the agenda for policy related to a critical national or regional problem. • Focus is on solving existing complex problems rather than building relationships for future problems. • Often emerges from information diffusion networks. • Relationships may be temporary, to address a specific problem, and then become dormant after the problem is resolved. • May be either designed or emergent.
Community Capacity Building Networks	• Primary goal is to build social capital in community-based settings. • Network purpose is both current and future oriented (i.e., to build the capacity to address future community needs as they arise). • May be created by participants (bottom-up) or by private and government funders (top-down). • Often involves a wide range of agencies with many emergent sub-networks to address different community needs that may arise.

A Manager's Guide to Choosing and Using Collaborative Networks

Networks and Partnerships Series

H. Brinton Milward
McClelland Professor and Director
School of Public Administration and Policy
Eller College of Management
University of Arizona

Keith G. Provan
Eller Professor
School of Public Administration and Policy
Eller College of Management
University of Arizona

COLLABORATION

COLLABORATING WITH CITIZENS

QUESTION: What are the different ways in which I can engage citizens?

ANSWER: To better understand how you and your agency can engage citizens, it is useful to segment the public into the five roles in which Americans interact with government:

- **As *consumers* of government information:** This is one of the oldest, most traditional roles of government—providing information for the public to use in a variety of ways. For example, citizens are major consumers of government statistics, as well as government information on safety and health.

- **As *customers* of government services:** During the 1990s, both the public and private sectors placed increased emphasis on "customers" and customer service. For example, in the federal government, agencies such as the Social Security Administration and the Centers for Medicare & Medicaid devoted increased efforts to improving the quality and responsiveness of their interactions with citizens.

- **As *citizens* participating in government decision making and policy making:** The challenge of this role involves moving beyond the traditional vehicle of voting as the primary mechanism by which citizens participate in government. New technologies—both face-to-face technologies and electronic technologies—have created new opportunities for governments across the world to engage citizens more directly in decision making and policy making.

- **As *co-producers* of services:** In this role, citizens are responsible for helping provide the services they use. In some cases, it can be serving as a volunteer in programs that help them. Neighborhood Watch programs are an example. In other cases, it is actually doing some of the "work," such as centralized post boxes in neighborhoods where customers go to pick up their mail instead of having it delivered to their door.

- **As *monitors* of government services:** In this role, citizens participate in the measurement and reporting of government service efficiency and effectiveness. Citizens in some cities collect information on street and park cleanliness. In other communities, there are user councils for neighborhood and school services that provide oversight and feedback. These approaches are spreading to other levels of government as well.

In the past decade, an increasing trend has been the creation of broader direct engagement with citizens in informing and making decisions that affect them. Technology is beginning to create a new set of forums that allows this on a larger scale. This technology extends from the traditional forum for citizen participation—voting—to new and innovative approaches, such as the use of surveys, wikis, and blogs.

In their report to the IBM Center, Carolyn Lukensmeyer and Lars Hasselblad Torres describe the changing landscape of citizen involvement in government worldwide. They describe a shift from the traditional "information exchange" model to an "information processing" model of engagement, where citizens are no longer just consumers of government programs and policies but actively engage in shaping them. They describe a spectrum of citizen engagement models, ranging from informing citizens of planned efforts, all the way to empowering citizens to directly make decisions.

What Is Citizen Engagement?

From *Public Deliberation: A Manager's Guide to Citizen Engagement*
by Carolyn J. Lukensmeyer and Lars Hasselblad Torres

Citizen engagement is part of a family of democratic reform ideas that includes public participation, public involvement, participatory democracy, deliberative democracy, and collaborative governance. When used in relation to the online environment, a new vocabulary is evoked, which includes e-democracy, digital democracy, e-government, and electronic governance. What is important to know about these terms is that, while they all make distinctions around the purpose, breadth, and techniques of participation, at base they recognize and build upon a fundamental right of all citizens to have a say in the decisions that affect their lives.

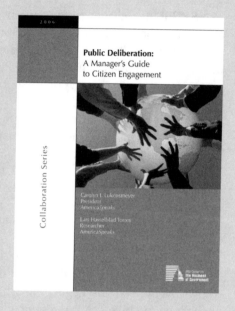

When we speak of citizen engagement, we will be referring to forums that bring the general, impacted public into partnership with decision makers through dialogue-based processes at points along the policy-development continuum, which is to say agenda setting, policy design, and implementation. In general, these kinds of forums are considered "deliberative spaces," characterized by face-to-face and online forms of discussion.

Characteristics of Information Exchange vs. Information Processing Models of Public Communication

Information Exchange Models (i.e., public hearings)	Information Processing Models (i.e., deliberative forums)
Speaker-focused	Participant-focused
Experts deliver information	Experts respond to participant questions
Citizens air individual ideas and concerns	Citizens identify shared ideas and concerns and assign them relative priority
Participants share anecdotal evidence	Participants use detailed, balanced background materials
Often engages the "usual suspects": stakeholders and citizens already active on specific issues	Reaches into diverse populations, including citizens not usually active, with efforts to reach under-represented
No group discussion of questions	Facilitator-led small group discussion

Source: AmericaSpeaks.

COLLABORATION

ACHIEVING NATIONAL OUTCOMES VIA COLLABORATION

QUESTION: My agency wants to work on national problems that are beyond our direct control. How should we go about it?

ANSWER: The challenge you describe is becoming common across all of government. While your federal agency may be facing limited federal resources, your agency is likely to be well positioned to establish a national network that can leverage the resources of nonprofit organizations and state and local governments. Because of anticipated future tight budgets, you should begin to reach beyond your own budget and programs under your direct control to form networks to work on national problems.

In his report to the IBM Center, John Scanlon describes how the Bureau of Primary Health Care (BPHC) in the Department of Health and Human Services created a national campaign to achieve a national goal: delivering quality health care to all American citizens and eliminating health-status disparities between vulnerable, uninsured Americans and affluent, insured populations. While the case study described is about health care, the model described is applicable to all government organizations faced with achieving national goals beyond their immediate reach. Success on national goals will require the creation of partnerships and networks working collectively to achieve a national goal.

Government now needs to increase its use of partnerships and networks to solve national problems. As noted above, there is little doubt that government budgets will continue to be tight in the years ahead. Thus, government must begin to marshal, coordinate, and inspire other organizations to collectively work on national problems. A key resource for you in creating these partnerships are the civil servants in your organization who can be creative in developing new approaches to national problems. The civil servants profiled in the Scanlon report all went beyond their job descriptions to provide leadership on a national goal in which BPHC had been legislated a relatively small defined role.

In describing how you and your agency can create networks to achieve national goals, Scanlon recommends the following actions:

- **Identify a national outcome that collaboration can help address.** In all agencies, there are government programs which are associated with higher national goals that, although beyond the reach of specific programs, can be achieved by a campaign deploying networks across the nation.

- **Begin to collaborate and network.** The challenge here will be to create a "space" where hierarchy can be set aside and collaboration can happen. As described on pages 148 and 150, government managers will need to begin to act like members of a network rather than traditional line managers.

- **Find the "hidden assets" in your organization.** In doing the "routine" work of your organization, it gains assets that are often not seen or acknowledged. Such assets include access to people in your field, knowledge of existing networks, influence, credibility, and a highly skilled, knowledgeable staff. All these assets can be used in creating a national network.

- **Operate in a campaign mode.** After you decide to create a national network to achieve a national goal, you must begin to work in a campaign mode. You must bring together a "campaign team" that can use social marketing and political skills to mobilize your network around a given national goal.

Bold, Audacious Goals: The Engine of Leadership

From *Extraordinary Results on National Goals: Networks and Partnerships in the Bureau of Primary Health Care's 100%/0 Campaign* by John W. Scanlon

Bold national goals startle and draw resistance in organizations. Introducing them takes courage and the willingness to deal productively with the resistance. The resistance is natural. Bold national goals always define a kind of performance that managers do not want to be accountable for, and often defy conventional wisdom.

In 1998, a group of managers in the Bureau of Primary Health Care, Department of Health and Human Services, launched what they called 100% Access/0 Health Disparities Campaign. The vision was to have every community in America provide 100 percent of its residents access to quality health care. In addition, every community would be eliminating health-status disparities, the severe and pervasive gaps in health status that show up in a community when vulnerable, uninsured populations are compared with affluent, insured populations.

In the Bureau, conventional wisdom was against 100%/0. The prevailing view was that 100% access called for more federal funding. Most felt the real solution was universal insurance coverage. The Clinton administration had failed to get health care reform in its first term and that was a dead topic. How the nation closes the gap in access to health care was considered a policy issue beyond the domain of the Bureau. The conventional wisdom said there was nothing to be done by the Bureau.

The campaign goals also went far beyond the program goals the Bureau managers and staff traditionally set, ones they could deliver with the program resources for which they were given responsibility. For example, developing so many new center grantees and National Health Service Corps (NHSC) placement sites. The 100%/0 team was making itself accountable on goals for which it did not have the required resources and was committing to find and secure those resources. That was a different kind of work than the traditional grant and program administration of the Bureau.

In May 1999, the 100%/0 team presented its goals to the Bureau executives and managers in the strategic planning process. The group was startled by these goals and resisted them. "Some felt that it was imprudent to set such ambitious goals, others felt it was not appropriate work for the Bureau. They were being honest and protective of Dr. Marilyn Gaston [BPHC director] and the Bureau."

Reasonable counter proposals were made by staff. The first was to move to a pilot approach, which involved selecting two cities and focusing on them, then doing a demonstration and evaluating it to show it can be done. Another proposal was to focus on the 10 neediest communities. The team saw these reasonable goals taking them down a different path into project management. They acknowledged the advice but stayed committed to enrolling 500 communities.

COLLABORATION

For Additional Information on Collaboration

From Forest Fires to Hurricane Katrina: Case Studies of Incident Command Systems (2007) by Donald P. Moynihan

This report describes the success of the Incident Command System (ICS) as a hierarchical-network organizational model in emergencies. The report examines the Hurricane Katrina experience and identifies the conditions under which the ICS approach can be successful.

Delivery of Benefits in an Emergency: Lessons from Hurricane Katrina (2007) by Thomas H. Stanton

The report examines the delivery of emergency financial benefits, such as pensions, Social Security, and Temporary Assistance for Needy Families, as well as payments relating to the disaster such as emergency food stamps, unemployment insurance, and emergency cash assistance. The report examines how government and non-government organizations worked together on providing emergency financial assistance in the aftermath of Hurricane Katrina.

The Blogging Revolution: Government in the Age of Web 2.0 (2007) by David C. Wyld

The report examines the phenomenon of blogging, which is being used increasingly as a tool for promoting online engagement between citizens and public servants. The report describes how members of Congress, governors, city mayors, and police and fire departments are now engaging directly with the public via blogging.

The E-Government Collaboration Challenge: Lessons from Five Case Studies (2006) by Jane Fedorowicz, Janis L. Gogan, and Christine B. Williams

This report examines five case studies of collaboration in the use of information technology. The authors assess the political, administrative, and technical challenges that occurred in each of the case studies and describe challenges faced and lessons learned. The report offers 10 recommendations to improve future cross-organizational initiatives that require using a common information technology system as the backbone of the collaborative effort.

The Quest to Become "One": An Approach to Internal Collaboration (2005) by Russ Linden

This report examines the efforts by three federal organizations—the Department of Veterans Affairs, the Department of Transportation, and the National Aeronautics and Space Administration—to move in greater concert toward the achievement of organizational goals. The three initiatives—One VA, ONE DOT, and One NASA—each faced distinct challenges. The report examines lessons learned from these experiences.

For Additional Information on Collaboration

Leveraging Collaborative Networks in Infrequent Emergency Situations (2005) by Donald P. Moynihan

This report reviews a highly successful model of network collaboration that contained the outbreak of Exotic Newcastle disease (a highly contagious disease among poultry) in California in 2002. The report describes the successful use of the incident management system approach and recommends its application in all infrequent emergency situations.

Cooperation Between Social Security and Tax Agencies in Europe (2005) by Bernhard Zaglmayer, Paul Schoukens, and Danny Pieters

This report describes the relationship between social security and taxation organizations in nine European nations—Austria, Belgium, Denmark, Estonia, Germany, Ireland, Italy, the Netherlands, and the United Kingdom. The report presents a series of observations about the potential of increased cooperation between social security and taxation organizations in the years ahead.

Restoring Trust in Government: The Potential of Digital Citizen Participation (2004) by Marc Holzer, James Melitski, Seung-Yong Rho, and Richard Schwester

This report presents three case studies which illustrate how government organizations are now using technology to enhance citizen participation. The report presents examples of how citizens can engage in a two-way dialogue on public issues and describes tools which allow citizens to participate in a dialogue with fellow citizens and government. This report presents recommendations to policy makers and government executives on ways they can increase the voice of citizens in the decision-making process.

Collaboration and Performance Management in Network Settings: Lessons from Three Watershed Governance Efforts (2004) by Mark T. Imperial

This report describes how performance measures and monitoring processes influence the collaborative processes used to develop and implement watershed management programs.

Leveraging Networks: A Guide for Public Managers Working Across Organizations (2003) by Robert Agranoff

This report examines the new challenges faced by public managers as they participate in collaborative undertakings with other governments and the non-governmental sector. The lessons presented in the report are derived from experiences in several Midwestern states, where many established networks operate.

COLLABORATION

For Additional Information on Collaboration

The Challenge of Coordinating "Big Science" (2003)
by W. Henry Lambright

This report examines the increase in cross-agency research and development projects. These initiatives include information technology, nanotechnology, climate change, global change, and bioterrorism. The aim of these and other interagency programs is to draw on the special skills of each organization and weave them into a whole that is greater than the sum of the parts.

Using Technology to Increase Citizen Participation in Government:
The Use of Models and Simulation (2003) by John O'Looney

This report discusses the use of decision support tools by citizens and community leaders to improve public decision making. The report identifies opportunities, examines existing attempts to use technologies, and presents research on simulation technologies designed to help citizens participate more fully in decisions about sustainable development.

Public-Private Strategic Partnerships: The U.S. Postal Service-Federal Express Alliance (2003) by Oded Shenkar

In recent years, postal services worldwide have been transformed, adopting private sector operational modes and efficiencies. This report reviews postal service alliances around the world to identify the best practices to guide future alliances. Postal services are now working with for-profit firms in delivery, logistics, and freight forwarding, and have established strategic alliances with them.

Communities of Practice: A New Tool for Government Managers
(2003) by William M. Snyder and Xavier de Souza Briggs

This report documents the creation and implementation of several intergovernmental "communities of practice." It traces the history of these networks and documents their structure, activities, and outcomes, as well as identifies a number of critical success factors related to these groups. Case studies include SafeCities, Boost4Kids, and 21st Century Skills.

Managing Across Boundaries: A Case Study of Dr. Helene Gayle and the AIDS Epidemic (2002) by Norma M. Riccucci

This report profiles Dr. Helene Gayle, former director of the National Center for HIV, STD, and TB Prevention at the Centers for Disease Control. The report is a case study of a public sector leader managing across boundaries. Dr. Gayle was responsible for working closely with the United Nations and other international organizations and nations in combating the AIDS epidemic.

For Additional Information on Collaboration

Leveraging Networks to Meet National Goals: FEMA and the Safe Construction Networks (2002) by William L. Waugh, Jr.

This report analyzes the Federal Emergency Management Agency's (FEMA) work with the private sector in implementing FEMA's goals via public-private partnerships. The project includes an assessment of FEMA's Project Impact Program. The report assesses and describes the achievement of national policy goals through private sector partnerships.

COLLABORATION

To download or order a copy of a report, visit the IBM Center for The Business of Government website at: www.businessofgovernment.org | 159

About the Authors

Mark A. Abramson is President of Leadership Inc. Throughout his career, he has been instrumental in establishing two cutting-edge organizations dedicated to improving management in government. In 1998, he helped create what became the IBM Center for The Business of Government and served as its executive director from 1998 to 2007. Earlier in his career, Mr. Abramson conceived and helped launched the Council for Excellence in Government and served as its first president from 1983 to 1994.

Mr. Abramson began his career as a public servant in the Office of the Assistant Secretary for Planning and Evaluation at the U.S. Department of Health and Human Services. In 1992, he was elected a fellow of the National Academy of Public Administration. Mr. Abramson is past president of the National Capital Area Chapter of the American Society for Public Administration.

Mr. Abramson serves as editor of the IBM Center for The Business of Government Book Series, published by Rowman & Littlefield Publishers. He is also the author or editor of 14 books and has published more than 100 articles on public management. He is a member of the editorial board of *Public Administration Review* as case study editor, and has served as a contributing editor to *Government Executive* and a member of the Board of Editors and forum editor for *The Public Manager*. He received a Master of Arts in Political Science from the Maxwell School of Citizenship and Public Affairs at Syracuse University, a Master of Arts in History from New York University, and a Bachelor of Arts from Florida State University.

Jonathan D. Breul is Executive Director of the IBM Center for The Business of Government and a Partner with IBM Global Business Services, where he helps public sector executives improve the effectiveness of government with practical ideas and original thinking. The IBM Center sponsors independent research by top minds in academe and the nonprofit sector, and creates opportunities for dialogue on a broad range of public management topics. Formerly senior advisor to the deputy director for management in the Office of Management and Budget (OMB) in the Executive Office of the President, Mr. Breul served as OMB's senior career executive with primary responsibility for government-wide general management policies.

Mr. Breul helped develop the President's Management Agenda, was instrumental in establishing the President's Management Council, and championed efforts to integrate performance information with the budget process. He led the development and government-wide implementation of the Government Performance and Results Act. In addition to his OMB activities, he helped Senator John Glenn of Ohio launch the Chief Financial Officers Act.

Mr. Breul is an elected fellow and member of the Board of Trustees of the National Academy of Public Administration, a principal of the Council for Excellence in Government, and an adjunct professor at Georgetown University's Graduate Public Policy Institute. He holds a Master of Public Administration from Northeastern University and a Bachelor of Arts from Colby College.

John M. Kamensky is a Senior Fellow at the IBM Center for The Business of Government and an Associate Partner with IBM Global Business Services. During his 24 years of public service, he played a key role in helping pioneer the federal government's performance and results orientation. He is passionate about creating a government that is results oriented, performance based, customer focused, and collaborative in nature. He is co-author of *Managing for Results 2002; Collaboration: Using Networks and Partnerships; Managing for Results 2005;* and *Competition, Choice, and Incentives in Government Programs.*

Prior to moving to the private sector in 2001, Mr. Kamensky served for eight years as deputy director of Vice President Gore's National Partnership for Reinventing Government. Before that, he worked at the Government Accountability Office for 16 years, where he played a key role in the development and passage of the Government Performance and Results Act. He is a fellow of the National Academy of Public Administration and a principal of the Council for Excellence in Government. Mr. Kamensky received a Master of Public Affairs from the Lyndon B. Johnson School of Public Affairs at the University of Texas in Austin, and a Bachelor of Arts from Angelo State University.

G. Martin Wagner is a Senior Fellow at the IBM Center for The Business of Government and an Associate Partner with IBM Global Business Services. A 30-year veteran of the federal government, he led initiatives that set the tone and direction for major changes in government management. He played a key role in promoting electronic government, embracing commercial contracting methods, and using performance measures. Mr. Wagner helped initiate FirstGov (now USA.gov), the government's Internet portal, and FedBizOpps, the gateway for all federal procurements. He established government-wide contracts for smart cards and electronic signatures, and co-chaired the federal government's first interagency electronic commerce effort.

As acting commissioner and later deputy commissioner of the Federal Acquisition Service of the General Services Administration (GSA), he oversaw the acquisition of more than $50 billion of goods and services for other federal agencies. His programs included the government's information technology and telecommunications contracts, the management of 200,000 motor vehicles, disaster relief for hurricane victims, equipment for the U.S. armed forces, travel management, and the use of charge cards. As associate administrator for government-wide policy at GSA for 10 years, he developed and implemented policies for internal government management.

As a member of the federal government's Senior Executive Service, Mr. Wagner received both a Meritorious and a Distinguished Presidential Rank Award during his career. He is a fellow of the National Academy of Public Administration. Mr. Wagner earned a Bachelor of Science and Engineering and a Master of Science and Engineering from Princeton University, and received a Master of Economics and Public Policy from Princeton's Woodrow Wilson School.

About the Contributors

Listed below are the titles and affiliations of the authors of the reports and other publications excerpted in this volume.

Michael Barzelay is Professor of Public Management, London School of Economics and Political Science.

Robert D. Behn is Lecturer, John F. Kennedy School of Government, Harvard University.

Lisa Blomgren Bingham is Keller-Runden Professor of Public Service, School of Public and Environmental Affairs, Indiana University.

Lloyd A. Blanchard is Associate Professor, Public Administration Institute, Louisiana State University.

Ray Blunt is a consultant, Annandale, Virginia.

Sandford Borins is Professor of Public Management, University of Toronto at Scarborough.

John Carnevale is President, Carnevale Associates.

Timothy J. Conlan is Professor of Government and Politics, Department of Public and International Affairs, George Mason University.

Ann Cotten is Director, Schaefer Center for Public Policy, University of Baltimore.

R. Steven Daniels is Professor of Public Policy and Administration, California State University, Bakersfield.

Thomas H. Davenport is President's Chair in Information Technology and Management, Babson College.

Kathryn G. Denhardt is Associate Professor and Policy Scientist, Institute for Public Administration, University of Delaware.

Charles H. Fay is Professor of Human Resource Management, School of Management and Labor Relations, Rutgers University.

Jacques S. Gansler is Roger C. Lipitz Chair in Public Policy, School of Public Affairs, University of Maryland.

Gary Hamel is Visiting Professor of Strategic and International Management, London School of Business, and co-founder, Strategos.

Harry P. Hatry is Distinguished Fellow and Director, Public Management Program, The Urban Institute.

Stephen H. Holden is former Assistant Professor, University of Maryland at Baltimore County.

Sirkka L. Jarvenpaa is James Bayless/Rauscher Pierce Refsnes Chair in Business Administration, University of Texas at Austin.

Philip G. Joyce is Professor of Public Policy and Public Administration, Trachtenberg School of Public Policy and Public Administration, The George Washington University.

Robert Klitgaard is President and University Professor, Claremont Graduate University.

W. Henry Lambright is Professor of Public Administration and Political Science, The Maxwell School of Citizenship and Public Affairs, Syracuse University.

William Lucyshyn is Research Scholar, Center for Public Policy and Private Enterprise, University of Maryland.

Carolyn J. Lukensmeyer is President and Founder, America*Speaks*.

Amit Magdieli is Managing Consultant, Public Sector Practice, IBM Global Business Services.

Lawrence L. Martin is Professor of Public Affairs and Director, Center for Community Partnerships, College of Health and Public Affairs, University of Central Florida.

Sharon H. Mastracci is Assistant Professor, Department of Public Administration, University of Illinois–Chicago.

Nicholas J. Mathys is Professor of Management, Department of Management, DePaul University.

Shelley H. Metzenbaum is Director, Center for Public Management, McCormack Graduate School of Policy Studies, University of Massachusetts Boston.

H. Brinton Milward is McClelland Professor of Public Administration and Policy, School of Public Administration and Policy, University of Arizona.

Elaine Morley is Senior Research Associate, The Urban Institute.

Patrick J. Murphy is Assistant Professor, Department of Politics, University of San Francisco.

Satish Nambisan is Associate Professor of Technology Management and Strategy, Lally School of Management and Technology, Rensselaer Polytechnic Institute.

Kathryn E. Newcomer is Director and Chair, Trachtenberg School of Public Policy and Public Administration, The George Washington University.

Rosemary O'Leary is Distinguished Professor of Public Administration, The Maxwell School of Citizenship and Public Affairs, Syracuse University.

Burt Perrin is a consultant, La Masque, France.

Keith G. Provan is Professor, School of Public Administration and Policy, University of Arizona.

Hal G. Rainey is Alumni Foundation Distinguished Professor, School of Public and International Affairs, University of Georgia.

Howard Risher is a consultant, Wayne, Pennsylvania.

Shelli B. Rossman is Senior Research Associate, The Urban Institute.

Barry M. Rubin is Professor of Public and Environmental Affairs, School of Public and Environmental Affairs, Indiana University.

Richard S. Rubin is Professor (Emeritus) of Public and Environmental Affairs, and Director, Center for Public Sector Labor Relations, School of Public and Environmental Affairs, Indiana University.

John W. Scanlon is Principal, JSEA Inc.

Mary Ann Scheirer is a consultant, Princeton, New Jersey.

Thomas H. Stanton is a Fellow, Center for the Study of American Government, Johns Hopkins University.

Fred Thompson is Goudy Professor of Public Management, Atkinson Graduate School of Management, Willamette University.

James R. Thompson is Associate Professor, Department of Public Administration, University of Illinois–Chicago.

Kenneth R. Thompson is Professor of Management, Department of Management, DePaul University.

Lars Hasselblad Torres is Founder, Global Peace Tiles Project, Cabot, Vermont.

Gregory F. Treverton is Professor, The RAND Graduate School.

Jonathan Walters is Staff Correspondent, *Governing* magazine.

Joseph S. Wholey is former Professor, School of Policy, Planning, and Development, University of Southern California.

Trefor P. Williams is Professor, Department of Civil and Environmental Engineering, Rutgers University.

Chris Wye is a consultant, Washington, D.C.

David C. Wyld is Robert Maurin Professor of Management, Department of Management, Southeastern Louisiana University.

Gary J. Young is Chair, Department of Health Policy and Management, School of Public Health, Boston University.

Index

Index of Departments and Agencies

Index of Key Topics

Index of Names

About the IBM Center for
The Business of Government

About the IBM Center for The Business of Government

Founded in 1998, the IBM Center helps public sector executives improve the effectiveness of government with practical ideas and original thinking. The IBM Center sponsors independent research by top minds in the academic and nonprofit communities. It focuses on the future of the operation and management of the public sector. Since its creation, the IBM Center has published 20 books and over 200 reports.

All reports cited in *The Operator's Manual* are available free of charge at the IBM Center website: www.businessofgovernment.org.

The IBM Center has earned a reputation for a deep understanding of public management issues—rooted in both theory and practice—during its 10-year history of providing government leaders with instructive ideas that inform their actions.

The IBM Center competitively awards stipends to outstanding researchers across the United States and the world. Each award winner is expected to produce a research report on an important management topic.

To find out more about the IBM Center and its research stipend program, to review a full list of its publications, or to download a Center report, visit the Center's website at: www.businessofgovernment.org.